GRAPE
BRITAIN
A Tour of Britain's
Vineyards

David Harvey

David Harvey

GRAPE BRITAIN
A Tour of Britain's Vineyards

www.angelshare.co.uk

The Angel's Share is an imprint of
Neil Wilson Publishing Ltd
0/2 19 Netherton Avenue
Glasgow G13 1BQ

Telephone/Fax: 0141 954 8007
E-mail: info@nwp.co.uk
Website: http://www.nwp.co.uk

A catalogue record for this book is available
from the British Library.

ISBN 978-1-903238-45-5

Typeset in Danubia
Designed by Mark Blackadder

Printed and bound by Oriental Press

Loose and dusty like the road,
each day I find a new place to see,
a new place to delve.
Amid thoughts of richer loam
and soil I become a vine,
trusted and tender.
Struggle to deepen.

They are not long, the weeping and the laughter,
Love and desire and hate:
I think they have no portion in us after
We pass the gate.
They are not long, the days of wine and roses:
Out of a misty dream
Our path emerges for a while, then closes
Within a dream.

Vitae Summa Brevis (1896), Ernest Dowson (1867–1900)

This book is dedicated to Silvio Berlusconi and Jacques Chirac
for their keen appreciation of foreign wines

CONTENTS

ACKNOWLEDGEMENTS

I would like to thank everyone at all the vineyards who put up with my questioning and made this book what it is. I had a fantastic time travelling round them all and received much warmth and enthusiasm wherever I went. In particular, I would like to mention George Bowden at Leventhorpe for first bringing Yorkshire wine, and hence UK wine to my attention.

I would also like to thank everyone who helped out with tasting wines (no great chore I'm sure) at home and gave me their encouragement and support. To all my family, especially Nikki and Mike, and Mum and Dad, thanks. Also, in particular, Martyn Newton in Shipley, who initially fired me with enthusiasm for wine and Anna and Jon (and all the staff at Oddbins, Chiswick) who egged me on in the venture. Cheers to Murray Wallace and Simon Oliver for their great cartoons – fame beckons

Finally, my biggest thanks of all go to Clare, for making me get stuff done and always being there. Without her, this book would probably never have seen the light of day.

2007 Vintage Report

With an early spring and a particularly warm and sunny April the 2007 vintage was set start earlier than ever before but a chilly start to the summer, followed by the rains in late June and July foiled any follow-up to the great previous years.

Many vines were hit just as they flowered and the effect was a much-reduced crop across most of the UK (up to 50% in many places). Despite these widespread problems, most vineyards used previous experience of bad weather to limit crops and maintain quality at the expense of quantity. As a result it is well worthwhile seeking out bottles of 2007 wine early to avoid missing out!

David Harvey, February 2008

INTRODUCTION

This book comes from a very British desire to champion the underdog. And let's face it, English and Welsh wine *is* very much still the underdog. Just as I was about to set out travelling to vineyards in February 2006, a customer at the Oddbins in which I used to work said, 'You don't have any English wine do you?' in a derisory tone, and then laughed nastily. I asked if he had actually ever tried any English wine. He replied rather indignantly, 'No, thank you very much.' Of course his was the most extreme of reactions; most people I spoke to were simply surprised it actually exists. When you mention the fact that there is a vineyard just outside Leeds, faces take on an aspect of disbelief, only increased by the comment that Yorkshire wines are actually rather good.

In all honesty *I* was surprised when after eight years in Leeds I discovered the presence of this improbable vineyard. Out of vague curiosity I decided to visit Leventhorpe and got not just a warm welcome, but a wander around the vines, a good natter, and a tasting of five different wines, all good with flavours unlike any other wines I had ever tasted, and all this among picturesque Yorkshire hills! I had caught the bug, and started visiting other vineyards in the UK. Finally, I decided that if I had found so much pleasure in and among the fields and hills of England and Wales, surely I should try to persuade others of the merits of the fresh, unique wines of Great Britain.

So why bother?

The best way to find out about wine, viticulture and winemaking is to grow your own grapes and make your own wine but to do this (and more importantly be any good at it) requires a life of devotion, heartache, back-pain and empty pockets. Perhaps a second, rather

'There is not the hundredth part of the wine consumed in this kingdom that there ought to be. Our foggy climate wants help.'

Jane Austen,
Northanger Abbey

'English wine is the world's best.'

Metro *of 21 July, announcing the results of the International Wine Competition 2006*

Young vines at Nyetimber in Sussex

I

less romantic option is better and that is to visit other people's
vineyards.

The more one appreciates the travails that a vine has to
endure, the more one appreciates the wine being consumed. As you
travel you will see that vines, like humans, come in all shapes and
sizes from young thin, twisty little fellers who'd break in a strong
wind to tough gnarly old dudes. Appreciating wine takes patience –
it is an area of life which demonstrates that, contrary to the general
rush and bustle of modern life, true excellence cannot be hurried.
It takes three years for a wine vine to produce grapes and another

20 before it is at its best and you might then need to age the wine for another six years or more before drinking it to allow it to achieve its true potential.

And vineyards are rarely *just* vineyards. Wine is not a profitable business generally speaking, so the owners have often come up with other means of keeping the visitor entertained. The scope of activities ranges from fairs to art shops, llamas to woodland trails, and cheese-tastings to Michelin-starred restaurants. Many of the vineyards are astoundingly beautiful places too, with the vines constantly changing through the seasons. A grand day out is there for the taking, and almost certainly a lot closer to home than you might think.

Woolly Alpaca at Nutbourne Vineyard

The British climate

The phrase *'cool climate'*, has become a marker of quality in the New World and there is no doubting that England and Wales possess this. At first glance then, the existence of so much good wine in such an unlikely climate seems almost miraculous. The cooler the vintage and the lighter and more acidic the grapes, the less complete will fermentation be in the autumn. This is a real problem in the UK (although light, acidic grapes are actually perfect for making sparkling wine), so the later the fruit is picked, the better. But producing the best possible fruit and harvesting it when the fruit is in prime condition and the fullest flavour has developed, is easier said than done when contending with early autumn frosts, rainstorms, drought, mould, mildew, hungry birds and ravenous badgers.

On the flipside of the coin, experts agree that the best wines are made in marginal climatic conditions. If a vine is overloaded with sun, heat and water the wines will taste over-ripe and out of balance. The beautiful subtleties and the finest aromas derive from cool weather and long slow ripening lasting well into the depths of autumn.

And if, at the end of the day, the raison d'être of wines from a given place is to produce wines that possess a taste, and a smell unique to that country then the UK succeeded a long time ago. Reading through the books that have been written on English and Welsh wine, there is a point at which they stop being compared to the wines of Germany and the Loire and are celebrated as unique. Not only this, but the white wines of Britain can have astonishing longevity and the capacity to age into something almost unrecognisable from the elderflowery herbaceousness of their youth. An

3

Pustular growths on vine leaves

Astley Kerner 1984 I drank in good company was astounding; fully fresh, yet developed into an intense honeyed, limey, minerally beauty. Clearly, even back in 1984 (the best vintage of the 80s) some people knew exactly what they were doing. As my brother-in-law put it as we sipped the Astley, 'I was still in shorts when this was made!'

The UK wine scene

The UK is at the start of a great vinous future. In 50 years it has gone from its first commercial vintage (1954) to seeing an English sparkling wine receiving the accolade of Best Sparkling Wine in the World. There are now roughly 300 commercial growers in England and Wales with some 2,000 acres under vine. Sounds a lot, but to put this in context, the region of Bordeaux has around 250,000 acres with 22,000 growers producing 44 million cases of wine per year. We currently produce more than 3 million bottles, which amounts to 0.5% of UK consumption, so on a global scale the UK wine industry is tiny. Having said this, it is expanding rapidly (production is expected to double over the next few years), and proof of quality is to be found in the fact that the UK is one of the only countries in the world where demand exceeds supply.

There are more and more good winemakers out there and many of the wines that are being made are superb. And it is not just the crisp refreshingly pure still whites, but frothy golden sparkling wine the equal of Champagne, vivid strawberry-ish rosés, and even elegant smooth reds. And my favourite bottle of all is a dessert wine, lusciously sweet with a haunting nose that you'll find yourself dreaming about. I cannot help but feel that this is a special time for British wine producers, that fleeting moment before the burgeoning industry is swallowed by larger companies. A spirit of excitement and exploration pervades these vineyards; a spirit often lacking in more established wine-growing countries. What grape variety? How to blend them? Where to grow and how? The prevailing mood among British winemakers is not one of competition between themselves but of co-operation, and of proving that UK wines can be world-class. Our wines are made by people who know and love what they do, the world of the amateur, of happy accidents and of genuinely bizarre experiments that should never work, but just occasionally do.

Finally, there is also a sense of capturing some vestige of the fading rural life and history of Britain, of engaging with a living world that is sadly drowned out by the sound of cars and too many people shoved together. The slow destruction of close-knit communities is a sad feature of modernity, and there is much to be learned from city dwellers like myself reconnecting with agriculture. My hope is that through adapting, the best things about country life might remain, flourish and change the way the city thinks. After all, Vine Street in London once had a vineyard in it.

What this book does and does not do

This book is intended to help you explore the world of British vineyards and wines for yourself. There is no point in me writing down every single good wine that I have tried – there are frankly, far too many to even make a start. I begin with some general help, how to taste wines properly, UK vintages, and grape types. For the experienced wine drinker the latter is one of the most exciting elements of UK wines: none of your Syrah or Sauvignon here, just fresh new names of which you'll probably never have heard.

The entries in the last part of the book, A Tour of Britain's Vineyards, are intended to give you a general impression of the vineyards that have visitor facilities, of which there are approximately 120, and are divided up by region and county. Having spent most of 2006 travelling around these vineyards and sampling both the ambience and the produce, I have tried to give an atmospheric description of each, rather than a rundown of technical details. I have included a few which are not generally open to the public purely because they are fascinating examples of differing techniques and wine-making philosophies. There is *no* substitute for going out and visiting a vineyard yourself, not least because my descriptions of the wines cannot enable you to taste them yourself. From a practical point of view too, the wines change with every vintage, and it is one of the marvels and frustrations of winemaking that a year's weather can change a bottle made from the same grapes and the same patch of ground so much. Still, I do draw attention to some of my favourites along the way (and hope there are still some bottles left for you to try).

The guide is punctuated with trivia, history, advice and general bits and bobs, so that if you *really* can't be bothered going outside you can always sit on the loo reading it, or order a case of wine on the Internet (see page 186). Having said that, I certainly hope that you will be inspired to go out and see for yourself, and to support our British vineyards.

PART
ONE

I

A BRIEF HISTORY OF BRITISH WINE

It is generally accepted that when the Romans invaded Britain in 43AD under the Emperor Claudius, they brought vineyards and wine to the UK in earnest. We do not know how many vineyards the Romans planted here, but there was clearly resentment back at home about new vineyards springing up in Roman territories and competing with established Roman winemakers. This eventually led to the decree of Emperor Domitian in 90AD ordering that no natives of conquered lands could plant vineyards. The Roman efforts spread as far north as Lincolnshire but the climate was considered too cold and wet to create an enduring presence. After the Romans quit Britain, winemaking fell into decline with only nominal production. The Normans certainly kept the activity alive and the monasteries were the main places of viniculture throughout England during the Dark Ages. There were over 40 vineyards mentioned in the Domesday Book of 1086, the first statistical census undertaken in Britain under the auspices of William the Conqueror. The Benedictine monks who had arrived before the Norman Conquest were followed by various other orders, most of whom planted their own vineyards to provide a homegrown supply of communion wine and to stock their own cellars.

At this time the vineyards were required to render one barrel of wine in every 20 to the king as a form of tax. In 1152, Henry, Duke of Normandy and Count of Anjou, married Eleanor of Aquitaine who was one of the wealthiest women of her day with considerable landholdings (including the vineyards of Gascony) in south-west France. Two years later, Henry succeeded to the throne of England as the first of the Plantagenet monarchs. At that time the English vineyards, although well-established, were of secondary importance to the trade in imported claret from Eleanor's Bordeaux. Wine, as a commodity, then cost a penny a gallon.

Bacchus, God of wine: Carter's Vineyard, Essex

9

When the Black Death came to Britain in the late 1340s many vineyards were ploughed up due to a shortage of labour. It is estimated that between a third and two thirds of Europe's population died from this pandemic with a total worldwide loss of 75 million people. After this, elderberries were often added to white wine to get right colour for communion (given the prevalent flavour of elderberry still present in British wines one might think they still did). Due to its preservative qualities it was not just elderberries that were used; wine was flavoured with a wide array of other ingredients including raisins, honey, herbs, spices and resin.

Between 1538 and 1541 the dissolution of the monasteries by order of Henry VIII together with the occurrence of a 'little Ice Age' in Britain, finally stifled what British wine production had remained from the Middle Ages.

In the 1630s one of England's most prominent citizens, Sir Kenelm Digby, developed a new type of bottle at his glassworks. It was globular in shape with a long, tapered neck and the glass was coloured to protect the contents from sunlight. It was not only durable, but stable to boot. He was eventually credited by parliament in 1662 with this invention, which was the forerunner of the modern wine bottle and it was around this time that wine gradually stopped being shipped in casks as the glass bottle took over. Another development was the arrival of sparkling wine at the court of Charles II. This happened after the Marquis de St Evremond, fell out of favour with Louis XIV and was exiled to England. He arrived with some casks of Champagne wine that were about to undergo spring fermentation after the winter months had stopped it. The English courtiers took to it immediately and St Evremond then set about importing casks from Reims to England. When the Champagne was then bottled with a cork that was attached by string, merchants were able to sell the wine all-year round in its fizzy state. It is this development in the wine trade for which the 17th-century English merchants can take full credit.

But despite these important developments and the publication of John Rose's *The English Vineyard Vindicated and The Way of Making Wine in France* in 1666, this was the low point in the production of wine in England and Wales. At this time the landed Scots were large consumers of claret and some of them even had landholdings in Bordeaux and drew their imports directly from France, the European country with which they had very strong religious, trading and cultural links. In effect, Britain's winemakers simply could not compete with the quality and quantity of wine available from France where all the ingredients along with the climate, existed in abundance.

At the beginning of the 18th century, the Methuen Treaty (1703) between England and Portugal meant that wine and port could be imported with a customs levy one-third of the equivalent French duty. France was involved at this time in the War of the Spanish Succession (1701–14) and imports from France became almost unobtainable; port imports, on the other hand, grew rapidly during this period and other sweet fortified wines such as Madeira and sherry from Spain were also popular. Due to their higher alcoholic volume, these wines travelled well and could cope with the long sea passages from Portugal and Spain. After the war the first evidence of a resurgence in wine production began as the landed gentry in England experimented with vineyards, many of them none too successfully. If you come across any pubs called The Vine it is a reasonable indicator of an historic vinous connection; most of them are in southern England.

The 19th century was one of upheaval in the French wine trade. After the Napoleonic Wars the British were partial to imported French wines, brandy and dessert wines. Many country houses established greenhouse vines and grew grapes for home consumption, although the vineyards of England gradually disappeared. The catastrophic effect of the phylloxera aphid which decimated French vines in the late 1800s had a curious effect on the drinking habits of the expanding middle classes. The most significant of these was the adoption of Scotch whisky as the post-dinner drink of choice in place of French brandy. As the French vineyards gradually recovered by grafting resistant root stocks onto the indigenous vines, winemaking was establishing itself in the New World with vineyards in America, Chile, South Africa and Australia growing rapidly. Britain, however, remained relatively dry.

In the late 19th century the Marquess of Bute did plant vines at Castell Coch in South Wales and five years after his death in 1900, there were some 63,000 vines there and at Swanbridge although after the First World War, it all seems to have fallen by the wayside. Between the wars, there was no winemaking at all in England and Wales and the modern-day industry is purely a post-war

ESTABLISHED 1836.

W. E. RANDALL,
(Late W. H. CHICK),

Wine and Spirit Merchant,
BRIDPORT.

Importer of PORTUGESE, SPANISH, RHENISH, and FRENCH WINES and LIQUEURS.

Agent for Max Greger's Hungarian, P. B. Burgoyne & Co.'s AUSTRALIAN WINES, and Superior BRITISH WINES.

Also Bass' Beers, Guiness' Stout in Casks and Bottles, and Jacob's Pilsener Lager Beer in Bottles only.

Single Bottles of Wine and Spirits Supplied. Price Lists on application.

CANADIAN CLUB WHISKY.

Early British wines for sale in Dorset

phenomenon. However, it is all really due to the efforts of certain pioneers that there is a British wine industry today. Edward Hyams planted a vineyard and also wrote a book on viticulture while Ray Barrington Brock researched grape varieties to see which were most suitable for the UK climate. After them came others. Sir Guy Salisbury-Jones established a vineyard at Hambledon in Hampshire and began selling his product in 1955.

Since then progress has been steady with the growth of some really big commercial vineyards counterbalanced by a plethora of smaller, 'lifestyle' operations on a much smaller scale. The combined adoption of modern farming practices and new-world winemaking methods has led to a massive improvement in the wines being made today. Over the last 30 years people have begun to recognise the distinctive UK style, herbaceous and crisp, and wines have stopped being compared automatically with their German or French counterparts. There were some tremendous vintages in the 1980s, and the climate generally has seen an upturn that has been shown most graphically over the past few years. The growing season is now much lengthier and warmer than before. With a vast increase in knowledge, and the invaluable contribution of Plumpton College (one of very few places in the world that has a specialist wine course) UK wines are now winning world awards as acreage under cultivation and production continue to expand yearly.

2

ENJOYING WINES

When it comes to talking about wine in certain company you can often come out feeling somewhat shell-shocked. Critics in particular tend to over-egg the pudding and leave the average wine lover feeling unexpressive and depressed. Kingsley Amis once commented on the ridiculousness of those engaged in verbose displays on the merits of certain wines. Amis believed that you should call wines simply red or white, dry or sweet, pleasant or unpleasant and take care over going any further than that.

Now, I know what Kingsley was saying here, but at the same time I can honestly say that I have *smelled and tasted* figs and even bananas in red wines. The exploration of wine is partly about being able to express what it is you are tasting. You should not feel embarrassed to say it tastes of something familiar to you, just as you should not be afraid to be excited by wine or its enjoyment. Indeed most inexpensive, decent wines do just taste pleasantly fruity, and are not in need of fulsome praise. At the end of the day, wine is, after all, just fermented grape juice.

But *what* grape juice! When I stop to think about the matter I am constantly amazed by the fact that the simple process of fermentation can produce the almost miraculous variety of wines that it does, very few of which taste like grapes. The enjoyment of different wines from all over the world is only enhanced by knowing about their history, geography, geology, how they are made, and by learning to smell and taste them properly. So a brief lesson ...

The deep gold of a dessert wine:
Eglantine North Star

Beautifully coloured rosé
at Three Choirs

The i-spy game

Colour is an integral part of any wine's loveliness and tells you an enormous amount about its age. Reds graduate from purple-pink in youth through brick-red to mahogany. Whites go from water-white with green tints to a deep golden colour (although a deeper colour is also a result of oak-ageing). Rosé shouldn't be left long enough to change colour! All wine browns with age, but if it actually does look brown, you probably shouldn't drink it (unless it's sherry). Finally, bubbly should have a fine, steady stream of bubbles, that you can feel fizzing vivaciously below your tongue upon sipping.

'Smell the wine'

It is important that you register the smell of a wine before tasting it – doing justice to good wine is about taking your time, and the aromas of this drink can be heavenly. When you nose a wine it activates the olfactory senses (basically, your sense of smell) which take a little time (roughly two minutes) to react properly. However it is possible to immediately smell another different wine since that will have another unique pattern. Taking a few deep, swift, sniffs of the wine after your initial attempt will help to determine the strength of character that the wine possesses.

Thick-skinned grapes – Cabernet Sauvignon for example – are more aromatic and have more colour extraction, while thin-skinned grapes are more prone to botrytis and these have great aromas. (See page 190).

Tasting

The juice of grapes is the liquid quintessence to concentrated sunbeams.   Thomas Love Peacock

When you take a good draught of wine in your mouth and swill it around it has an effect on your tongue which detects varying types of taste. The tip detects sweetness, the sides sourness (which in winey terms is called acidity). In drawing in air over your tongue, the volatile characteristics of wine at the back of the throat are magnified allowing you a greater ability to analyse the wine. This accounts for the somewhat bizarre slurping sound that you hear at tastings. It is important to remember that smelling and tasting wine is all down to personal preference; violets and roses have different aromas but it is a purely subjective matter as to which one you prefer. Larger berries produce more elegance than concentration while smaller berries yield more intense flavours, Pinot Noir being a notable exception to this rule. The constituents of wine are acidity, alcohol, tannins, sugar, esters, aldehydes, alcohol and residual sugar which in correct proportions produce balance.

So what in that case is good wine? In no particular order, it should be balanced, lengthy and show good character within its own type or style. What is exciting about UK wines is that they have not yet been rigidly defined so there is room for winemakers to experiment; they can be flexible. On the downside of course, this makes our wines less easy to market as the consumer never knows quite what they are going to get, especially with radically differing vintages.

Good wine deserves care and attention; my experience is that more expensive, better wines take time and air to open up, they change mood and character over the course of an evening, and equally bring about changes of mood and character in ourselves. My old housemate Adam once commented, 'time seemed to take a step back in this house, and everything seemed to take a little longer', and that is how good wine should be appreciated and should make you feel.

Here is wine,
Alive with sparkles – never, I aver
Since Ariadne was a vintager,
So cool a purple.

Endymion *(1818), John Keats (1795–1821)*

Finish, or aftertaste is the lingering effect that remains on the palate after a good wine has been swallowed. It can be dry or flowery, sweet or soft or various other combinations. Many people complain that they dislike the aftertaste of a wine, but this only means that they haven't yet found the wine for them, since a long finish is simply a hallmark of quality. Once you have discovered a wine with good aftertaste, it is sometimes hard to move on to try others.

Varying shades of vine leaf

3
NOTES ON GRAPE VARIETIES

White Grapes

Auxerrois

Can produce fresh creamy-rich wine that fits well with oaking, and can also be a useful part of sparkling wines. Granny Smith apple flavours predominate.

Bacchus

One of the UK's success stories, Bacchus is actually very versatile. When ripe, it has many of the characteristics of Muscat, the wine world's 'grapiest' grape. It is also sometimes lighter and Sauvignon-like but can be too grassy and herbaceous in cool years. High sugar levels make it a successful grape for the UK. It is a Riesling/Sylvaner cross. When aged the Riesling characteristics show more, with fuller peachier flavours. Fourth most-planted variety. Grows high and treelike. Basic flavours and aromas are of nettles and elder-flower.

Chardonnay

Shows increasing promise in England, mainly for sparkling wines. This most flexible of grapes adds lovely full lemony and nutty characteristics to wine, and may well prove to be the creamy contrast to Britain's plethora of unoaked, Sauvignon-like whites in future. At present, ripens fully only in hot years.

Huxelrebe

Herby, grapefruity, elderflowery and easy to drink. Can be quite spicy. Can be too green. Large grapes. Ageworthy. Susceptible to botrytis so can make good dessert wine.

What is man, when you come to think upon him, but a minutely set, ingenious machine for turning, with infinite artfulness, the red wine of Shiraz into urine?

Seven Gothic Tales (1934)

The Dreamers, by Isak Dinesen aka Karen Blixen

Kerner

Takes its name from a 19th-century writer of German drinking songs. Kerner is a useful part of a blend as it buds late (avoiding spring frosts) and has very high acid levels and good aroma. Floral and grapey (like Riesling). Ages well. A pain in the vineyard as it is leafy in the extreme and grows sideways. Has large pale berries.

Madeleine Angevine

Sometimes known as the 'English Grape'. A staple of more northerly vineyards in the UK, but also of the west and southwest, this can be fantastic with lovely apricot flavours in warm years and the ubiquitous elderflower in cooler ones. Also has a lovely, ethereal, floral nose. Crisp acid when correct. Ripens in first week in October. Ages well and usually takes time to develop flavours (four years).

Madeleine Sylvaner

A favourite of some up north. If treated right, not stung by the wasps' appetite and left on the vine this variety is extremely prone to noble rot, and is ideal for those wanting to make dessert wines.

Müller-Thurgau

Can be good with real body and flavour: sweetness combines well with this variety. Unfortunately it is also often thin and overly grassy. Lower acidity than Seyval. Adds grapeyness to blends and still good for marginal climates. Was once the most planted grape in the UK, but much has been grubbed up in the past few years.

Orion

Fruity, aromatic, heavy-cropping and gaining in popularity.

Ortega

Named after the Spanish philosopher, Ortega y Gasset, this can be fat and jammy (zesty too), making splendid pudding wines in the right conditions. As usual, it can be flabby and unripe in cooler years. Adds body and middle to blends. Bad resistance to disease. Bushy-looking vine. Distant cousin to Gewürztraminer.

Phoenix

Full and fruity with a crisp finish. Very disease-resistant. Sauvignon-like.

Pinot blanc

Easy-drinking and tasty in the right conditions. Blackcurrant leaf flavour in youth.

Pinot Gris

Can be flabby and bland, but with enough acidity can be deliciously fruity and does well with or without oak. Should be spicy when good. Tawny coloured grapes and spectacular burnished leaf hues in autumn. Sedate grower.

Reichensteiner

Good blending grape and cropper. Has good sugar and resists rot but flavour-wise is rather bland. Early budding. Reichensteiner seems to develop tropical fruit flavours, or limeyness with age. Third most popular grape. Low acidity.

Schönburger

Can be lovely, with stone fruit flavours and a hint of spice, but can also be dreadful, acidic and green. Highly identifiable in the vineyard during the ripening season as it turns from light lime green to light pink, and when ripe to a tawny brown colour. This aids picking, as the ripest bunches are very recognisable. Difficult ripener further north and birds and wasps enjoy this variety too much.

Seyval Blanc

A staple of the English and Welsh vineyards. Good Seyval Blanc is often similar to Loire Sauvignon Blanc, with delightful, crisp flavours of gooseberry, grass, creamy apple and elderflower, though it ages much better and works with judicious oak-ageing too. Not particularly aromatic. Very late but plentiful cropper (known as 'Save All' in the West Country). Two years' development needed. Rhubarby when young and makes superb English-style bubbly.

Siegerrebe

This can make wines with good body and tangy citrus/orange fruit and a slight spritz. High sugar, and can make both Bacchus like dry wines and dessert wines. Can be flabby. A neat, compact vine. Early (sometimes as early as 2 September) low cropper with sweet, aromatic golden pink-skinned grapes.

Red Grapes

Once, all grape varieties were red, to attract birds in order to spread seeds. The mutant albino strains were cultivated by humans as they were more productive.

Acolon

New red grape. Only just starting to produce grapes in many vine-yards.

Dornfelder

Can make lovely light- to medium-bodied reds, like tinned straw-berries with a silky, treacly texture. Perfumed nose.

Dunkelfelder

Produces highly-coloured blood-red juice. Useful for blending to add colour to reds. Beautiful foliage in the autumn.

Gagarin Blue

Decent Russian red grape. An amateur winemaker's variety reputedly smuggled over here during the Cold War by an Embassy civil servant in return for a box of Biros!

Pinot Noir

An ancient variety known as the 'Heartbreak grape', because it is so hard to get right, both in the vineyard (especially with the English rain and Pinot Noir's tendency to rot) and the winery. Yet we are producing some superb, light, smooth, cherry- and raspberry-flavoured reds in good years. Also a component of many very good sparkling wines. Colour can be a problem in cooler years.

Regent

New red, with good colour and matures well with oak.

Rondo

This has spread massively since its introduction here in 1983. Important red blending grape, for both rosé and red wines. Very early ripening. Skins have somewhat strange taste so perhaps better for rosés than reds. Bizarre history: crossed from Manchurian non-vinifera variety (*Vitis Amurensis*) and Austrian varieties (among them the excellently named Précoce de Malingre). Has dark red skin, ageing potential and sits well with oak. Also high natural alcohol and yield. Soft juicy Merlot/Rioja style.

Triomphe (D'Alsace)

Sweet, small, red-fleshed grapes which can occasionally make earthy Pinot Noir-like wine, at best when displaying hints of coffee. Can be awful and taste rather like dirt, and often best when blended. Provides intense colouring. 'Springers', as Richard at Glyndŵr calls them: massive growth.

Wrotham Pinot (Pinot Meunier)

Named by Edward Hyams at Wrotham in Kent, the grape known as Wrotham Pinot is now definitely known to be one of the Champagne grapes, Pinot Meunier. Fantastic for making sparkling wine in partnership with other grapes. Also known as 'Dusty Miller', probably due to the powdery fleece it has on its leaves.

Picking times at Glyndŵr vineyard: Last week September: Madeleine Angevine. End September–1 week October: Siegerrebe. 1–3 weeks October: Triomphe, Leon Millot, Reichensteiner, Regent. End October: Seyval Blanc.

4

A BOOK OF DAYS:
A YEAR IN THE LIFE OF A VINE

January

Winter pruning. A bit of an art form really. Vines are usually reduced to two to four primary canes. Good pruners know each vine as an individual.

February

Winter pruning.
The weeping vine hanging like gossamer wounds, spider-thin tears. A single vine cane can lose up to four and a half litres of sap during pruning, if it is done while the sap is rising. This does not harm the vines at all.
1 Feb: Partridge and pheasant hunting season ends.
28 Feb: Hind stalking season ends.

Newly planted vines at
Wernddu in Winter

Planting new Phoenix vines
at Thornbury

March

Pruning continues and the vines start to come to life. Over March and April the sap begins to rise and buds begin to form on each stem.

14 March: Coarse fishing season ends.

April

Annual St George's Day Trade Tasting. Look out for reviews of new vintage UK wines around this time.

The canes that have been kept on the vines are now tied down in the direction required. Vines are still dormant. With no leaves to obscure anything this time of year is perfect for those who wish to see how the vines are trained in different manners.

1 April: Fox hunting season ends

13 April: Stag stalking season ends

Leafburst

May

With swifts and swallows arriving on the northerly breezes, the new canes and shoots begin to grow. Shoots, foliage and then tiny flowers appear in a six-week period. Spraying. Vines still dormant in more extreme parts of country. Leaf-burst evident.

Frosty nights in May can nip off the little flowers in the buds which will mean a small harvest. Many producers spend this time of year with anxious eyes on the thermometer and find themselves rushing out at any hour to light the little smudge-pots which keep

Tied down vines at Wernddu

the buds from freezing. The irritating thing is that if the temperature is hovering just around freezing and then rises just the tiniest bit you can end up getting leaf burn which isn't particularly helpful. Add to this the temperature differences between different parts of a slope or vineyard, or even differences between areas of single vines and potential problems can arise.

It is no wonder this time of year is known as the time of the Ice Saints and of the Cold Sophie. If there is a spring frost, costs tend to quadruple and yields are drastically reduced. A -3°c air frost at Tas Valley on 11 May 2005 led to the loss of the entire crop.

June

After the slightly tense period when the Ice Saints could wreck the potential harvest come the long evenings, the beautiful song of the pesky blackbirds, a certain soft smell in the air after light rain. June is the time when the long wait for the vines to progress suddenly takes on a new dimension and the shoots begin to grow by an inch a day after doing almost nothing since bud-burst.

Flowering, spraying, pruning. The vines flower as spring turns to summer but don't expect tremendous leaves; the flowers are really incredibly unimpressive, more like tiny dots. Last year's

The Ice Saints (or Frost Saints)

The feast days of St Mamertius, Pankratius (Pancras), Servatius (Gervais) and Bonifatius as well as St Sophie are known for a cooling trend in the weather. The days used to be from 12–15 May until Pope Gregory VIII altered the calendar in 1582 in order to correct the difference of the Julian calendar to the Sun years, so the feared dates became 19–22 May. These days are the most likely to bring a late frost. This period is also known as The Blackthorn Winter, a phrase mentioned in Thomas Pynchon's *Gravity's Rainbow*.

In olden days farmers and wine growers burned wet wood, green twigs and soil which rose to form a thick, smoky, fog over the valleys. This helped to protect any new growth and blossoms from the frost. Many gardeners and farmers still wait until mid-May has passed before planting seedlings.

Vines flowering

Opposite. Canes growing at Ickworth Walled Garden

Left. Trellising at Three Choirs

Right. Pinot Noir grapes ripening at Ridgeview

Below. Grape bunches begin to form at Tiltridge

newly bottled vintage traditionally goes on sale at around this time of year. The vines are pollinated by the wind, so dry breezy conditions are essential at this point. Summer pruning involves stopping the flowering shoots, usually at the point about 14 leaves beyond each bunch. Side shoots are also removed.

English and Welsh Wine Week

This is usually first week in June. Many of the vineyards across the country hold events to focus attention on the industry giving the visitor the chance to visit places that are not generally open and sample English and Welsh wine. Visit www.englishproducers.com for more information.

July

Flowering continues as pollination does. Rapid cane growth, bunches of grapes start to form. Spraying. At this stage the grapes are still bitter and sour, but the grapey flavours are definitely beginning to develop.

August

Trimming of leaf canopy to allow maximum sunlight to reach the fruit. With any luck the red grapes will start changing colour at some point in the month. Vineyard maintenance continues, the

vines have now been trimmed and look wonderful. With their new slimline profile more light can get to the grapes and the more air that can flow through the canopy, the less chance there is of disease and the better chance of riper grapes.

Spraying weeds and vines to keep disease at bay is also a constant activity. Finally, removing weeds and mowing take place to stop thistles and other unwelcome guests from seeding themselves.

September

Leaves are removed from around the fruit to let in air and sunlight. The grapes swell, ripen, soften and become translucent. Red grapes take on a true red colour. Final spraying.

Wonderful autumn weather means clean, very ripe grapes with high sugar levels. The heat in a preceding year sets the potential cropping for the next year, so a hot year often means a higher crop yield the next. However, this does not dictate the quality of the crop. Ivy flowers at the same time as the grapes and this attracts wasps which is a blessing.

October

The vintage. Harvesting. Pressing and winemaking often keeps people up until midnight or later, particularly in wineries with small presses as they have to make room for the next lot of grapes.

Left. Early Autumn, Sedlescombe

Right. Wheat is harvested just before the wine vintage (overleaf)

Below. Harvest at Thornbury

The Anglo-Saxons called this month Wynmonath, for obvious reasons.

November

The end of the harvest. Vineyard maintenance is now a priority. This is also the time to rest and take a holiday. The vines die back and leaves disappear after the first frosts.

December

Sap levels fall at the first frost which is also needed to kill off any over-wintering diseases. The wine is left to settle in the vats, ready for bottling, usually the following spring. A good hard winter is best for this.

5

VINTAGES

It is hard to describe the excitement of knowing whether a vintage will be good or not. Somehow, the Old World's unpredictability, its wary wait on the weather, and its ability to make great wines in the face of awful conditions, mirrors the vagaries of life itself. This might seem a curious way to put it, but wine has been an integral part of everyday human life since the days when the Pharaohs ruled Egypt. That said, we all crave a little consistency and the unpredictability of wines can be infuriating, particularly if they are expensive!

'Wine, like life, is a fleeting beauty.'

Jonty Daniels,
Astley Vineyard

Recent Vintages

The recent run of warm late-summer and early-autumn weather has ensured good ripening over the last six years, with most vineyards, particularly those using early-ripening Germanic varieties starting to harvest earlier than normal. 2003 was an exceptional year, and is now seen as a turning point for UK vineyards. There is no sign of the good conditions letting up either, my vines on the balcony in London were in full leafy growth by the end of April 2007, and a hot, dry summer was predicted.

2006

Near-perfect growing season. Cold start but no spring frosts. Driest July since 1911 and the sunniest since 1990. An Indian summer. Should be good to exceptional. 20,000 bottles expected at Warden. Hurricane in Leeds. Occasional torrential rain.

2005

Wonderful autumn weather with good ripe grapes. Despite a rather unpredictable summer (very dry), many vineyards had a good quality harvest of reasonable quantity. A few vineyards through

Top. Winter snow at Thornbury

Bottom. Full cycle: young vines at Wernddu

south-central England were unfortunately hit by late frosts which decimated the final crop; some also experienced difficulties at flowering due to the inclement weather. This was not a widespread occurrence and most vineyards were very pleased with the overall quality and quantity of their crop. Sugar levels were moderate to high. Some vineyards reported acids that were a little low: 1.7 million bottles as opposed to average of 1.9 million.

2004

Unseasonable winds in late June, not much spring frost, mixed, rainy (mildew problems) but warm. High yield. Somehow out of this weird mixture came an almost uniformly brilliant year, with high yields (one of the largest ever) and quality. Bizarrely enough, and in sharp contrast to the way things work elsewhere, in the UK a large crop seems to go hand-in-hand with high quality in the grapes.

2003

Hot all summer, a little spring frost. Moist soils. A year that has changed the boundaries for English and Welsh wine. Still, it may actually have been too hot, certainly several winemakers had problems dealing with such ripe grapes. High sugars, luscious wines. The wines typically show a ripeness and a degree of elegance and complexity that has often been lacking in UK wines previously. The vintage also attracted unprecedented levels of press and public attention. Some great reds.

2002

Cold, wet, and wind delayed flowering (end of July) despite good bud-burst and a fine autumn. Good in most places, and many wines worthy of ageing.

2001

No spring frost, but fine summer weather with good flowering in early June. Wet, windy autumn which caused some to harvest early. Those who waited reaped the rewards with excellent wines. Perfect year at Chilford. Good at Astley.

2000

Not a good year, with autumn floods and a wet, pallid, summer. Poor flowering. High yield at Painshill. Halfpenny: first two weeks of July 11–12°c average daytime temp! Later than average harvest into November. Not really a cold enough winter.

Ripening grapes in
A' Beckett's vineyard

1999
Light spring frost, June and July helped things, August damp with hailstorms. Good September. Standout year at Shawsgate, but some disease elsewhere. Generally good quality. Typical mixed-up British weather really.

1998
Rain during flowering and lots of mildew. Good autumn. Highest quality at Llanerch. Better in west than east generally.

1997
Very cold January. Late frosts common, low yield. Bad year at Chilford (one-tenth of usual crop). Good year at Bow-in-the-Cloud. Terrible frosts at Sedlescombe. Those that avoided frost were good.

1996
High yield, average ripeness but superb wines. Largest crop ever at Astley and Llanerch.

1995
Bad spring frosts at Wroxeter, Tiltridge and Halfpenny. Good generally. Hottest summer on record. Excellent quality.

1993
Bad at Tenterden. Coldest winter on record.

1992
Very good year, set up by the previous good summer.

1991
Big, good vintage at Wissett, incredibly late sharp frosts (4–5 June) at many places. Very damaging.

1990
Very sunny July.

1987
Superb at Chilford.

1986 and 85
Bad winters.

1984

Terrible at Chilford, excellent at Chevelswarde. Great year in general.

1983

Superb, really warm year with record harvests.

1975 and 76

Hot summers but wet autumns.

1911, 1947 and 1968

All good years.

Tuesday, 11 April 2006

The year after a great vintage usually brings a good harvest (1983, 1992, 1996, 1904 being examples). 1977, the year of my birth, was a miserable, rainy exception to the rule, coming as it did after the great baking heat of 1976. Much like today really. Spring has descended back from warm beginnings into April showers with cool temperatures (as I write, I have to stop every now and again to warm my hands), hail and even snow outside London. Strange really, that my sales today consist mainly of cigarettes and Champagne.

6

GROWING GRAPES

Grapes need moisture to swell, acidity for flavour and sunshine to develop sugar which turns into alcohol during fermentation. Ideally grapes require the correct combination of heat, sunshine, rain and frost. The following section describes some of the ideal climatic factors that affect viticulture. Bear in mind however that here in the UK many of the theoretical requirements for growing good grapes have been disproven.

Heat

Grapes will not be suitable if the annual mean temperature is less than 10°c (50°f). The ideal mean temperature is 14–15°c with an average of no less than 19°c in summer and -1°c in winter.

Sunshine

Light is required for photosynthesis. There is actually often sufficient light even in cloudy conditions for this to take place. Approximately 1300 hours of sunshine are required and 1500 hours are preferable although most places in the UK do not come near these levels. Short days retard the canes' growth in favour of fruit maturity, an advantage after the vines reach maturity.

Rainfall

A vine needs 68cm of rain per year, ideally mostly in spring and winter, but some is needed in summer too. The less rain in autumn the better, although a quick shower before harvest rinses off chemicals and is ideal if followed by sun and a gentle, drying, breeze. Vines need less water if the temperature is higher, though rain in warm conditions is more harmful than in cool. Torrential rain leads to split berries and fungus, and is becoming much more common in the UK. Close proximity to forests and mountain ranges protects the vines from too much rain, and forests and large masses of water can also provide humidity in times of drought (through transpiration and evaporation) but can also encourage rot.

Frost

Frost in winter hardens the wood and kills pests and spores in the bark, but it can also kill vines particularly at bud-burst and flowering.

General Topography

Aspect

You will often hear owners announce proudly that their vineyard is on a south-facing slope. This is because these slopes attract more hours of sunshine in the northern hemisphere. Because of the angle, vines on a slope absorb more of the sun's rays as it is never directly overhead. Lake and river valley slopes are especially good for vines because the water also reflects the rays. The surface of the water acts as a heat reservoir that releases heat at night, so reducing frost risk and sudden temperature drops. Slopes also provide natural drainage. However, hilltop areas are also harder to work, and are exposed to wind and rain whereas forested hilltops absorb the worst of torrential rain.

For every 100m (330 ft) above sea level, atmospheric temperature falls by 1°c! This can mean 10–15 extra days are needed for the grapes to ripen fully for each extra 100m. Because of the extra time required, acidity increases in the grapes.

Soil

The most important type of soil is the subsoil type which is always determined by the rock base below it. The vine's main roots penetrate several layers of subsoil the structure of which influences drainage, the root system's depth and the ability to absorb minerals. The ideal medium for the vine is a thin topsoil and easily penetrable (well-drained) subsoil as vines don't like 'wet feet'.

In short, warm soils will advance ripening (gravel, sand, loam), good mid-soils would be chalky, cold soils (clay) retard ripening and dark, dry soils are warmer than light, wet soils.

Different types of grapevine respond very differently to different soils, the perfect example being Pinot Noir, Pinot Meunier and Chardonnay, the grapes that make Champagne flourishing on the chalky soils of Sussex and Kent.

Friday, 24 March 2006

It is with some trepidation that I begin.

In exactly one month, I am leaving my job in order to write this book and travel around the vineyards of the United Kingdom. I am filled with doubts. Will I get it published? Have I saved enough money? Do I have the knowledge required? Will my bad back be in agony after six months of constant driving? And why would anyone in their right minds want to write a book about English and Welsh wine? Come to think of it, why would anyone want to *make* wine in the UK?

It is a particularly British madness that drives us to do these things. The very unpredictability of what I am embarking upon is the same thing that drives the people who have started vineyards here in the UK, the challenge of making something unlikely and rather wonderful work, the transformation of unpromising land into a vineyard and of the grapes into wine.

PART TWO

7

WEALD AND DOWNLAND

Kent, East and West Sussex, Surrey and Middlesex

If you were to trace the same chalk seams that form the basis of the soil in the Champagne region of France, you would descend into a basin which falls below the English Channel and rises again at Dover to form those spectacular and famous white cliffs. This region is also known as the Garden of England which might also make a regional appellation name. It is probably the most promising wine region in the UK, with lower rainfall than the West Country and lacking the bitter winds of the east coast, though not as warm as the Thames and Chiltern region. Soils range from clay to chalk, the latter producing the sparkling wines that are just beginning to challenge Champagne's position as the premier sparkling wine of the world. In fact, this fantastic region lies just one degree further north than Champagne.

The best sites for buying Weald regional wines are at www.englishwine.co.uk and www.highdown-vineyard.co.uk

Kent

Tuesday, 25 April

An inauspicious start. Bearsted: closed, Harden: not open to the public, Pembury: not a winery at all but a fruit farm (thank you www.bbc.co.uk), Meopham Valley: owners away until Friday (frustratingly the day I return to London), Penshurst: closed and a sad sight with its fine French-style gate, name wrought into the metal, standing in front of derelict, once proud vines. The now inappropriately named Vine House stands forlornly beside them.

The man who tends the vines at Leeds Castle is not there, so I find myself sitting in the drizzle, with a humungous peacock staring at me from behind one shoulder. Funnily enough, none of this bothers me as it just feels good to be out of London, ever since

The view from Ditchling Beacon, East Sussex.

Penshurst … all quiet.

the slow, grey, drawl of the M25 sloped suddenly into chalk cut-out cliffs with expansive views over the green downs. Anyway, it is a salutary lesson in terms of visiting UK vineyards, always check beforehand that they are still open and that someone will be around before you visit; smaller ones are often run by only one or two people. One bad vintage can be all it takes to wipe out a smaller vineyard; a glance at older UK wine sources proves this fact, though vineyards are tending to stick around rather longer these days.

Anyway, I bought some *Leeds Castle Dry White 2004*, a blend of Schönburger and Seyval Blanc and tried it at my cousin's house. It was clearly aimed at the tourists with its high price, and was still very young and too sharp, but in a year the mouth-watering grape-fruit and citrus flavours will have a chance to shine through. It is one of the few places where a vineyard is planted on roughly the same ground as an historical vineyard; one acre is recorded as having been planted at Leeds by William the Conqueror's brother, Bishop Odo. The vineyard was maintained for at least a couple of centuries, but then lay fallow until 1980. As well as being a fantastic visit with its maze, aviaries and history, Leeds Castle also hosts an annual Festival of English Food and Drink in May.

Peacock at Leeds Castle

Leeds Castle, Broomfield, Maidstone ME17 1PL
Telephone: 01622 765400
Open: daily 10.30–16.00 throughout the year
www.leeds-castle.com

Barnsole

At Barnsole vineyard, much care is taken over canopy management. Large leaves are encouraged in order to gain higher sugars from solar radiation, and vines are placed close to the ground to make the most of soil warmth and give better protection from the elements. This is particularly important as Barnsole is in eastern Kent, near Sandwich, far from the more sheltered Kentish Downs vineyards clustered to the west. This distance is perhaps also a reason for the fact that Barnsole's grapes are not shipped off to Chapel Down vineyard like so many others in the region. Their wine is made and bottled at their own winery, thus retaining all the freshness of grapes just picked. Frost is not a problem here, the coastal breezes mean they have only suffered spring frosts once, in May 1997.

The three acres are capable of producing up to 10,000 bottles a year, an amazing level even after 14 years of production. John Danilewicz has been working in UK wines a lot longer than this though, and 28 years of experience have led him to be particularly fond of Reichensteiner (for consistency) and Huxelrebe (for flavour). Red grapes have recently proven successful, with Rondo, Regent and an early clone of Pinot Noir planted. All the wines have quality status and their *Canterbury Choice* wines are consistently good. That said, the *Kent Classic 2002* and *2003* (Huxelrebe) and the *Red Reserve 2003* have been particularly excellent. One very unusual fact is that in the exceptional 2003 vintage the wines here reached 13.5% alcohol, which in the UK is astonishingly high. Perhaps it is a feature of being one of the closest vineyards to France.

Visitor facilities are good. Free mini-tours and wine tastings are available, along with full guided tours showing how vines are tended and wine is made. Prior arrangement is needed for larger groups.

Fleming Road, Staple,
Canterbury CT3 1LG
Telephone: 01304 812530
Open: 10.30–17.00 every day
April–October. Winter: open most days
10.30–16.00 depending on the weather.
Contact by phone first
www.barnsole.co.uk

Biddenden

Biddenden Vineyard & Cider Works lies down the quaintly named, and indeed quaint-looking Gribble Bridge Lane. On a lovely mid-spring morning I wander through the vines, following the free tour leaflet as rabbits scamper around. At this point in the year (April), the Ortega vines (which comprise half of the plantings) look like dark wiry beings ranked for war, bare-boned with no foliage except the red-budded eyelids that have opened just recently. The base of each vine is kept relatively free of weeds, while the grass between rows is allowed a to develop a plusher shade of green.

Acreage

I've chosen to use acres despite the general tendency to use hectares partly because most UK viticulturalists do and partly because of its historical interest. An acre was fixed by Edward I in 1305 as the amount of land that a man with two oxen could plough in a year. It can support four sheep for a year. A football pitch is about 1¾ acres. 2½ acres = 1 hectare.

At the top of the vineyard there is agricultural land, while the bottom is bordered by a gorgeous pick and mix of trees, including holly and white-blossomed hawthorn. Cuckoos, cockerels and sheep are audible, and flowers deck the dip at the bottom ... this truly is a beautiful site and I can feel my back pain melting away. The grape types listed on the map at the top of the upper field are no longer accurate and it is intriguing to note the ones that they no longer grow, Sauvignon Blanc and Müller-Thurgau. They do still persist with the Beaujolais grape Gamay, though the long-term owner, Julian Barnes commented that it wasn't exactly their most successful.

Biddenden has been going for as long as most, since 1969, and it shows. With their lovely café, plenty of cider and wine-related stuff to look at and a welcoming tasting table with proper tasting glasses, this has to be one of the best vineyards in the country to visit. Julian's parents diversified Biddenden away from apple growing, though the cider making (all with Kentish apples) continues. Their ciders are thoroughly delicious and have won CAMRA awards, and their ordinary apple juice tastes like no super-market apple juice I have ever tasted.

Looking down the vineyard
at Biddenden in April

Julian reckons that the ripening date of the grapes in his vineyard has come forward massively since he started, perhaps by as much as three weeks. He is very proud of their many awards and particularly by winning English Wine of the Year with the *1986 Ortega*. Biddenden Ortega has an intriguing fairytale label of a Hansel and Gretel cottage that came courtesy of an old cinema artist, Dudley Pout, who had retired next door. Back when it was designed, the fashion was to hide the Englishness of English wine with Germanic labelling and bottling, and by contrast to the more modern Gribble Bridge labels the old Ortega design has a historic feel that suits the place.

The *Ortega 2004* is deliciously soft, off-dry, with crisp summery tropical fruit and well-balanced alcohol and acidity. One for a picnic methinks. Also good was the *Dornfelder 2004*, all ripe plums, medium body, slight sweetness and a wisp of smokiness. You should unquestionably try the ciders too. The vintage, Monk's Delight and Special Reserve (matured in ex-Scotch whisky hogsheads) are all lovely and utterly different.

Little Whatmans, Gribble Bridge Lane, Biddenden, Ashford TN27 8DF
Telephone: 01580 291726
Open: March–December, Monday–Friday 10.00–17.00.
Saturday: 10.00–sundown, Sunday: 11.00–17.00, bank holidays: 11.00–17.00.
January–February, Monday–Friday, 10.00–17.00, Saturday: 11.00–17.00, Sunday closed
www.biddenvineyards.co.uk

Chapel Down/Tenterden/English Wines plc

I never know quite which of these names to use, since each means something slightly different. Tenterden vineyard itself was started by Stephen Skelton (one of the godfathers of English wine and indeed English wine-writing) back in 1977. He successfully grew grapes and made wines here at what was called Spots Farm, the Seyval Blancs being particularly good. The large barn was turned into a decent tourist facility and a herb garden was established. The impressive legacy of all this hard work is plain to see despite various changes in ownership, the last of which was the takeover by Chapel Down in 1995. Chapel Down were originally formed in order to source grapes from other vineyards and make wines more professionally than most English vineyards were then doing. The name was taken from Chapel Farm vineyard on the Isle of Wight, but after working first from Rock Lodge then from an industrial site in Burgess Hill, the business became too big to handle and the company ended up buying Tenterden Estate. Recently, Chapel Down has paired up with various other vineyards (notably Lamberhurst) to form English Wines plc, one of the biggest, and most successful wine producers in the southeast.

I pondered this history as I walked along a lovely vineyard trail through the estate after a rather lacklustre reception, the tardy and rather bored response of the staff contrasting unfavourably with

Tenterden Vineyard Park, Small Hythe, Tenterden TN30 7NG
Telephone: 01580 763033
Open: January–February, Monday–Saturday 10.00–17.00.
March–December, Monday–Sunday 10.00–17.00.
Guided tours by appointment
www.chapeldownwines.co.uk

Further Reading

For those who want a much more detailed overview of the UK's vinous history, of grape types and the more technical aspects of the trade, read Stephen Skelton's *The Wines of Britain and Ireland: A Guide to the Vineyards* (Faber & Faber, 2001). Alan Rook's *A Diary of an English Vineyard* (Wine and Spirit Publication Ltd, 1971) is a great little description of what was then the most northerly vineyard in Europe and gives a good impression of how the pioneers operated. For old but detailed and well-written history go to Hugh Barty-King's books about the UK wine trade, *A Taste of English Wine* (1989) being a particularly interesting snapshot of the past state of the trade.

If on the other hand you want more details about how to grow your own grapes then go to your regional association and get the UKVA's advice (see www.englishwineproducers.com/ukva.htm for local contact details) and publications. Alternatively, the following books are pretty good, though both are occasionally confusing; *Successful Grape Growing for Eating and Wine-Making* by Alan Rowe (1998) and *Growing Vines to Make Wines* by N Poulter (1998).

Biddenden's warmth. Still, Chapel Down is smaller and less imposing than Denbies (its main competitor), better cared for and they've actually bothered to produce something worth reading as you wander, in particular the section on grape types. It has a more youthful wine-oriented feel, rather than the chintzy, tea-set feel that grabs you at Denbies.

Fresh herby smells drift from the garden; the vines are weeping sap, the fields all around are bright with rapeseed and huge bumblebees drone by. The vineyard path becomes a little confusing at one point past the tall youthful Chardonnay, up near where the red vines dominate. These 25 acres (a large site for the UK) provide the grapes that go into the Tenterden Estate wines, but are dwarfed by the 180 acres of vineyard in Kent, Sussex and Essex that produce grapes for Chapel Down (the four shields on their wine labels are the emblems of these three counties and St George). The consistent excellence of their wines must then come from something other than good grape growing, though they pay for grapes according to quality, and haven't had a truly bad vintage since the early nineties.

Beyond careful monitoring of grape quality there is one obvious answer for their success, and that is Owen Elias, UK Winemaker of the Year several times over. This blue-eyed, characterful man is a delight to talk to, just as his wines are a diverse delight to splash down the back of one's throat. Personal favourites of mine are the *Chapel Down Bacchus 2004* and *2005*, which are utterly different, the first all gooseberry and grapefruit, and the second deliciously complex with something indefinable on the nose and peachy, nectarine flavours. (My auntie Moira's tasting notes: *Lovely bouquet, slightly petillant, fresh Riesling like taste, refreshing, gd summer drinking and gd with salmon*). On the red front the *Chapel Down Pinot Noir 2003* compares favourably with Pinots from elsewhere in the world, all mellow summer fruit with medium body, soft silky tannins and vanilla finish. The 2004 and 2005 versions of the Pinot will be as good but need a little cellaring to attain their full loveliness. Finally, the *Chapel Down Extra Dry* is a very English sparkling wine, a touch of sweetness, elderflower, appley and light ... perfect for a picnic.

Owen Elias is a frank man, not taken to mincing words and puts it to me, affectionately but with some exasperation, that the English and Welsh wine world is 'run by enthusiasts and lunatics'. His favourite time of year is harvest, in which period he travels around 2–3,000 miles testing grapes and seeing what that year's wines will be like. Owen reckons Bacchus is the one to age, taking on a slight Riesling character after three years or so. He laughs at odd moments, like when I ask if he has noticed the effects of climate change, to which he answers that sugar levels have remained similar but that the harvest times have changed, though he had thought springs were generally getting warmer. He laughed because the 2006 spring was one of the coldest he could remember! Owen and the team at English Wines have been very effective in promoting and producing quality English Wine on a mass scale. They continue to help move the entire industry outside the bounds of what has previously been thought possible, both in quality of wine and in promoting and selling it. Quite apart from all this Chapel Down is a damn good day out as well, especially combined in a 'Garden of England' wine tour with Biddenden and Sandhurst.

Young vines at Chapel Down

Groombridge,
Tunbridge Wells TN3 9QG
Telephone: 01892 861444
Open: 31 March–3 November,
11.00–dusk
www.groombridge.co.uk

Groombridge Place Gardens and Enchanted Forest

Beneath a tree-topped hill above the Kentish weald lies the small Groombridge vineyard, part of a set of beautiful gardens that lie on the Kent/Sussex border. The vineyard is not a key part of the estate, and one suspects that many of the grapes get eaten by tourists rather than getting turned into wine. Planted with Schönburger and Seyval Blanc, the vines have not yet been tied down and I suspect they are not the gardener's first priority, which is no great shame given the lovely condition of the *gigantic* estate as a whole. They will look lovely enough in the summer too, especially the trellised tunnel (currently bare and rusted) through which you can walk. The verges between the vines are covered in daisies and the views are truly stunning. The house is well worthwhile as well and you can also enjoy the canal boats, bird of prey demonstrations, tepee, secret gardens, giant swings, assault course ... the list is endless. There is no official free tasting but I did get to try the *Groombridge Place Dry White*, which was from 2001 and was crisp, decent but a bit old. Still, a lovely place, and make sure you see the giant rabbits and the zedonk (a cross between a zebra and a donkey!)

The sloping vineyard at Groombridge

Gusbourne Estate

Another recent vineyard, planted with the traditional Champagne grapes: 50% Chardonnay, 30% Pinot Noir and 20% Pinot Meunier. This Kentish vineyard has just had its first harvest of 30 tonnes of grapes. Like other bubbly specialists, they intend to mature the wine for some time and the expected release date of *Gusbourne Sparkling* is around 2009–10. The plan is to open to the public and to build a winery, though for the time being the wines will be made at Ridgeview so quality should be high. The vineyard manager Jon Pollard used to work for Majestic, then studied at Plumpton College and is looking forward to producing some good sparkling wines.

Griffin Farm, Appledore, Ashford TN26 2BE
Telephone: 01233 758666
Not yet open to the public

Harbourne

The first UK vineyard to have a website (lovely photos, well worth taking a look) has had some great press over the years. This is particularly impressive given its small size and the fact that all the wines produced are grown, made and bottled by the owner Laurence Williams at Harbourne. Only hand-picking and manual basket presses are used and traditional methods are employed throughout the grape-growing and winemaking processes. Planted in 1979 in an area of southeast England that was noted in Roman times for the quality of its wines, Harbourne is also a part of a designated Kent Wildlife Site. The vineyard is 15m above sea level, 10 kms from the English Channel on a gentle southeast slope at High Halden. The soil is a medium loam over Wealden clay. A high-trained, double-curtain system permits good air circulation and maximum exposure of the fruit to the sun allowing maximum ripeness of fruit. Because of the height of the fruit, frost is less of a problem and the vines are able to take full advantage of the beneficial climate. The long growing season allows the grapes to assimilate the delicate flavours and aromas that are the hallmark of Harbourne wines. The vines are always pruned hard to reduce the crop and ensure good quality.

Wittersham, Tenterden TN30 7NP
Telephone: 01797 270420
Contact beforehand to check they are open
www.harbournevineyard.co.uk

In the winery manual basket presses are used to gently squeeze the juice from the hand-picked and selected grapes avoiding the risk of off-flavours in the wine caused by crushed pips and stalks. The wine is gently filtered and aged in bottle for at least two years before being released for sale. The range of wines for sale is impressive, and Harbourne specialise in long-period bottle ageing. They have many old vintages (some 10-year-old wines), and UK grapes really do age particularly well, acids and flavours balancing beautifully as they grow older.

Hush Heath

Hush Heath Manor,
Cranbrook TN17 2NG
Telephone: 020 7479 9500
www.balfourbrut.com

Hush Heath Manor have just released the first vintage of their one and only vinous product, Balfour Brut Rosé 2004 and it is stunning. Not many get things so right first time, but then with Master of Wine Stephen Skelton, and Owen Elias (Chapel Down's winemaker) helping out, there is no doubt that the 9,000 bottles of Balfour Brut being produced each year should continue to be high in quality. Salmon-pink in colour, and racing with lasting flavours and aromas of strawberries, raspberries and subtle yeastiness, it is the best pink bubbly in the UK. Not to mention the fact that it knocks the spots off most rosé Champagnes, many of which I have found to be incredibly lacking.

Spectacular Hush Heath Manor is perched on high with the whole of Kent in its view. Founded in 1503, the Tudor timber-framed manor is soaked in English history and is the home of property mogul Richard Balfour-Lynn who set out to begin the only UK vineyard dedicated to the creation of rosé sparkling wine, one he wanted to be 'uniquely light, entertaining and fun'. The Wealden Clay that overlies the Tunbridge Wells sands gives the vines ideal conditions for establishment and fruiting, with enough moisture even in dry seasons. A system of underground drainage pipes was initially installed to remove excess spring rainfall, and the topsoil was meticulously prepared to break up compacted areas and remove any old tree roots. Luscious gardens, statue-lined terraces, Japanese ponds and ancient oak woodland provide the backdrop to perfectly manicured vineyards and orchards. Pinot Noir, Pinot Meunier and Chardonnay grapes flourish amidst orchards blossoming with Bramleys, Cox orange pippins and Egremont russets – each apple is individually tended, handpicked at perfect ripeness, pressed and bottled as their delicious Hush Heath apple juice.

Lamberhurst

Ridge Farm, Lamberhurst TN3 8ER
Telephone: 01892 890000
Tours daily 10.00–17.00
www.newwavewines.com/vineyards/
lamberhurst.asp

Lamberhurst will forever be associated in my mind with leaping about in excitement on a hilltop in Kent after being told that my friend Anna was pregnant. There is no tour as such which is a shame as Lamberhurst Priory (as the vineyard was once known) has an illustrious place at the forefront of England's vinous history. You are able to wander around the fenced-off vineyard, which tumbles over the edge of a (very unusually for the UK) north-facing vineyard that is sheltered from the prevailing south-westerly winds, and is prettily situated above green fields filled with dairy cattle. Established in 1971 by a member of the McAlpine construction company it has since passed to numerous other owners, most recently becoming part of English Wines plc. They seem to be using it more as a source of grapes albeit with a great restaurant (the Swan at the Vineyard) and a grimly-painted pink tearoom, than as an attraction for visitors.

This seems particularly sad given Lamberhurst's historical position as an innovator, although admittedly not always for the better. Lamberhurst's 'British Wines' of the early eighties, which included imported grape juice from Germany were a precursor to today's boxed British wines which are actually made from poor quality Cypriot grapes and have nothing to do with true English and Welsh wines. Lamberhurst followed this damaging idea with the decent home-grown *Lamberhurst White* in the early 80s at an unbelievable £1.99 and for the first time, true English wine was on the shelves of supermarkets across the country. Good harvests brought success and the vineyard was also one of the first to buy in grapes from other vineyards to bolster its own supply. It was, during this period, not only the largest UK producer but also won many awards for the quality of its wines. After the nineties, one hopes that the new partnership with Chapel Down may improve their tourism operation and help them to re-establish the professional operation that helped push our wines into the mainstream UK market.

As for the wines, well, quality is very consistent, as ever with Owen Elias's wine. Mind you it is hard to separate out the wines from Chapel Down's as the Lamberhurst label may well not mean that the grapes were grown on that specific estate so don't expect any hint of *terrior*. Still, all three wines are tasty, the lemon-yellow *Sovereign* is easy-going, peachy and just off-dry with a hint of limey Australian riesling, while the Rondo is a great food wine, with dry dark cherry flavours, spicy wood and good length. I would drink it with some kind of a stew, or perhaps herb-crusted chicken.

Meopham Valley

You may go straight past Meopham Valley vineyard as it is situated in the middle of Meopham village and is practically invisible, just one house among many with a sharp turn in to the drive. Once there, you will receive a warm welcome from David and Pauline Grey who are passionate about their wines. Herein lies the chance to try unusual grape types, including single varietal Chardonnay and Pinot Gris. The vineyard grows organic grapes too, and has had some very successful wines over the years.

Norway House, Wrotham Road, Meopham DA13 0AU
Telephone: 01474 812727
Phone beforehand. Open Friday and Saturday 11.00–dusk, some Sundays
www.meophamvalleyvineyard.co.uk

White blossom beside the vines

Sandhurst

Sandhurst is a lovely little place, with its thatched guesthouse, traditional-style wine-tasting barn and wandering hop fields and vineyards perfect for a meander (beware of the bird-scaring shots). The hops under their criss-cross wiring are a bizarre sight, akin to giant cat's cradles. It is worth going right to the end of the dirt track just for a look at the cherry blossom in full bloom when I visited. Mrs Nicholas is a lady of the old school, slightly patrician but very friendly and down to earth. If you prebook as a group you can get your hands on her delicious ploughman's lunches. Her son has taken over ownership of the farm nowadays and the wines are made, as they have been for almost 20 years at Tenterden. The sheep that once roamed may have disappeared but the hops have not and Sandhurst still also make two of their own beers, Legend and Tradition. The former is named after a story about the bridge just down the lane, referred to by locals as the White Lady Bridge.

Legend has it that many years ago, a bride was thrown from her husband's horse at the bridge after an argument on her wedding day. She was found floating in the stream the next day in her wedding dress. Prior to machine picking, cockneys who picked hops at Hope House Farm would frequent the inn at Link Hill, Sandhurst over the weekends. One Saturday night a young farm worker told the story of the white lady to the Londoners. Leaving the pub a few minutes early he waited in the dark at the bridge wearing suitable attire and when the Londoners left the pub in good voice, they were accosted by a vision in white which ran wailing and shrieking down

Crouch Lane, Sandhurst,
Cranbrook TN18 5PA
Telephone: 01580 850296
Easter–Christmas, Monday–Friday
14.00–16.00; Saturday 11.30–18.00;
Sunday 12.00–15.00

the rows of hops near the bridge. The next day all the talk was of seeing 'the White Lady!'

The older wine labels which show Sandhurst clocktower were drawn by the art master down in the village school and have a certain faded English elegance that suits the locale. The wines themselves are excellent, each one very different from the last and very reasonably priced. They also make a late-harvest dessert wine given the right conditions. Picking wines out is difficult, but I'd plump for the *Kentish Medium Dry 2003*, which is – rather unusually – a top-class winter-drinking white, all spicy apples and hints of butterscotch. Fantastic value for money is the Pinot Noir 2003 which is packed with smooth cherry and strawberry fruit and has a bright lengthy finish.

Smoke drifts from above the Sandhurst vineyard

The Mount

The Mount is a new vineyard, planted in 2004 with seven different varieties and their first small crop arrived with the 2006 vintage, when the weather was hot and dry apart from the wet August. I'm particularly intrigued to see whether the large local population of ring-necked parrots causes them any problems – if they prove to have the same tastes as parakeets (see Painshill Park), then there may well be some friction!

Church Street, Shoreham, Sevenoaks TN14 7SD
Telephone: 01959 524008
Open by appointment only

Throwley

Duncan Wilson's lifelong interest in wine became rather harder work when he purchased his house in Kent in 2000, as the property came with a vineyard. It was originally planted in 1986 with Pinot Noir, Chardonnay and Ortega, the old Pinot Noir vines producing a lovely red in the warmth of 2003. The bottle-fermented bubbly they make is probably consistently the best wine though. Like others I spoke to, Duncan drew attention to the strange counterpoint of viticultural life, the contrast between the quiet loneliness of pruning changing to the noisy camaraderie of picking as something he relishes.

In the sixties and seventies there was apparently no question of what the biggest pest was, the same response could be heard every-where ... starlings. While I found that starling populations elsewhere in the UK have declined dramatically, and they are now rarely cited, here at Throwley flocks of up to 10,000 starlings still decimate the fruit. In 2005, they were so bad that they were left with no Chardonnay at all.

The Old Rectory, Throwley, Faversham ME13 0PF
Telephone: 01795 890276
Open by appointment only

57

EAST SUSSEX

Barnsgate Manor

Herons Ghyll,
near Uckfield TN22 4DB
Telephone: 01825 713366
Shop open: daily 10.00–17.00
(or dusk if earlier)
www.barnsgate.co.uk

The manor house at Barnsgate is 500 years old, and the vineyard itself is rather older than most in the UK. When it was planted in the seventies Barnsgate was one of the biggest British vineyards, though it turned out to be something of a white elephant with production not matching expectation in the damp, poor summers after start-up. Still, it has survived in scaled-down form and is now part of a complex that puts on events, weddings, conferences etc. It's worth popping into the shop on your way down to the more visitor-oriented vineyards of East Sussex.

Battle Wine Estate

Leeford Vineyards,
Whatlington TN33 0ND
Telephone: 01424 870449
Open: by appointment only
www.battlewineestate.com

Battle Wine Estate is located at Leeford Vineyards, not much further than an arrow's flight from Battle and its historic abbey and battlefields. The vineyard was established by the Sax family in 1982 and is larger than average, stocking various quality outlets such as local Waitroses and the National Trust. Saxon Red is easy, light and deliciously fruit-driven with a rich cherry palate, while the whites are distinctive and easy-drinking. The name Saxon is part historical, part to do with the family name. Battle wines are well-regarded as being good-value and decent year in, year out. Finally worth a mention is the distinctive arched label with its Saxon helmet.

Breaky Bottom

Breaky Bottom is probably as close to an English pastoral idyll as vineyards get. It is quite simply, a magical place. It has a cracking name, simultaneously traditional and humorous. Though your car may struggle up the steep broken farm track that leads to it (I wouldn't recommend trying it in poor weather), you'll probably stop several times just to admire its beauty. The view stretches for miles, and on hitting the top you descend and a sudden dip to the left reveals the very edge of a vineyard buried in a fold between the hills. This is the scene that the elegant label displays, an elegance matched by the wines.

Rodmell, Lewes BN7 3EX
Telephone: 01273 476427
Open: 10.00–18.00 or dusk, phone first
www.breakybottom.co.uk

UK Wine Labels

English and Welsh Wine labels are very rarely dull. In sharp contrast to the predictable château labels that grace almost every French bottle, or the unimaginative labelling of most European countries, UK producers have, as a rule, adopted with gusto the idea of telling stories, portraying stylised images, and generally making their labels as interesting and colourful as possible. Of the labels that are sadly no more my favourites were the art-deco labels of Hidden Spring vineyard in Sussex, as collectible as the wines were tasty. Eccentricity runs throughout the UK wine trade and labelling is no exception.

A selection of UK bottled wines

A feature of Breaky Bottom wines is their longevity. Tasting their *1999 Sparkling Seyval* was a revelation; gone were the crisp fresh apples of youth and in their place came an astonishing Champagne-like flavour, particularly on the finish. If anything, though it was less heavy, less yeasty, but fresher and just as fine. Proof yet again that many of these much-derided 'English' grapes are capable of incredible beauty and complexity after a few years in bottle. Breaky Bottom are also deservedly regarded for their still *Seyval Blanc*, and while the nose of the 2003 was delicately elderflowery and nutty, the palate had something indefinably lovely, almost austere about it. And as if to add to my impression of varietals that are the *bête noire* of most critics, even the *Müller-Thurgau 1996* was good, all orange and nut flavours, a good one for a snowy post-Christmas day with left-over turkey and fruit begging to be eaten up. You could follow it up with a drop of the lightly-honeyed *Late Harvest 1999* too, if you've got a bit of Wensleydale to munch.

The reason that these wines have so much to offer is clear; Peter Hall, the grower and maker knows exactly what he is doing. Letting the grapes ripen fully, and with minimal winemaking interference he shows what these supposedly inferior grape types can do. This is especially so with regard to Seyval Blanc, the grape which seems to find a true expression of greatness here on the chalky soil of the downs. Perhaps the vines, first planted in 1974, appreciate the great efforts of their keeper, who over the years has had to put up with just about every type of calamity, from flooding and drifting chemical sprays to pestilential badgers. He has persisted and it really does show in this exceptional vineyard.

The wonderful view from
Breaky Bottom

Carr Taylor

Carr Taylor is an old vineyard renowned for its sparkling wines which are frequently mentioned in the esteemed company of Ridgeview and Nyetimber (though it also produces four fine still wines). It dates back to 1971, and is a large vineyard with just under 40 acres. Back then, the decision to grow grapes was made simply on the basis that the land around the farmhouse was too small to give them a good rate of return on cereals. Of the other options, vines seemed to be one of the better, despite being relatively untested at that time.

The warm summer of 2003 has proved a high point thus far, with exceptionally ripe grapes and lovely clean wines. Other years that stood out were 1986, when the vineyard produced around 186,000 bottles, around three times as many as normal, and 1996 with its high yield, and a harvest that stretched well into November. That year produced Winery Manager Alex Carr-Taylor's personal favourite wine, the *Alexis 1996*, a Würzer/Bacchus cross with a touch of Ortega, a beautiful grassy, Sauvignon-like wine. More recently, the *Brut Sparkling* possesses lovely fruit and subtle toastiness. Regarding climate change he comments that historically harvest began within the first week to ten days of October, with picking continuing through to early November. Over the last five years however, it has moved earlier and earlier until in 2005 they began on 20 September, and in 2006 on the 19th, almost three weeks earlier than they used to. In the same way 2006 picking finished on 19 October, again the earliest finish ever.

I can put the state of the UK wine scene no better than to use Alex's own words, and anyone thinking of starting a vineyard would do well to bear the following in mind:

> We have been involved with English wines right from their very early days and have seen more trials and tribulations than most. Growing and making wine in the UK is not the romantic continental idyll that many people might imagine. It is bloody hard work. We have weathered recessions, worked an awful lot for love and not money, been the butt of jokes, tolerated the amateur retired Major image in the early years and fought tooth and nail to keep the business afloat.
>
> However, for the first time in those 30 years we are beginning to see a change in people's attitudes to English wines. They are being taken more seriously by the critics, the press and the public, we no longer feel

Wheel Lane, Westfield, Hastings TN35 4SG
Telephone: 01424 752501
Open: seven days a week throughout the year (10.00–17.00) except between Christmas and New Year. There is a shop and tours and tastings can be organised
www.carr-taylor.co.uk

the need to justify ourselves or prove that it can be done in this country. The tide is subtly changing. We now have a viable business in which all the family are working and the future for English wines is looking very bright.

Davenport

Limney Farm, Castle Hill,
Rotherfield TN6 3RR
Telephone: 01892 852 380
www.davenportvineyards.co.uk

Will Davenport is one of the UK's finest winemakers, not only of his own wines but those he successfully produces for other vineyards. While the winery is in East Sussex, Will's original 15-year-old Horsmonden vineyard is in Kent (hence the confusingly named but gorgeous *Horsmonden Limney Dry White*). Davenport now comprises 12 acres of organically grown grapes on the original site (which somehow manages to avoid any spring frosts) and at Limney Farm near Rotherfield. At the former they grow aromatic varieties, while the Sussex site (where the Romans once smelted iron ore) concentrates on grapes for their bubbly.

The modern winery, which is in an old dairy farm, is well-equipped though in keeping with his general organic sustainable bent, treatment of the wines is minimal. All this professionalism does not stop Will from being passionate about his wines and it shows in the gorgeous flavours that shine like sunshine from his wines. The Davenport website is well worth a look if you interested in organics and growing, the past newsletters being particularly informative.

While the *Limney Estate Sparkling* has a nutty goodness, for me it is the aforementioned *Horsmonden Dry White* that stands out. It is utterly different from any other wine, the 2006 vintage possessing an intense autumnal, faintly smoky nose together with a beautiful, deep, lengthy palate that I really can't put into words. Try it, and be blown away.

The English Wine Centre

Sunday, 3 September 2006
The 32nd English Wine and Regional Food Festival

Christopher Ann is not only the owner of the English Wine Centre, a shop devoted to English Wines, but also the organiser of the English Wine Festival, the first of which took place back in 1975. He has been heavily involved in all aspects of wine since the seventies, especially as part of the UK Vineyard Association. Attending the

Festival on an autumnal day in September with grey mists and fog rolling across the Sussex Downs, and occasional bursts of rain and sunshine, I can see that it will be a lasting memorial to his years of effort. It has recently returned to Alfriston and the EWC where Christopher held it back when precious few people had ever heard of English wine. The festival has helped to provide an annual event to focus attention on the UK wine industry through the years.

The EWC shop sells a magnificent range of wines (and other assorted goods) from the UK. The staff are excellent, I was warmly received, offered a tasting (which I gratefully accepted of course) and was treated to knowledgeable chat about the different wines and producers. Also part of the complex is a very small museum, containing historical artifacts from UK wine production which could perhaps be expanded and overhauled to give it a more modern and informative look. On the other hand, it is free. The museum is part of Walton's Barn, a 1670 Surrey edifice that was rescued from demolition and moved here wholesale. It is now a venue available for functions and has a bar and good food available. The EWC is now up for sale, and I'll be interested to see what innovations the new owners come up with. I just hope they maintain the standard of good service to the UK wine trade that the centre has shown over the past 30–40 years.

As for the festival (running from Saturday–Sunday), it is not only the site of much frivolity, over-consumption and purchase of

English Wine Centre,
Alfriston BN26 5QS
Telephone: 01323 870164
Open: 2 January–23 December,
10.00–17.00
www.englishwine.co.uk

Autumn mist settles over Sussex on the day of the Wine Festival

The Booker's stand at the
Wine Festival, 2006

all sorts of food and drink, but has its very own wine competition.
This includes not only a professional panel tasting, the results of
which are announced on the Saturday afternoon, but also a
visitor's choice, the chance for the ordinary punter to have their
say.

The seasonal showers did not deter people from attending, not
when there was a bubbly bar with live jazz, a hog roast, grape-
treading and a host of stalls with everything from the most astonishing single-estate olive oils to Indian pickles; home-made ice
cream and traditional English fruit wines to keep them going.
There was also a second-hand book stall with a fantastic collection
of old food, drink and UK wine-related material, and the Sussex
Churdle stand selling pies made to a historic recipe baked in the
shape of a Bishop's Mitre. As for vineyards, there were 13 different
exhibitors with a host of great wines. Another important point ...
the signs for the toilets were brilliant!

2006 Wine Festival Winners

Wine of the Show	Biddenden Ortega 2005
Dry White 1st	Biddenden Ortega 2005
Oaked White 1st	Warnham Vale The Gap 2004
Medium Dry 1st	Iron Railway Old Tramway 2005
Sparkling 1st	Kemps Brut
Rosé 1st	Biddenden Gribble Bridge 2005
Red 1st	Bookers Pinot Noir 2004
Dessert/Late Harvest 1st	Breaky Bottom Late Harvest 1999
Public Wine of the Show	Warnham Vale The Gap 2004

Opposite.
Grapes ready for treading

Henner's

Church Road, Herstmonceux,
East Sussex BN27 1QJ

This is a newly planted vineyard which will be producing sparkling wines. The first wines are expected to be on sale in late 2011, a good indication of the length of time vines take to get going, especially if you want good fizzy wine.

Hobden's

Wellbrook Hall,
Mayfield TN20 6HH

Another new Sussex vineyard, Hobden's is about to come into production of … you've guessed it, sparkling wines. It grew from the combined wish for a working countryside life, a tangible product and bubbly. I look forward to sampling some of the wines when they appear in a couple of years.

Plumpton College

Plumpton College, Ditchling Road,
Plumpton, near Lewes BN7 3AE1
www.plumpton.ac.uk

For more information on
Plumpton's Wine Studies Courses
contact Chris Foss
chris.foss@plumpton.ac.uk

Plumpton College, founded in 1926, has been at the heart of the improvement in UK winemaking and grape growing. There are not too many people with vineyards who have not attended some Plumpton course or taken advice based on Plumpton research. The wine courses taught are only part of what is a fully-fledged agricultural college which has practical applications and teaching at the centre of all its activities. Various wine-related courses are run and the ever-increasing acreage of the vineyards (several sites have been planted under the looming rain-shadow created by the Sussex Downs) are taken care of and then vinified by the students under the careful eye of Chris Foss (Head of Wine Studies), Peter Morgan (Winemaker) & Kevin Sutherland (Vineyard Manager). There is a new, well-equipped winery and a dedicated tasting room, and the wines seem to get better every year.

Winter pruning at Plumpton College

Plumpton's 2006 harvest began on 3 October (a week earlier than in 2005) with the Regner and Triomphe varieties and finished on 26 October with the final loads of Seyval Blanc. In spite of the onset of cooler weather and some heavy rains, the six hectares yielded 20.5 tonnes, breaking the 17-tonne record set the previous year. This should make up to 18,000 bottles of wine. Initially, some excellent quality fruit was harvested, particularly Pinot Noir and the aromatic white varieties (Bacchus & Schönburger), but as the vintage progressed, weather conditions became increasingly wet and humid, increasing levels of botrytis especially in the Ortega, Reichensteiner and some of the Seyval Blanc. Selective picking in the vineyard made sure that sugar levels, acidity and flavours were still good in the latter part of the harvest.

In the winery, fruit is lightly pressed to optimise quality while varieties destined for sparkling wine (Pinot Noir, Chardonnay and Seyval Blanc), are pressed uncrushed. Red wine varieties are given gentle pump-overs and short skin contact times during fermentation to optimise soft fruit character, and are matured in oak in order to fill out flavour and depth. Aromatic whites are left on their lees for a few weeks to give them extra body and flavour while red and sparkling base wines undergo malolactic fermentation, which produces an easier-going acidity and increases complexity. In 2005 the College winery produced its excellent first vintage of American-oaked Ortega, which sells exclusively in Hakkasan's Michelin-starred restaurant. Their *Cloudy Ridge* range is also particularly decent (especially the *Rosé* and *Red*), and new plantings are currently concentrating on Champagne varieties and reds.

Ridgeview

Ridgeview Wine Estate lies in the shelter of the Sussex Downs, sloping gently southwards towards them. These high hills keep things comparatively dry, with mild winters and hot summers combining with the limestone and chalk soils to produce some truly lovely wines. Often talked of in the same breath as Nyetimber when quality English sparkling wine is discussed, Ridgeview's

A tractor at work in the lower field

Right. Spraying the vines

Below. Mike Roberts with the new
Coquard wine press

Bloomsbury 2002 won International Sparkling Wine of the Year in 2005. Mike Roberts, the joint owner (with his wife Christine) and winemaker is a singular character who used to work in the computer industry and believes fervently in the future of Merret. Merret is the name he would like to see used internationally for English Sparkling Wines of a certain quality, with the same stringent controls applied as for Champagne.

Ridgeview began commercial sales in 2000 and immediately began to pick up awards for their traditionally made wines, which use the classic blend of Chardonnay for backbone and finesse, Pinot Noir for body and depth, and Pinot Meunier for richness of fruit. Mike comments that the latter grape is often underrated, and is the secret weapon of Champagne, with its early ripening and capacity for ageing gracefully, the latter being something often attributed only to the other two grapes.

While the climate is generally good here, Ridgeview still struggles with disease but a thorough spraying program generally deals with it. As for animals, they encourage foxes to keep the rabbits off, while there isn't much to be done about the birds making origami from the vine leaves. Mike chooses to ignore his two Labradors' fondness for grapes and lets them have their share. 2006 had been good so far when I visited. No frost, and flowering over and done within a week, though warm nights and humidity meant extra care and attention against the downy, powdery mildew (the latter being a problem for the Chardonnay grape in particular). Still, he comments that people used to say you couldn't even grow Chardonnay in this country. The problem was they weren't asking whether you could grow it for sparkling wine, because acidic, bland Chardonnay makes terrible still wine, but great sparkling wine.

And great wine it certainly is and it really depends on what you're doing as to which of the wines you pick. Personally I like the *Grosvenor 2001* (100% Chardonnay) with its bready, richly delicious palate and light floweriness, it would be good with food. If on the other hand you just want to sit and swig and chat, I'd go for the *Cavendish 2003*, with a slightly sweeter touch, and lovely citrus and tropical notes.

The various Ridgeview products are widely available and currently sell from Waitrose, Laithwaites, the *Sunday Times* Wine Club and various other stockists. Being so near to the capital helps, and the vineyard even has its own Circle of Merret, a club for fans of the wine. Everything about Ridgeview wine is carefully considered, from the distinctively shaped label ('We wanted it to be instantly spottable, like Brown Brothers wines.') down to the recent dropping of the word 'cuvée' from the Merret bottle, to make it more English.

They now have a brand-new Coquard press, a massive beast of a thing and the same top-quality equipment that is used in France. It is, as one might expect, ferociously expensive. Mike thinks that we are currently on the same curve as the New Zealand wine industry was with Sauvignon Blanc in the 80s. He anticipates that by 2015 there will be around 4½ million bottles of British bubbly produced every year and exports will rise accordingly. Champagne houses have already started buying up land here, always a sign that things are really going somewhere (a similar situation when New Zealand, Australia, Chile and California became prominent). I can't see how this driven man can fail to succeed really, and I'm certain his business acumen will see Ridgeview through to many more successes.

Sedlescombe Organic

Sedlescombe vineyard is a fantastic day out. It is the largest organic vineyard in the UK and also produces cider, apple juice and fruit wines, all of which are as tasty as its wines. It is also one of the oldest, founded in 1979 (Chevelswarde in Leicestershire pips it by four years). Only natural manures and mineral sprays are used to

Fragbarrow Lane, Ditchling Common, Hassocks BN6 8TP
Telephone: 04258039
Open: by appointment all year round
www.ridgeview.co.uk

Dr Merret vs Dom Perignon vs Blanquette

The birth of sparkling wine traditionally revolves around a French monk, Dom (Father) Perignon who is supposed to have invented the art of bottle-fermented bubbly in the 1690's. Legend in Languedoc, however, suggests that he stole the technique while travelling north from Spain from the monks of the Benedictine abbey of Saint-Hilaire, near Limoux, who had been producing a bottle-fermented sparkling wine since the 1530s. Today this is sold as Blanquette. Furthermore, in 1662, Dr Christopher Merrett compiled *The Mysterie of Vintners* and presented it to the Royal Society in London as a guide to the treatment of wines in bulk. 'Our wine-Coopers of later times use vast quantities of Sugar and Molasses to all sorts of Wines, to make them drink brisk and sparkling ... '

Is it any surprise we Brits drink so much of it?

stave off disease from their large holding (several acres of which of are at nearby Bodiam Castle). One thing you may wish to consider doing is joining the Willing Workers on Organic Farms scheme (www.organicenglishwine.co.uk), which means you can go and help out with the running of the vineyard. Sedlescombe itself is fantastically set up with a lovely tour of the vineyard, ancient bluebell-filled woodlands with a nature trail, plentiful wildlife and well-marked points of interest.

The whole place has something fantastically eccentric and English about it which is ironic as a key part of the equation after the inimitable owner Roy Cook is his friendly German wife Irma. Mind you she comments that she doesn't actually like German wines much and prefers the drier English styles of wine. In keeping with this 'try anything attitude' is the fact that they built their house themselves through a succession of heavy rain, electricity cuts and gales. Even the site is different; Roy featured on a history program uncovering the anti-tank defences (there are still pill boxes around the vineyard) placed at Cripp's Corner in case of German invasion. He inherited the farm from his grandfather, and grew organic vegetables before grapes. Things have definitely got easier lately too, with five of the hottest summers in recorded history in the last 12. Picking gets later every year, giving the grapes maximum sugar levels. Autumn is often the loveliest time of year,

Cripps Corner, Sedlescombe, Robertsbridge TN32 5SA
Telephone: 01580 830715
Open: Easter–Christmas 10.00–18.00;
Christmas–Easter: weekends 12.00–17.00
www.englishorganicwine.co.uk

Through the trees to the lower vineyard

Opposite top. Sunlit vines from Pine ridge

Opposite bottom. The tasting room

71

with amazing sunsets to add to what is already an appealing vista with its rolling green hills and view out over trees all the way to Battle. Sedlescombe used to be called Pine Ridge.

The wines are not cheap, but given the amount of effort it takes to make the wines to organic standard on such a large holding, this is not surprising. What may surprise people is the standard of the wines that are here, from the delicious *Bodiam Harvest Medium Dry*, which has weight, length, and a lusciously tangy, lemon-curdy palate. It is one of my girlfriend's favourite English wines, and with its drier finish sits well with a range of foods. The other wines range from a smoky, apple-flavoured dessert wine to a grassy, dry white, rosé and white sparkling and a delicious bramble and tobacco *Regent* red. A new *Pinot Noir 2004*, with dark morello cherries is chompy and good. The reds will age nicely too, and will be even better in a couple of years.

The difficulties of organic growing should not be underestimated, and Roy Cook's achievement in establishing this vineyard is a model to be followed. Perhaps at the end of your visit you might care to try and guess the number of bottles that the antique 1912 vertical basket press holds (they actually used it up until 1991).

Sol Solis Leo Vinting

www.sslvinting.com

John Murison is a winemaker without a vineyard, a fairly unusual venture for the UK. But if you taste his *Albesco*, a 100% Schönburger from grapes grown at Nutbourne, you wouldn't know it. The bottle, for a start, is astonishing with its vivid double-sided label on one side so that it shines through the golden wine. The flavour is definitely not your typical English wine either, with lovely, fierce, lemon herbaceousness, more Mediterranean than English country garden.

WEST SUSSEX

Booker's

The steady patter of rain began to hammer on the roof as I sat in the Booker's café/tasting room sipping hot coffee. 'So much for the weather forecast,' said Samantha Linter as she walked in. Sam has been responsible for Booker's vineyard for the last five years or so, taking over from her parents, who started it up in 1972. Even in the super-enthusiastic talkative world of UK wines you will rarely find a more effusive person than Sam. With girlish wonder, she will talk one moment about the technicalities of winemaking and the next

Top. The far Downs

Bottom. Spindle sticks

Foxhole Lane, Bolney RH17 5NB
Telephone: 01444 881575
Open: Monday–Friday 10.00–17.00;
Sunday 13.00–17.00 (not Saturday)
www.bookersvineyard.co.uk

Hurricane Wine

It was October 1987, three days before the Booker's folk were due to harvest the grapes when the great hurricane that the BBC weather presenter Michael Fish refused to believe was imminent, hit the vineyard during the night, waking all from their sleep. The next day, the bunches of grapes lay scattered on the ground. Resigned to the situation, they salvaged the unbruised grapes, took them straight for pressing and produced a few hundred bottles of wine from them. The strangest thing was that when the wine tasted it had a salty tang to it; it turned out that the storm had raged so hard and long that the crop had been drenched in seawater despite being a long way inland. Curiously, a lot of people seemed to like it and they sold out of their minimal stock of *Hurricane Wine* quickly.

of how she loves budburst, 'when the baby leaves unfold like strings of fairy lights.' She was followed into the homely café, with its wicker chairs and forest-green colours, by a racing pigeon which has adopted them and likes to be stroked and fed. Having cajoled it outside again, we continued our talk.

It all began when Sam's father visited Germany and got caught up helping out with the vineyard at which he was lodging. As soon as he returned home, the Linters transformed Booker's from a pig farm into a vineyard and used the pig manure to fertilise the vines. Unfortunately, the pigs had been eating dock leaves, and the seeds that they ate grew along with the vines leaving them no option but to kill the vines and the dock leaves and start again. Since then the site has grown from three acres of Müller-Thurgau to 23 acres with ten varieties and there is the potential to expand onto another ten-acre site. Storms were predicted on the day I visited and as we sat sweltering in grey humidity Sam said that being in the middle of flowering, a storm could affect fruit-set, particularly if the showers were heavy and developed into hail. Still, climate change has generally been favourable here, with the last few years being warmer and sunnier, and always reaching the 100 days of sunshine (from budburst) needed to ripen grapes enough for good wine.

Booker's are experimenting with Merlot at present, something almost no-one else has done, but it isn't ready to be released yet, being a bit thin, though recognisably plummy. Still, I don't think I've tasted an English Pinot Gris as good as theirs. My tasting note from the day read: 'Bloody delicious! Pear nose, complex, fresh, slightly minerally. Yum. Piercing acidity, spice and delicious creamy texture.' Terry Wogan's togs (tired old geezers ... or listeners) like Pinot Grigio and Sam was considering sending him some of their Pinot Gris (same grape, different name) to try. I think it would probably be wasted, this is miles above the stuff his listeners probably go for (although I expect he'd love to have a bottle as a prop for some Europe-baiting during the Eurovision song contest).

I also love their *Bart's Bubbly*, which is a pink sparkler that I think should get sponsorship from the Simpsons. This despite the fact that it actually gets its name from Bartholomew and Eleanor de Bolne who give their name to the village of Bolney, beside which Booker's is sited. In fact if you look closely at the Booker's labels, you will see the lychgate of Bolney Church. They could have used the vineyard itself mind; if you climb to the top of the main field, there is a terrific view of the Sussex hills and wiry vines, a great view for a great vineyard.

Highdown
(Centre For English Wine)

Highdown vineyard is also the Centre for English Wine and is the labour of love of young Ross and Karin Hay. Ross used to be a manager at Deloitte and Touche but hated commuting so when he spotted the vineyard up for sale a year and a bit ago decided that this was the life for him. Being from a farming background, he wasn't averse to hard labour and since the vineyard had not seen much of it in the previous three years, he set about it the only way

Littlehampton Road, Ferring BN12 6PG
Telephone: 01903 500663
Open: Monday–Saturday 10.00–17.00
and Sunday 11.00–16.00
www.highdown-vineyard.co.uk

Above. Poppies, vines and horses

Left. The CfEW shop and tasting rooms, a fine modern complex

he knew how. However, despite his best efforts the 2004 crop was tiny due to the previous neglect. In addition to the varieties already at Highdown they planted 1000 Chardonnay vines by hand; backbreaking work and they have since added a large number of extra red vines. Mild winters and warm summers are the rule due to Highdown's proximity to the sea, and because of this the intention is to produce fantastic English still reds and sparkling from Rondo, Dornfelder and Pinot Noir. Ross himself loves reds and would also love to be able to grow Riesling and Gewürztraminer, but it takes a long time to experiment with grape growing.

It must also have helped that Ross's first degree was in geology, this being a key to successfully identifying viticultural potential. The vineyard consists of 12 acres on South Downs chalk soil (genuinely the Champagne type), this being double the size it was when they took over. The names of the wines are all fossil- and rock-related, such as *Helix*. Much of the rock layer that the grapes are grown on is composed of fossils. Problems at Highdown include major thunderstorms which can reduce the crop by half. When asked about the peskiest animal in the vineyard, Ross replied straight away 'starlings', and then laughingly, 'and don't you dare tell me they're endangered'. Apparently, they recently left their Pinot Noir grapes until last to pick, and the pests stripped 12 entire rows of grapes in 20 minutes flat. At least if he keeps the starlings off he should get some good wine; Ross tasted the *Highdown 1998 Pinot Noir* and it had aged superbly.

The Centre for English Wine which sits beside the vineyard in the splendid modern facility, stocks a large range of UK wines and is an excellent provider of local Sussex wines. The facility came about because of the Hay's frustration at the paucity of outlets selling UK wines and is the perfect place to enjoy a free taster of wines from different vineyards. There are also event facilities, guided tours and tea and coffee available. Of the wines, the best so far is the *Bacchus 2005*, fresh and lengthy with a little more weight than some. But bear in mind this is a young vineyard, and I believe that the wines here will get better and better over the next few vintages.

Nutbourne

The wines of Nutbourne are served in London at the Guildhall, the Foreign Office and at Buckingham Palace on state occasions. They deserve to be and Nutbourne thoroughly deserves a visit. It is, without a doubt, one of my favourite vineyards, oozing character

Top. Under the vines

Bottom The sweeping views over the vineyard

from the carefully restored windmill that serves as its tasting room to the vines that fill the grounds of Nutbourne Manor. Reputedly, a Roman villa and mill existed here; the new mill was built in 1850. The vines were planted 27 years ago, and Bridget and Peter have been running the place for ten of those. You are free to walk through the grounds on a well-laid out trail. Stop at the lakes where wildfowl and swans glide; here, a cascading little waterfall gushes while llamas and alpacas gaze superciliously from their pasture. There are even wooden chairs so you can bask in the sunshine of the lower rows of vines as the sounds of clucking waterbirds, distant barking dogs and cooing pigeons lull you into a sense of deepest satisfaction. An old windmill, rare llamas, swans, little cottages straight out of the *Famous Five* ... I love it!

Nutbourne is also extremely friendly, with an easy welcoming atmosphere and is beautifully laid out for visitors. You can even help with the harvest, but think carefully before you put your name down, as it may not feel so idyllic after a backbreaking day's work, especially as all the grapes are hand-harvested. Given they make 40–60,000 bottles a year that is a heck of a lot of grapes to pick. You could just take a wander instead, enjoy the ½ hour plus walk, fresh wind in bright sky, over greensand soil, and take a picnic if it's a nice day. My only complaint (and it is a small one) is the tiny plastic glasses used for tasting.

All the Nutbourne wines are excellent but my favourite is the *Bacchus 2002*, deliciously aromatic, with a long, slightly sweet finish. It would be perfect for drinking whilst watching cricket, though maybe that was just the idyllically English setting speaking to me. The *Late Harvest Dry 2001* was also good; Schönburger grapes picked late but not made into a sweet wine as is usually the case. The lovely deep pink-skinned grapes produce a wonderful golden wine that smells of honey and tastes of rhubarb and pink grapefruit.

Gay Street, Pulborough RH20 2HH
Telephone: 01798 813989
Open: May–October weekdays, 14.00–17.00;
weekends and bank holidays, 11.00–17.00
www.nutbournevineyards.com

Nyetimber

Just down Gay Street from Nutbourne Manor lies Nyetimber, probably the UK's best known winery. The name Nyetimber is ancient as the manor is recorded in the Domesday Book and was once home to Anne of Cleves. Ironically, Nyetimber vineyard was started by an American couple, is owned by a Belgian and their winemaker is Irish. Here, only one product is made, sparkling wine and it is exceptional. Luscious gold-coloured flutes of frothy frivolity, all creamy-textured and with (in the case of the as yet unreleased 2000 vintage wines) a subtle orange blossom tint to them. The *Blanc de Blanc* was light and lithe with fabulous length, while the *Classic* blend was breadier with bright acidity and a crisp clarity, and pure zesty orange fruit to it.

Nyetimber was founded in 1988 by Americans Stuart and Sandra Moss, who felt that the UK had missed the trick when it came to the planting of grapes. They noted the similarity in soil and climate between the Champagne region and Sussex and decided to plant Chardonnay, Pinot Noir and Pinot Meunier. With the aid of French advisors, a new winery and a refusal to release anything until they were happy with every detail, they ignored the detractors and persevered. The first vintage was finally released in 1996, when Nyetimber's *1992 Première Cuvée Blanc de Blanc* won an international gold medal. A year later Nyetimber was again the toast of the town, quite literally, when the *1993 Classic Cuvée* won a gold medal, the English Wine Trophy and International Trophy for best non-Champagne Sparkling. Nothing much has changed since then

Gay Street, West Chiltington RH20 2HH
Telephone: 01798 813989
www.nyetimber.com

Dermot Sugrue by the pond

except the owners and the *Nyetimber 1998 Classic* won the International Trophy again in 2006. I have little doubt that it could have won the Champagne section trophy as well were it allowed to enter against French efforts. Without the Mosses we might well not have what is now the great white hope of English wine, and making quality sparkling wine is now all the rage in the UK.

Dermot Sugrue, the young flame-haired, trainer-wearing Irishman who is the current winemaker at Nyetimber began his career making beer and wine at home as a teenager. By the time he was 16 he knew that winemaking was the life for him and he has worked his way up through Bordeaux and Suffolk to his current esteemed position in an astonishingly short time. His will be an increasingly important position as Nyetimber have just planted another 200 acres, and their new owner is rumoured to want to have a quarter of all UK sparkling wine production by 2010. Dermot loves July after flowering, as it feels like the end of a cycle, when the bottling of the previous vintage is completed, and he has a good idea of how the new vintage might turn out to. He is a top bloke,

The sea of vines at Nyetimber

enthusiasm for the job leaking out in his cheeky smile, despite being ill the previous day, and you can tell he will be a fixture in the UK trade for some years to come.

Unfortunately, there is one hugely disappointing feature of Nyetimber vineyard, which is that it isn't open to the public. I still find it incredible that such a beautiful estate with such a great product should be closed. On the positive side, Nyetimber is probably the most widely available English wine, sold at Waitrose, Morrisons, Berry Bros & Rudd, Fortnum & Mason, Harvey Nichols and loads of independent wine stores. There are strong rumours that it will be opening to the public in the very near future, which given the expansion plans of the new owner seems a likely outcome. Fingers crossed. In the meantime go and pick yourself up a bottle for a special occasion and drift into bubbly perfection ...

Southlands Valley

A newcomer to the established Sussex wine scene, the Giberts are no stranger to wine, he (John) being from the Champagne region, while Pamela Gibert's grandfather was the first commercial grower of grapes in England (under glass). They are producing a Champagne-style bubbly, and in proper fashion are not going to be releasing it until 2007 at the earliest. Good sparkling wine is worth waiting for, and with any luck, given good vintages since 2003 and a very good local precedent we should find that to be the case when the cork is finally popped.

Mitchbourne Farm, Malthouse Lane, Ashington RH20 3BU
Telephone: 01903 892203

Warnham Vale

The Old Barn, Northlands Road,
Warnham RH12 3SQ
Telephone: 01306 627603

This small two-acre vineyard is a recent venture planted in the early nineties mostly with Seyval Blanc, but also some Schönburger and Reichensteiner. Award winner *The Gap 2004*, was lightly oaked with a light nuttiness, and a slight, sweet, lemony-citrus flavour. Interestingly *The Gap 2003* had too high an alcohol level to be entered into the UKVA competitions, not a familiar problem to most British producers. Will Davenport (of Davenport vineyards) also works his winemaking magic on their *Happy Valley* which has a lovely gooseberry and grass nose and palate. Doug and Kay Macleod now plan to add a sparkling wine to their range, and if their previous success is anything to go by, it is something to look forward to.

SURREY
Denbies Wine Estate

London Road, Dorking RH5 6AA
Telephone: 01306 876616
Open: January–March, Monday–Friday
10.00–17.00, Saturday 10.00–17.30,
Sunday 11.30–17.00; April–December,
Monday–Saturday 10.00–17.30,
Sunday 11.30–17.30. Closed Christmas
Day, Boxing Day and New Year's Day
www.denbiesvineyard.co.uk

Denbies is one of the largest vineyards, with some of the most reliable and available wines in the UK, and is also one of the easiest to access from London. It is a shame then, that the visitor experience there leaves me a little underwhelmed. With its pebble-dashed oversize visitor centre plonked in the middle of its large acreage (not far off 300 acres in the Surrey Downs), and its expensive visitor tour, this is the apotheosis of the passion found in most British vineyards. I acknowledge that it is hard in a large visitor operation to maintain real passion for the produce, but here the wine seems less important than the food or the garden centre. What is really lacking is a self-guided tour around the vineyard. Nothing is marked up, no boards or signs to show you around the rather beautiful valley, though at least you are free to walk around it. Instead you get a visitor 'experience' with a film and a 'people mover' which are decent enough, but not awe-inspiring considering the price. It could be brilliant mind, with a little more thought and staff who cared more about wine.

On the other hand we have the evident passion of Denbies (one of the few family-owned large vineyards in the UK) for the quality of their wines, and the massive impact that they have had in making good English wines available to a wider market. Denbies experiment with and grow a massive range of grapes. It was planted in the late eighties on a previously unheard of scale that many thought was madness. The land comprises a variety of terrain, from fairly steep slopes to flatland where frost gathers in spring.

Denbies wine estate

The latter problem was solved for a while by rather noisy frost propellers which stir up the air until the local residents complained. Now, as in many places, oil burners are used.

At the fantastically well-equipped winery, they now produce undoubtedly some of the best (and best value) wines in the country, from their consistent award-winning lightly-oaked whites to pudding wines that are always some of the best in the UK, and more recently some very good reds. Both *Yew Tree Pinot Noir* and the *Cellarmaster's Choice Redlands* wines are excellent, and show what can be done in the UK with red grapes. Denbies is clearly successful and always seems busy, and I have no quibbles with the quality of its products, indeed very much the opposite, but if they are to gain a younger set of devotees the visitor experience does perhaps want a rethink, especially given they are within easy reach of London.

Greyfriars

On the south-facing chalk of the Hog's Back Ridge is a small one-and-a-half-acre yard growing Chardonnay and Pinot Noir. From here Bill Croxson and Philip Underwood have grown, made and sold their own still white and sparkling wines since 1989. The sparkling wines are particularly good, with balanced crispness, acidity and fruit, and in the case of the 2001 vintage (interestingly 10.5% abv in contrast to 2000's 12% abv) Bill describes as 'mindblowingly good'. They accompany white meats and fish well,

The Hogs Back, Puttenham,
Guildford GU3 1AG
Telephone: 07970 525377/01483 813712
See website for visiting hours.
An open weekend is held each year
in early December
www.greyfriarsvineyard.com

and after ageing the wines all go a deep golden colour, a result of the Pinot Noir used to make it. They have slowly expanded the operation, one which began very small scale as an act of 'bravado', and are likely to expand further in the future, particularly in view of their selling grapes on to other sparkling producers in recent years. Theirs is a particularly elegant label with its grey-clad monk riding contemplatively through English countryside.

Painshill Park

Painshill Park, Portsmouth Road, Cobham KT11 1JE
Telephone: 01932 868113
Open: April–October, Tuesday–Sunday and bank holidays, 10.30–18.00 (last entry 16.30), November–March. Phone beforehand
www.painshill.co.uk

The smell of wet trees drifts across Painshill Park, a beautifully restored landscape garden that was originally created by Charles Hamilton in the mid-18th century. A huge lake fed from the river by a giant waterwheel lies below the steeply sloping small vineyard that has been carefully reconstructed with the advice of Stephen Skelton. Nowadays, it is planted with half Seyval Blanc, one third Pinot Noir, and the rest Chardonnay. It is the former variety that causes the most problems in a vineyard that is the bane of Mark

Painshill vines beside the ruined tower

84

Ebdon's life. This amiable man ended up taking care of the vineyard because no-one else would take it on, and says that he loves November after the vintage because he can stop battling the elements for a bit. That is the hard reality of vineyards in the UK, especially in sites that may not be ideal. There is also the difficulty of balancing the presentation required in a steep show vineyard with the need to get decent ripe grapes to make wine with. Apparently, the Pinot Noir made a pretty awful red so they are now making a rather good sparkling out of it instead (at a bargain price too). They also do a white and a rosé.

Mark, who does a bit of everything on the estate, gave an interesting response when I asked about climate change. He suggested that the main difference occurring is that we get more *lumpy* weather. By that, he means instead of getting a day or two of rain, then sunshine, then a bit of cloud like we used to, we are getting concerted lumps of weather, whatever that might be, baking heat, tropical rain, fog etc. I think he may be correct too, worrying for his grapes if there is the wrong lump of weather at the wrong point in the year. Anyway, Painshill is a magnificent project, with beautiful spacious grounds and it is a great family day out. There are many follies with a ruined abbey, Roman temple and a Turkish tent. Best of all is the tale of the Hermitage for which Charles Hamilton originally hired a hermit on condition that he lived there all day every day. The Hermit was sacked shortly after he was discovered down at the local inn!

The Iron Railway Vineyard/Old Tramway Holdings

The vintage of 2003 sticks out at The Iron Railway, you can taste the clean ripe grapes, the sweet glorious sunshine in the wines. The *Medium Dry* and *Dry Oaked* wines from this year were particularly fine. Based at Merstham, the Iron Railway sell their wines mainly at farmers' markets around the region. The name comes from the fact that the site contains the longest existing stretch of the Old Surrey Iron Railway, which was the world's first public railway, opening in 1804. Now all that remains as evidence is a third-of-a-mile-long gully. Their quaint, almost rudimentary, children's-picture-book-style wine labels seem to dwell in another more bucolic age too.

Despite 'expert' advice they have found that rabbits will eagerly attack not just young plants but mature vines as well and they have had to put collars and guards around them. Moving from being amateur makers of parsnip and rhubarb wines (in 1-gallon demijohns) to planting six vines experimentally on an allotment,

11 Vincent Road, Coulsdon CR5 3DH
Telephone: 01737 551829
Visits by appointment only

85

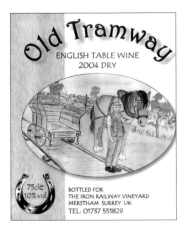

Old Tramway
ENGLISH TABLE WINE
2004 DRY

75cle
10% vol
BOTTLED FOR
THE IRON RAILWAY VINEYARD
MERSTHAM SURREY UK
TEL: 01737 551829

they have never looked back. Iron Railway still grow a wide range of fruit to eat and apples for cider production as well as the grapes.

Idiosyncratic labels usually disguise really good cheap wines. The Old Tramway wines are made by Will Davenport and range from the delightful fresh elderflowery *Orion* to the heavily orange and citrus *Late Picked Dry 2004*, not a trace of herbaceousness in the latter. They hold only two acres and are currently experimenting with reds. Finding the wines may be a problem, I happened on them only at the English Wine Festival and by chance at Fanny's Farm Shop, near Redhill in Surrey, at which I screeched to a halt, having seen vines growing just past it. Turns out those vines were not Iron Railway nor are they used for wines but I did pick up a bottle of excellent Iron Railway there for only £4.50. They also sell at farmers' markets and agricultural shows, so keep an eye out.

LONDON

Friday, 21 April
St George's Day English Wine Trade Tasting
Great Hall, 1 Great George Street, London SW1

The Greek *Agiorgitiko* grape means literally St George, though to my knowledge no-one has been foolhardy enough to try growing it in the UK so far.

> *AFTER DRINKING CURE FOR THE HEID-AKE*
>
> *Take green hemlock that is tender, and put it in your Socks, so that it may lie thinly between them and the Soles of your Feet; shift the Herbs once a Day.*
>   The Hon Robert Boyle, *Medical Experiments* (1692–4)

I trudged into Westminster nursing a rather sore head (and stomach) as a result of an Oddbins blind-tasting competition the previous evening. It was my last week of work and I hadn't exactly gone easy. A pub had beckoned me into its beery embrace afterwards too. Passing the Houses of Parliament on the left I came to No 1 Great George Street, a grand old building and a very apt place for a St George's Day tasting. Entering the Great Hall I was rather daunted by the sight of a long table in the centre filled with bottles of wine and around the edges of the hall, display stands from various UK wine companies. There were also representatives of the Vineyard Associations, a rather old-fashioned British term which

The Vintners' Company of London

Before the Norman Conquest, trading groups would meet in their local church, in the case of the Vintners, this was St Martin in the Vintry, so the origins of the name of the Guild are actually not related to the wine trade. In medieval London, persons of similar trades lived in the same area and so these local groups soon took on an economic element, later becoming known as Guilds or Mysteries. There are 12th-century references to London merchants fixing the price of wine, one of the earliest indications of an official group governing trade. The Vintners' first charter in 1364 gave far-reaching powers to the Guild, including duties of search throughout England and the right to buy herrings and cloths to sell to Gascony. Wine made up nearly one-third of England's entire import trade and was a huge part of the economy. After the date of charter it was the Vintners who presided over this trade in a monopolistic arrangement.

By the 16th century, the Company's importance was in decline, with the loss of its religious duties and severe curtailment of the Vintners' countrywide right to sell wine. Having supported Charles I, it suffered from penal taxation when Cromwell's parliament came to power in the 1640s. The further removal of privileges by Charles II and James II badly damaged the Company's influence. During the Great Fire of London in 1666 the Vintners' Hall was destroyed along with many of its other properties. The Guild was financially crippled and never recovered its former dominance.

The Livery Companies of the City of London came under sustained political attack during the 19th century. Fortunately, the Vintners were able to show that it was caring for its estates and spending more on its charities than was legally required. It also managed to hold onto some of its once enormous power, namely the privilege of selling wine without licence in London's vicinity and in certain other specified ports and thoroughfare towns. The 20th century was marked by the Company's renewed interest in and support for the wine trade, culminating in the granting of a new Charter on the 20th August, 1973. Until 2006 the Company still exercised the right, granted by Royal Charter by James I in 1611, to authorise certain members of the Company to sell wine without a Magistrate's Licence. This was known as the 'Vintners' Privilege'. Take a virtual tour of the Vintners' Hall at www.vintnershall.co.uk *

* Text is reproduced by courtesy of the Vintners' Company of London

The Swan with two Necks

I had always wondered where this bizarre pub name came from, assuming it was some kind of weird legend, or perhaps just that sometimes from the right viewpoint, two swans can look as if one swan has two heads! The Vintners gave me the real answer. In medieval times it was within the gift of the king to allow Livery Companies the right to what was known as 'a game' of swans on the Thames. In effect, this meant that a certain number could be culled for the Company's feasts. Their right to own swans on the Thames continues today, as it does for the Dyers' Company. It is therefore an urban myth that the queen owns all the swans on the Thames, although the crown does have ownership of all unmarked birds. This marking is where the pub name originates, as a swan has a certain pattern notched into its beak to denote ownership, the sign of the Vintners being two nicks in the beak.

Even today, the Swan Warden displays a swan feather in his Tudor hat on ceremonial occasions and is responsible for the organisation and execution of 'Swan Voyage' when the Court and Livery observe Swan Upping. In November each year the Company holds its famous Swan Feast when a stuffed swan is paraded into the Hall and presented to the Master.

equates to the French appellations.

I spent the first half of the afternoon moving along the central tables tasting a good selection of wines, and despite spitting them all out, I still felt slightly drunk after about 50, a salutary warning to any of you driving to several vineyards in one day. Later, I engaged in conversation with producers from the south-east and vineyard association reps from all over the UK; fortunately there was the bonus of delicious cheeses from Heart of England Fine Foods. One thing obvious from my conversations was that there is actually a shortage of grapes for the big wineries to use, a healthy sign for the UK industry, provided we can increase supply. That there should be an EU cap on how much the UK is allowed to produce seems ironic, as unlike their foreign counterparts British producers have no problem selling their stock each year.

Vinopolis: The Museum of Wine

Vinopolis, No.1 Bank End, London SE1 9BU

Open: February–November, Monday, Thursday, Friday, Saturday 12.00–21.00; Wednesday–Sunday 12.00–18.00; Tuesday closed. December: Monday–Sunday 12.00–18.00 except Tuesday. Closed, 24–26 December inclusive, 30 December–1 January inclusive.

Closest tube stations: London Bridge, Cannon Street, Monument, Borough www.vinopolis.co.uk

Situated on the South Bank of the Thames beside London Bridge, Vinopolis is a museum devoted to the appreciation of wine. The wine-tasting part of the tour offers a rare opportunity to explore and sample different wines and spirits of the world under one roof. Each tour includes a minimum of five wine tastings, a specially prepared Bombay Sapphire cocktail and a Vinopolis Tasting Notebook. Additionally a 'How to Taste Wine' Session, Champagne, Premium Wine, Whisky, Absinthe and Beer are also available depending on your chosen tour package. The Vinopolis wine tours are laid out around the traditional wine-producing regions of the world but it is the opportunity to try some wines from lesser known regions such as Thailand, Russia and indeed the UK that is particularly welcome.

You are free to wander around whilst you drink ... and that is where Vinopolis really falls down, as the actual museum is pretty poorly done. Unimaginative displays and neglected exhibits fail to grab your attention, and given the price of your ticket you might reasonably expect all the displays to be up to the standard of the excellent South African section. Instead, you find yourself paying extra to sample a few more of the interesting wines in the tasting room. The other problem is it can be very busy, particularly on a Saturday. There is also a particularly well-equipped bookshop and a Majestic Wine Warehouse next to Vinopolis in which you can buy single bottles, where normally you have to buy at least a mixed case of 12. And there are often special events going on here, so it's worth checking out the website below too.

8

EAST ANGLIA

Essex, Suffolk, Norfolk, Cambridgeshire, Bedfordshire and Hertfordshire

When I think of East Anglia I think of Oliver Cromwell's New Model Army, formed of dour farmers, which was based around the Eastern Association counties. Stand on the east coast of Norfolk and the chances are you will feel the bitterly cold easterly or north-easterly wind that scours this, the flattest and most exposed wine region of the UK. A hardy breed of farmer is perhaps to be expected. On the other hand the area does have fertile soils which encourage higher yields (but not necessarily quality wine grapes) than most other areas, and the viticulturalists I met were very far from dour, they were, in fact a most welcoming bunch.

A variety of East Anglian wines is available at the excellent www.winehub.co.uk.

ESSEX

Bardfield

Like Nyetimber, Bardfield was once in the ownership of Anne of Cleves. Alan Jordan has established a small vineyard beside the impressive barn. Planted with Bacchus and Reichensteiner, three still wines and a bubbly are produced. Visits here include tastings in the walled garden (weather permitting), tours of the 17th-century Great Lodge and the 16th-century barn, and good food.

The Great Lodge, Great Bardfield, Braintree CM7 4QD
Telephone: 01371 810776
www.thegreatlodgeexperience.com

Carter's

Carter's Vineyard is a real treat of a visit; well set out, welcoming and good value. You can tour the vineyard and winery, ramble through the wildflower meadows, lakes and woodlands, see their alternative energy program and receive a generous tasting of various good wines. Clare and I were there just after picking, and

Green Lane, Boxted, Colchester CO4 5TS
Telephone: 01206 271136
Open: Easter–end October 11.00–17.00
www.cartersvineyards.co.uk

The vineyard entrance

the autumn colours were stunning although the wind was less than welcoming. If you want to see vines at their most lovely, it's worth a bit of a nip in the air. About 30 ducks serenaded our blissfully (almost) unsupervised tasting of *Colchester Rosé 2005* (Dornfelder and Phoenix). It has a beautiful reddish pink swirl with light off-dry strawberry flavours, and a touch of herbs and white pepper that would make it a good match for barbequed food. Summertime here we come.

The luscious *King Coel 2004* is £3 cheaper than its award-winning 2003 counterpart but just as good. This is a red made from four varieties that tastes like a good Beaujolais, all berry fruit, medium body and lush elegance; fun in a glass and with just a hint of woodsmoke; one of the UK's best reds. In fact, given that another of my favourite red wines is also grown in Essex (though you wouldn't think so given the vineyard name on the bottle), I reckon Essex must have a certain affinity with red grapes. Older teenage girls should try *Vodka Fusion*, they'll love it.

There is more to look at here than just the vines. Carter's is a large 40-acre vineyard dedicated to using renewable energy sources, with no mains electricity, water or drainage required. Rather graceful wind turbines sit above the vineyard, adding character to the well-kept rows that surround it. At one point you are guided down a row by a cheeky little statue of Bacchus that sums up the jolly atmosphere of this place. Other good indicators are the detailed tour leaflet you get and the picnic often held in English Wine Week, where you bring your own food and free half bottles of wine are given out to the punters. So if you happen to be passing that way, a trip to Carter's comes highly recommended.

Autumnal vines

Castle Vineyard

A quick mention for Castle Vineyard seems appropriate despite its sad demise due to the death of Mr Paniel in 2006. The vineyard was for many years the only co-operative vineyard in the UK, with a unique training method devised by Mr Paniel in order to make the vines struggle more in the over-fertile land. It is small-scale innovators such as the Castle co-op who have made the UK wine scene what it is today.

Autumn avenues

New Hall

I drive through alternating small hills and rich agricultural land that probably was once marshland. The small villages have names like Gay Bowers and Cock Clarks, and roads like Great Gibcrack's Chase. The houses are the kind that might have a small wood for a back garden or a helicopter sitting beside them. If you ever fancy wine tasting and food shopping at the same time then this would be a top place. I see signs advertising free range eggs, turkeys, pickled onions, rare birds, fresh fish and numerous other delights.

New Hall Vineyards, Chelmsford Road, Purleigh, Chelmsford CM3 6PN
Telephone: 01621 828343
Open: Monday–Friday 10.00–17.00, Saturday–Sunday 10.00–13.30
www.newhallwines.co.uk

Understandably, New Hall instruct you to slow down in case of animals crossing the little track that leads to the farm houses at the centre of the vineyard. This mention of animals doesn't quite prepare you for the menagerie of animals that one encounters here: two friendly Labradors and one tiny Jack Russell which I think might have my fingers off but ends up rolling over to have his tummy tickled. Then there are the croaking black crows that live in the nearby woods, the raucous Guinea fowl lording it through the vines as if they own them, the two wild cats and a chicken that thinks she's a dog (all mentioned in the free tour leaflet). This is not a place for those afraid of animals.

That said it *is* a fantastic, slightly ramshackle place for an afternoon visit. Apart from being rather too flat (though there is some slight terracing) it is in a superbly dry site (only 43cm average annual rainfall) which avoids storms and rarely attracts the dreaded budding time frosts. This is mainly due to the black storm clouds being split asunder by the nearby Danbury Hill, with the rain coming together again well past the vineyard over the River Blackwater, and then following it down to the sea. Even the great hurricane of 1987 didn't cause much damage here, except for casting most of the netting into the sea.

New Hall no longer bothers with netting; the vineyard area is so huge that they don't mind losing a few grapes to the noisy birds. Their free tour of the vineyard is one of the best around, with many points of interest beginning with the church on the nearby hill at Purleigh. This is where Mr Greenwood's father first went upon purchase of the farm in 1969 to see what he should try and grow on his new acquisition. He discovered that as far back as the Domesday Book there had been a vineyard on the hill below the church and decided that grapes were the way to go, a spur of the moment decision that turned out to be an eminently sensible one as New Hall is now one of the largest and most successful vineyards in the country. This same Purleigh church was where a certain George Washington's great-great-grandfather was Rector, until he was removed by Puritans for alcoholic overindulgence! Turning to face north the land flattens out as Essex slopes down into the sea with its cold east-coast winds.

The Greenwoods sell on the majority of their grapes to other major vineyards but retain a good number to make their own reasonably priced and consistently decent range of 11 still wines and one sparkling. They also rent out vines to people who wish to have their own wines made at the New Hall winery. Grape varieties are wide-ranging, and the harvests here are generally large, aston-

A Menagerie of Drunkenness, by Thomas Nash (1592)

Ape-drunk, who leaps and sings and hollers.
Lion-drunk, who is quarrelsome and rude.
Swine-drunk, who is sleepy and lumpish.
Sheep-drunk, who is wise in his own conceit, but unable to speak.
Maudlin-drunk, who declares he loves all mankind.
Martin-drunk, who drinks himself sober again.
Goat-drunk, who is lascivious.
Fox-drunk, who is crafty like the Dutch, who bargain when drunk.

ishingly so in 2005, the largest harvest yet, when they collected 435 tonnes of grapes (it is normally 270 tonnes) The vineyard also hosts an arts and crafts show (with belly dancing) on the first weekend in September, spring wine sale in mid May, and runs prebooked group guided tours. With medium sweetness, and light flavours of strawberries and cream, balancing acidity and a refreshing finish the *Pinot Noir Rosé* is a top barbeque wine, particularly good with sticky ribs, and price-wise compares very favourably with Pinot rosés from other countries.

Sandyford

Sandyford Vineyard is part of a 400-acre family farm based in the village of Great Sampford in rural North West Essex. As well as the two-acre vineyard, Sue and Mike Lindsell grow wheat, barley, sugar beet, oilseed rape, beans *and* rear free-range turkeys for the Christmas market. The idea to set up Sandyford was made down at the local pub over a glass of red where the Lindsells decided that grape cultivation would be an exciting diversification project. After much research involving wine-tasting trips to numerous vineyards in the UK and Europe, vines were purchased from Germany, planted in May 1999, and left to mature for two and a half years. The 2,000 vines enjoy long hours of sunshine and very low rainfall and lie on a sheltered southwest facing slope.

In September 2001 an army of willing helpers from the local village helped the Lindsells harvest their first crop and in May 2002 *Clover Hill*, Sandyford's first white wine, was ready for drinking. A range of white, red, rosé and sparkling wines are made, the latter (a Bacchus/Reichensteiner blend) being especially good. The bubbly has also achieved 12.5% alcohol, a high level for England. There is a good tour and tasting here, together with eating facilities and traditional English farm fare.

Sandyford Vineyard, Salix Farm, Great Sampford, Saffron Walden CB10 2QE
Telephone: 01799 586586
Open for wine tasting all year by appointment
Tours are available by appointment from May–September
Evening tours are conducted Monday to Thursday between 19.00 and 21.00
www.sandyfordvineyard.co.uk

SUFFOLK
Gifford's Hall

Hartest, Bury St Edmunds IP29 4EX
Telephone: 01284 830559
www.giffordshall.co.uk

Growing from small beginnings into one of the largest producers of Madeleine Angevine grapes (see Kemp's entry for a brief history) Gifford's Hall is located in the village of Hartest. They currently have 12 acres of vines under cultivation with four grape varieties; Madeleine Angevine, Reichensteiner, Bacchus and Rondo. Like many vineyards in the UK Gifford's Hall are growers only and do not produce wine for retail, but top wines are made from the grapes produced here. While it is no longer open to the public, people are welcome to join in the picking at harvest, and refurbishment of the former café/shop has being undertaken. They hope to let a small holiday cottage soon as well.

Ickworth House

Ickworth House, Hollinger,
Bury St Edmunds IP29 5QE
Telephone: 01359 251173
Vineyard open on first Sunday of
month, June–October, 11.00–16.00
Ickworth House is closed on
Wednesday and Thursday
www.nationaltrust.org.uk

Don't know whether it's just the time of year, but the fly spatter on the windscreen seems particularly bad in Norfolk and Suffolk. I feel oddly at home here around the Norfolk/Suffolk border; perhaps some weird collective memory is prompted by the sights and smells; my dad's family were from Watton just to the north.

Ickworth's huge house, run by the National Trust, is dominated by a massive dome, somewhat akin to a Victorian version of the Pantheon, and is a beautiful day out for all the family. Its Secret Garden-esque walled vineyard (which was once the estate's kitchen garden) is a few hundred yards southwest of the house. Honking geese beckon you on in the correct direction, past the little church and down to the sleepy river Linnet, where the vineyard rests encased in its red brick shroud. The garden was first enlarged and converted by John Hervey, later first Earl of Bristol, and his summerhouse lies at the bottom of the restful vines. It is advisable to visit Ickworth on the first Sunday of the month from June to October as the vineyard is open for self-guided tours and a tasting (with grape juice for children). The vineyard has a mock-Roman feel, moveable heaters (to warm the air at ground level in case of a really bad frost), and a restfully grand atmosphere.

One can see very easily the lush fertility of the soil at Ickworth; the gardens are quite astonishing and it is a good place to view wide-planted vines. The reasoning behind this is that since fertile soils provide all the necessary nutrients for the vines there is a tendency for them to become like a jungle, too much foliage preventing the sun from ripening the grapes and stopping the

Top. Ickworth House.

Bottom. The Walled Garden

94

The anti-frost heaters at Ickworth

breezes which help prevent rot. They use the popular Scott Henry vine-training system (named after an American who was originally a rocket scientist), which is a version of Double Guyot whereby half the shoots are pointed downwards in early July so that the leaf canopy is opened up to sunshine and breezes. Fascinatingly, the strangely jutting wall that spikes from the garden down toward the river appears to be a Victorian frost channel to guide frost away from the garden.

Wine-wise, Ickworth make a red, the *Earl Bishop's Reserve Rondo*, the *Walled Garden Bacchus*, the *Suffolk Pink Sparkling* since 1999 and a sparkling white since 2001. These are made using the Champagne method with Auxerrois and Pinot Noir grapes. The *Walled Garden 2003* is fabulous too, pale gold in colour with hugely long peachy, citrus, summertime flavours; crisp and almost Viognier-ish. I'd drink it on its own on a lengthy sunny afternoon.

Kemp's

Shimpling, Bury St Edmunds
Not open to public

'The most fearsome animal here is the mole. Aren't we lucky? He just messes around in the roots and disturbs new plantings.' John Kemp has a glint in his eye and is a cheerful talkative character. The vines were planted in the winter of 1985 to combine John's favourite hobbies of 'gardening and boozing' and the enterprise slowly grew into the 14 acres of Gifford's Hall Vineyard, well-known as one of the better vineyards in East Anglia. The site is high up for Suffolk (300metres) and is therefore well protected from frost attack. Apparently the starlings that used to pester him have 'buggered off to Birmingham' these days. Now he has sold the bulk of that estate retaining just the original two acres, on which a new winery sits. This is where he makes wines such as the *Sparkling Bacchus* which beat off esteemed competition to win best bubbly at last year's English Wine Festival. All John's wines are good, and a particular favourite of mine is his vibrantly coloured *Rosé*, close to a red in colour and flavour.

Theoretically retired, and relishing the peace and quiet of only selling from shows and not being open to the public, he makes me realise what hard work it must be to be open to people *all the time*. As he puts it in his own inimitable fashion; 'If I learned anything about the wine industry it is that we are mostly a minor branch of show business. As soon as you open your doors to visitors you have to be prepared to amuse and look after them. And don't expect to get any serious work done until they have all gone home or before they arrive in the morning.'

This should not be misunderstood for unfriendliness, as John is in fact an incredibly personable guy, and is clearly passionate about wine as he couldn't bear to give up his vineyard entirely. The new winery was his retirement present to himself. Here, where they use an elderly Maerelli screw press that gives best results when the stems are left intact, the gentlest way of preparing the grapes is to routinely tread them, a practice rarely seen these days but entirely in keeping with the philosophy of Kemps. Try the wines if you get the chance, and see if you can catch John at a show.

The Kemps

Staverton

This small old vineyard established in the mid-seventies had its best year in 2002 when they filled 3030 bottles. They grow Reichensteiner, Müller-Thurgau, Schönburger, Sylvaner (usually blended into a single medium-dry wine), and Bacchus, which makes a good floral-tinged varietal wine. Not only that but they also make an extra dry sparkling wine (meaning, in a typically obtuse French way, off-dry, or with more sweetness than Brut, which also means dry). Staverton is named after the family who were lords of the local manor back in the 14th century, but the Sheepshanks family have owned Rookery Farm, with its sheltered and gentle slopes since 1925. It was formed initially from a redundant vegetable garden and now extends to 1.3 acres, all trained in traditional Guyot style.

The Rookery, Eyke,
Woodbridge IP12 2RR
Telephone: 01394 460818
Open by appointment

Willow Grange

Street Farm, Crowfield,
Ipswich IP6 9SY
Telephone: 01449 660612
Call before visiting

Willow Grange was planted 25 years ago and has three varieties of grape, Müller-Thurgau, Ortega and Optima. The latter grape is a favourite as it suits the Suffolk conditions, despite being susceptible to wasp damage. Wasps have proved a real nuisance here, especially after heavy rain or when the grapes have been affected by botrytis. Despite this distraction, Peter and Jill Fowles have had some excellent harvests with the high volumes of 1996 being excelled only by last year, although the quality is yet to be seen. A smaller yield, but excellent in terms of flavour was 2004. The vineyard was started as a result of a village-twinning scheme with a wine-growing area in Germany.

Unusually for a small one-acre vineyard, Willow Grange has its own small winery. Rigorous spraying is needed here to contain a mildew problem that is a continual threat to the growing vines. One year was particularly disastrous, not due to mildew (for once) but probably from wind-drifted clouds of weed killer, a known problem for many vineyards, and one that very little can be done about. That year, the tender growing tendrils suddenly collapsed, the vines followed suit and the grapes dried up in mid-August with no nutrients coming through to give them sustenance. Typically, they will pick over two weekends here, with 'indentured' labourers who get a hard-earned vendange lunch for their hard work.

Willow House Vineyard/Oak Hill Wines

Willow House Vineyard, Fressingfield,
Eye, Suffolk IP21 5PE
Telephone: 01379 586868
There is an Open Gardens weekend
in June. Guests staying at Oak Hill
Granary also have admission
www.oak-hill.co.uk

The Oak Hill wines, produced by Willow House vineyard in the centre of Fressingfield village are named after a small wood that once crowned the hill. All that remains today is one 800-year-old oak which now overlooks one acre of Bacchus. Originally planted in 1987 by Marta Stevens, the choice of grape was rather prescient, as this variety is generally considered to be one of the best varieties in the UK and it does seem to flourish here in East Anglia. The current owners, Carol and David Spenser have been here for three years and last year's vintage (October 2006) was the biggest ever; they harvested an amazing 3,000 bottles from that one acre.

Even more impressively, three wine varieties are produced from their single grape variety, dry, medium and oaked (French oak fumé-style), the last of which is the Spenser's personal favourite. They have won many awards over the years, and may expand upon retirement as they own another seven acres of land. At the moment the wines can only be found locally, in the village shop, local pubs and local restaurant, The Fox and Goose.

The village has an open gardens weekend in June at which the vineyard put on tastings. There is also Oak Hill Granary, a restored agricultural building in which you can stay and the perks include a welcome pack of basic groceries, including a bottle of the latest vintage. A good incentive I reckon.

Shawsgate

A hazy, warm May day with the sun attempting to break out of its thin pale prison. Heart of London FM begins to break up around Colchester, which pronounces itself 'the oldest town in Britain'. Here perhaps even the resentful air resists London's cultural push outwards. The land flattens, down to the sea, which I can almost smell. A sharp turn to the north and I am in Suffolk, where if you

Badingham Road, Framlingham, Woodbridge IP13 9HZ
Telephone: 01728 724232
Open: 15 January–24 December, 10.30–17.00
www.shawsgate.co.uk

The barn.

find yourself on a higher hill you can see for miles around over the relatively flat Suffolk farmlands, swathed in bright yellow rapeseed flowers, their sickly-pungent smell wafting into the car as I drive past. Through Earl Soham, an almost implausibly pretty village and by an owl sanctuary. Somewhere near here lives a man who still makes gallows and sells them to third world countries. Through Framlingham ('Fram' to the locals) with its medieval castle to the well set-up and friendly atmosphere of Shawsgate.

Shawsgate was planted in 1973, added its own winery in 1987 and has 15 acres comprising three white varieties and two red. Greeted by a pretty converted barn, somewhat akin to Chapel Down, the whole place is carpeted in the most beautiful arrangements of flowers. The East Anglian winds are disrupted by windbreaks spaced well enough apart to reduce the start and spread of rot and disease. The deep ditch running beside the vineyard encourages flies, but walking the pretty vineyard with your free tour sheet you won't mind that. The buds are out, it being May, and some are very big indeed. Walking down to the end of the vineyard, I am surprised by how long it is; each time I think it's about to end there is more. Finally, reaching the ancient Seyval Blanc vines that look as shabby and ragged as a wizened old sorcerer, I turn to the right to see more gnarly vines, looking even blacker beside the trees in bright blossom and the daisy-strewn floor. These are some of the oldest vines in the country, grown through all the ups and downs of the UK wine scene. A prime picnic place sight.

Back at the buildings I pause to take a quick look at the winery. Rob Capp, Shawsgate's winemaker recalls being drenched in wine

Top. Spring

Bottom. Autumn

'that came up like a New Zealand geyser', whilst attempting to de-acidify the wine without a sufficiently large tank. The deluge ran the length of the winery and went mouldy, stinking to high heaven. The last two vintages here have produced wines needing less and less added sugar due to the grapes achieving natural ripeness levels. After the wet summer of 2004, there was a long, lovely autumn, while the 2005s, which were being bottled on the day I visited, had had a long ripening period and were expected to be very good. The last three years have also seen exceptionally high yields.

In fact the main problem experienced at Shawsgate has been wasps, which are particularly fond of Rondo grapes which they suck the moisture out of. They destroyed 38 wasp's nests in 2005. The hand pruning of just under 16,000 vines is carried out by a lovely group of ladies who help out, and everyone at Shawsgate seems genuinely happy to be there. They have a good reciprocal arrangement whereby New Hall vineyard (in Essex) make red wines for Shawsgate and vice versa. The shop offers grape juice and other bits and bobs and tasting is very much encouraged, though if you look vaguely young take some ID with you!

The winemaking style has changed considerably after a change of winemaker. Previously the wines were made with incredibly high acidity, and have consequently aged very well. The 1992, '93 and '94 vintages of Müller-Thurgau have just been stabilised and rebottled and have apparently stood up to the test of time and the *Venus 1999* I tried still had high acidity and was all crisp, bright, apple flavours. Rob's more modern, younger, drinking style is showcased really well by the Riesling-like *Harlequin 2003*, which managed to satisfy two of my friends who *never* like the same wine. It is grapey, minerally and medium sweet, but with a bracing acidity to balance. If you want something very different give their Apple dessert wine a try, with a sweet smell and a drier, smokey-apple flavour.

Wissett

Valley Farm Vineyards, Wissett, Halesworth, Suffolk IP19 0JJ
Telephone: 01986 785535
Open: daily 08.00–14.00
www.wissettwines.com

Back when they lived above the Vale of Oxford 25 years ago, Jonathan Craft was allowed a plot of land in the flower garden by his wife Janet, and decided to experiment with 30 different vine varieties. Finding that he was actually able to make decent wine he began the search for a good site on which to try it out on a larger scale. He found this at Valley Farm in Suffolk where soil samples were compatible and it was confirmed as their new home. The Crafts offer B&B accommodation and a self-catering cottage called

Noah's Ark with all mod cons, a games room with table tennis, a lovely rose garden and a barbeque.

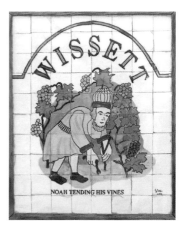

You can also get good food if you stay, and might well end up taking the farm spaniel Daisy with you as you wander along the wine trail with the informative Walkman that comes with the tour and which you can stop and start as you like. Ponder the woolly headed alpacas that make a bizarre noise like buzzing flies crossed with a sheep's 'baa'. The air is cooler here being well east towards the coast with its biting winds. Windbreaks are formed by lines of elegant Italian alder which not only stop the rushing wind (leaf-fall occurs well after the grape harvest) but also fix nitrogen imbalances in the soil (much like broad beans do). Wissett is planted mainly with Alsace varieties; Pinot Gris, Auxerrois, with some Pinot Noir, Pinot Meunier and Madeleine Angevine. Müller-Thurgau had just been grubbed up when I was there, due to poor ripening, yield and disease.

Behind the house is a small area of vineyard known as Le Clos, which is the oldest part planted and means 'enclosed'; an apt name as a large thick hedge surrounds it. If you want to feel a real example of a meso-climate, just walk into Le Clos and feel how much warmer and more still it is compared to the rest of the vineyard. Here the grapes are mainly Auxerrois, the climate giving encouragement to these late-ripening grapes.

One of the Wissett alpacas

A Noah theme permeates this whole vineyard, from weathervane to wine label. The latter was adapted by Jonathan's daughter from a detail on the roof of Norwich Cathedral of Noah tending his vines after the flood was over. The Dean of Norwich used to come and bless the wines and sample the vintage on St Swithin's Day (15 July) in order to keep the harvest from 40 days of rain. This caused mild controversy as Wissett is actually in the diocese of Bury St Edmunds. And in 1993 a not quite biblical flood took out all the vines in the bottom field, but by handpicking selected grapes from each bunch they managed to make an outstanding thousand bottles of wine that Jonathan named *Noah's Flood*. Now, his favourite wine of the year is always known as *Noah's Flood* (currently a Pinot Gris).

Sparkling Auxerrois is a speciality here, though apparently the 1994 still Auxerrois was drinking superbly after 12 years and was a treat with local oysters. Their *Brut Non Vintage* was a beauty if you like mouth-puckering Granny Smith apples as I do. The *Mostly Madeleine 2004* was a great easy drinker – dry, crisp and zesty. I would have loved to try *Noah's Flood* but they had run out, so you'll have to let me know ...

Wyken

Wyken Hall, Stanton,
Bury St Edmunds IP31 2DW
Telephone: 01359 250287
Open: 12 January–24 December,
Wednesday–Sunday; bank holiday
Mondays 10.00–18.00
www.wykenvineyards.co.uk

Human settlement at Wyken (pronounced Wicken) reaches back over 6,000 years, and even the name reeks of something old. As a place to visit, however, it is a great mix of modern efficiency whilst retaining the traditional connection with the land. If you want a day out with masses to do for everyone, I think this might be the perfect day with ancient woodlands, rare sheep, an Elizabethan manor house, rose gardens, vineyard and a fine restaurant (featured in the Michelin and Good Food Guides). I would choose to include a little shopping too, as a farmer's market is held here on Saturdays from 9.00–13.00, and maybe a quick gander at the art exhibitions which are often held, followed by a long wander round the gardens, woods and finally the vineyard. Here, just past the woods and away from any main roads, the vineyard, planted in 1988, is beautifully quiet, nothing disrupting the faint clucks of the game birds.

John Carrier, one of the pioneers of the TV celebrity chef phenomenon, used to present some of his shows from his old home

An interview with Charles Macready (who with his wife Jillian looks after the vineyards at both Ickworth House and Wyken)

With his cowboy hat and easygoing friendliness, it would be hard to dislike Charles Macready. He started working here in the vineyards employed by his wife-to-be Jillian, after his previous wine-related businesses had gone bust. He seems to have found his niche here, producing superb wines and flitting happily between subjects recalling that 'there was frost at Ickworth on the day it was planted', then on to talk of the best vintages that he has seen. Charles disputes the popular view of 2003 as the best year of recent times (a view confirmed by other winemakers) and thinks if anything it was too hot. For pretty much the first time he saw sunspots and evidence of heatstroke on the vines, and also thinks that winemakers in the UK were unused to dealing with such ripe grapes. He points to 2004 as the year to beat, with both high yield

and quality (25,000 bottles by comparison with 15,000 in 2003). Unfortunately, as is the way with vines, 2005 will be a much smaller vintage as the vines had cropped so heavily in the previous two years. He is also unconvinced by early clones of some grapes, notably Pinot Noir, which to him just doesn't taste quite right somehow.

Apparently, the deer at Wyken like eating roses, which are a delicacy for them, but they're okay about grapes. Indeed, the main problem in terms of animal life is the wasps, which, as is the case all over East Anglia, seem to have a love of Rondo and Madeleine Angevine grapes. Still, Charles recalls, that when picking the latter in 2000 the buckets were brim-full with bunches, but they still felt astonishingly light. It turned out the wasps had sucked out a good deal of the juice, but what was left was incredibly high in sugar and flavour and

made fantastic sweet wine. As he puts it, 'the French have Pourriture Noble, we have wasps'. He enjoys the quiet of winter pruning and also September, when everything should be in order ... 'unless it's pissing down with rain'.

They'll soon be producing a free run rosé wine from the Rondo, because the skins seem to impart a strange taste to reds that many people do not take to. Wyken changed from Double Guyot training to Scott Henry to avoid the jungle-like summer growth and massive amount of pruning that was required, and in the vineyard you can see that the posts used to be considerably shorter. The owners of Wyken, Kenneth and Carla Carlisle love the hares which live in considerable numbers around about the house, and have placed them on all the labels and named their restaurant The Leaping Hare.

The Leaping Hare

here, the gorgeous Vineyard Cottage in the bright bluebell woods. Carrier's shows included the 1970's Carrier's Kitchen, Food, Wine & Friends, The Gourmet Vegetarian and Carrier's Caribbean in the 1990s.

Winewise, Wyken do four whites, all of which are good. If you visit head straight for the *Madeleine Angevine 2002*, possibly the best Maddy I have tasted and their cheapest wine to boot. It possesses a faint honey smell and something else indefinably lovely on the nose with a fresh delicate flavour that tastes like a thousand years of English countryside heritage. Suitably over the top as usual. Mind you, if there's none of that left the rest of the bunch are all great, and there's always *Wyken Moonshine*, which is not – as you might think – bootleg whiskey but a sparkling wine made from Auxerrois, Pinot Noir and Chardonnay. Or then again perhaps a drop of *Good Dog Ale* with its slogan 'Makes you want to Sit Down and Stay'. All of these come with some of the best UK labels, originally taken from a woodcut by Margaret Preston.

NORFOLK

Tas Valley

Forncett St Peter is the unique home to the edible European marsh frog which resides in the attractive ponds in the dell at the bottom of Tas Valley vineyard. Loud cuckoos awoke Mike Smith, the owner this morning, and he curses them forthrightly in his faintly burred voice. He reminds me of Michael Eavis, the co-founder of Glastonbury Festival. Mike is probably one of the most forward-thinking vineyard owners in the country, railing loudly against woolly romanticism and lack of business acumen, though it is equally evident that this friendly talkative man would be deeply out of place in a 9–5 Monday–Friday job. After obtaining the land, Mike chanced across an article describing the conditions needed for vineyards: 'south facing slope, sheltered by trees and no more than 300 feet above sea level', which described his land to a tee. So he ordered in 4,000 vines from Germany (Bacchus, Müller-Thurgau and Reichensteiner (which does particularly well here)) and Bob was his uncle.

Mike hates doing shows and has recently worked hard and spent a lot of money on updating the website from which he had sold six bottles in four years, all to a woman half a mile away! Since November 2005, when he finished gearing his site to a very professional and well-handled personalised wine gift service, he has had over 300 orders in six months.

The vineyard itself is attractively sited within trees, by a little wooden tasting hut and a marquee tent, although these may soon be replaced by a small winery and more appropriate shop and

Mike Smith

Forncett St Peter NR16 1LW
Telephone: 01953 789445/
07850 609062
Open: March to September, Saturday,
Sunday and bank holidays,
10.00–19.00. All other times by
appointment. Booking is essential
for groups
www.tasvalleyvineyard.co.uk

reception. The picnic table beside the aforementioned pools is a fantastic place to sit and lunch whilst looking up at the neatly kept vine rows and listen to the huge march frogs make their loud and peculiar chirrup. Indeed, it is available to hire out for camping, and with the buzz of dragonflies nearby would be a very pleasant place to mooch, especially with a bottle of Tas Valley wine lulling you to sleep. Talking of wines, the *Triomphe d'Alsace Medium Dry Rosé 2004* isn't oversweet, but is fantastically fresh with strawberries and cream that would be super with anything from scones to a barbeque. The *Bacchus 2003* is far too young at the moment but will be grand in a couple of years with all the requisite sharp acidity for ageing and masses of bright gooseberry and citrus fruit to boot.

Thelnetham

With its magnificent oak standing watch over the front gates of the farm, Thelnetham was originally planted in 1985; the current owners decided to continue the vineyard when they bought the house. Two wines are made for them at Shawsgate, and thus far the best vintages have been 2002, with a small yield but really ripe grapes, 2005, and 2006 which should prove to be good too. The biggest problem so far has been mildew blowing in from the surrounding farm land.

Lodge Farm, Thelnetham, Diss IP22 1JL
Telephone: 01379 890739
Open: daily by appointment

The majestic oak

CAMBRIDGESHIRE
Chilford Hall

Balsham Road, Linton CB1 6LE
Telephone: 01223 895600
Open: 1 March–1 November,
11.00–17.30
www.chilfordhall.co.uk

Lying just south of Six Mile Bottom, Chilford Hundred combines a modern pristine conference centre with what is probably the strangest, most idiosyncratic vineyard and winery in the UK. A cluttered assortment of bits and bobs pilfered from various places: Romanesque arches; old agricultural machinery; a wine barn made from bricks that used to be the floor of one of the other buildings. There is enough bizarre stuff here to suit the most curious of people, even down to the wine labels themselves (which range from looking like someone has puked up on them to clean, elegant, modern designs). This vineyard is more like an inventor's playground than any normal vineyard I have visited. The winemaker himself described his winery as being like 'Steptoe's front room'.

Unusually for the UK the wines here are part-made using old oak barrels, which have previously contained alcoholic liquors of some description; this accounts for the rather peculiar and unusual range of smells you will encounter at the tasting table. That said, the wines do seem to age very well, and may start out unpromisingly but often bloom with four or more years of bottle age. This is perhaps partly the oak-ageing and the maturity of the vines, some of which are 35 years old.

Inside the winery …

108

Chris Durrant, a pig farmer turned winemaker, is as singular as the wines he makes. He chatters fantastically about all sorts from the early leaf burst (on their Pinot Noir vine the growth is so unbelievably early that you can already see how many bunches of grapes there will be) to his favourite bottle bank driver and how much he hates harvest time. At that time of year, he is so focused that he loses weight, forgets to wash, has no social life and sometimes doesn't eat. He will make up for this at the end of harvesting by eating a gigantic chilli con carne, having a couple of beers (definitely no wine) and heading to bed.

Chilford is well worth a visit, with its beautiful 18th-century buildings, lovely sun-kissed site and aforementioned curiosities. It runs group visits and tours on the hour during the tourist season, and is a friendly informative place with an easy fun feel suitable for all types of people. I discovered that if the leaves are too vigorous, some people nick the vine, to trick it into thinking it is dying, so that it produces grapes to ensure survival in some form.

Chilford's *Brian de Scarlariis Medium '02* is gorgeous, with a sweet peapod and honeysuckle nose, and a palate like Gentle Ben's hug. It has a honeyed finish too ... in response to which tasting note my companion commented 'pompous twat!' Meanwhile, the *Aluric de Norsehide Rosé Sparkling 2001* was toasty with delicate strawberries, deliciously easygoing, and would be perfect on a summer's evening, just as the sun is setting.

CHILFORD HUNDRED

Brian de Scalariis

Juror of the Chilford Hundred, 1086

2001

Medium

e75cl   English Table Wine   10% vol

Estate bottled at Chilford Hall, Cambridge, UK
Produce of the United Kingdom

... and outside.

Chilford lions

BEDFORDSHIRE
Warden Abbey

> To happy convents, bosomed deep in vines,
> Where slumber abbots, purple as their wines.
> *The Dunciad*, book IV, Alexander Pope (1688–1744)

Sunday, 10 September 2005

Near Old Warden, Southill Park,
Biggleswade SG18 9LJ
Telephone: 01462 816226
Open: one weekend in September with
a wine-selling day soon after and
tasting days in June and December
www.wardenwines.co.uk

Warden Abbey Vineyard is open to the public only once a year, on one weekend in early September just before the vintage begins. It is well-regarded, with its wines recognised as consistently merit-worthy. We had agreed to meet my sister and her husband there at roughly 2.30pm. After a journey that started well, we jammed on the brakes and slowed to join a queue of traffic and then ... we stopped, moving an inch or so every few minutes. A journey that should have taken an hour took two and a half. Once through to the other end we were beset by a deluging torrent of rain, hurtling along roads that had become floods, the darkly pretty Bedfordshire countryside shrouded in deep grey squalls. Warden Abbey is not easy to find, round bending roads that all look rather similar in the wrong weather.

We arrived in the muddy field with its damp marquee at 4.05pm (4.00 being closing time) just as my sister's car was leaving. The moral being that if a vineyard is open for only two days a year then you should set off early. Anyway, Nikki and Mike told us that they were given a little talk and tour by Jane Whitbread who was very informative, approachable and friendly. The abbey vineyard dates back to the medieval abbey founded in 1135 by Walter Espec, though originally the field upon which the annual marquee now stands was also the site of a second Great Vineyard of ten acres. Lower down in the dip, there were also orchards. The abbey was famed for its tiles, which are still to be found on the floor of the Cathedral at Ely in Cambridgeshire. Unfortunately the monks did not stick to their celibacy vows or the Benedictine limit of one pint of wine per day and were to be found 'frolicking' regularly with the local girls. Some of the monks were described as 'common dronkerds', so the abbot of Warden asked that it be closed down in the 16th century.

Warden send their grapes to a winery near Chelmsford, but the Warden winemaker determines the final blend. 2005 has been good though cold and then they suffered a little from May frosts. This frost points to a reduced crop, but after a wet September, a bright hot November will help to salvage a typically British up-and-down year. Generally they try to avoid Chaptalisation (the addition of sugar prior to fermentation) and it has been unnecessary for four to five years in a row now, a sign both of good crop control and a changing climate. Because of the latter, pruning now takes place in January rather than February. While the 2003 vintage was harvested in November, the 2005 would be gathered in mid-October.

Warden wines seem to have quite a different, almost tropical passion-fruit flavour to them; they also seem to be fuller in body than many other English wines. The quality of the wines is universally good, but the *Warden Abbot Sparkling 1998* is particularly good value for money. It is deep gold in colour, with a hazelnut nose, fine beads and a tingly, toasty citrussy palate. It goes magnificently with salty nibbles like olives.

Sunday, 17 September 2006: one year later

I actually made it on time this year during a weekend that typified how late the summer is becoming in the south of England.

In 1846, the *Bedfordshire Times* asked of the site of Warden Abbey, 'would any modern ever think of planting either a "greate or lyttel" vineyard in England?' Clearly, someone did. Nowadays, the owner is Jane Whitbread, and since its reestablishment in 1986 a decision was made to try planting a large quantity of what was then

Warden House and the field which used to be the abbey's larger vineyard

a fairly unknown grape in UK terms, Bacchus, which now makes what might well be called the nation's signature wine. Other grapes are grown too, including a few token vines of Madeleine Angevine, because of its similarity to the variety the monks used to grow here all those years ago.

Generally, Warden expect to make around 10–20,000 bottles from their site, but after a great crop in 2003, the 2004 vintage was an absolute wipeout, powdery mildew setting in at the wrong time and ensuring a zero harvest. Hoping to recover in 2005, things were going well, then an unexpected outbreak of botrytis late in the season meant that they only managed to produce around 4,000 bottles. On the positive side, this year Warden is looking at 24–25,000 bottles, and at the open day they were desperately trying to round up anyone who wanted to help them pick on 1 and 2 October.

The open day itself is fantastic, totally free and with a fantastic guided tour and tasting, on which you will learn more and see more than many of the paying vineyard tours that you get. There is a magnificent cheese stall, with produce from all over the country, and the cheese man also does delicious mixed nibbles: stuffed olives, chilli peppers and the like. All delicious. Add to that a cake stall and the Bedford Museum stand for those who want to know more about the area, and you have yourself a magnificent day out.

Opposite.
No problems with the crop this year!

HERTFORDSHIRE
Frithsden

Hemel Hempstead HP1 3DD
Telephone: 01442 878723
Phone for details of opening times

Planted in 1971 on the site of a steep five-acre barley field between Berkhamsted and Hemel Hempstead, Frithsden vineyard is situated in the beautiful Chiltern Hills. Like many of the early vineyards it was planted with Müller-Thurgau, but after three decades of successful growth the owners retired and grubbed up the vines in 2001 leaving the horses to graze.

In 2005 the Tooleys discovered the lost vineyard and gave it a second lease of life, bringing in a team from Luxembourg to plant Solaris, Phoenix, Rondo and Seyval Blanc. After the magnificent growing season of 2006 they are expecting a small crop next year and are in the process of re-equipping the winery and refurbishing the shop. Problems encountered so far have chiefly revolved around deer (mainly small Muntjack) eating the first vine-shoots. They have come across a rather bizarre but apparently thus far effective solution, the strategic placement of bars of cheap soap around the perimeter. The theory is that deer don't like the smell as it makes them think humans are around, though Simon Tooley does say it could be coincidence.

Simon has been growing vines since the early 1980s when his parents bought a ramshackle house containing a conservatory with six mature vines. Having managed to produce a healthy crop every year, and keeping vines in all his houses after this, he and his wife decided to go the whole hog when they found Frithsden, and this despite both having full-time jobs. Frithsden is definitely a vineyard to keep an eye on.

Hazel End

Bishop's Stortford CM23 1HG
Telephone: 01279 812377
Open: by appointment

Growing grapes at Hazel End began as an experiment after the long hot summer of 1976, but the vineyard proper was not established until the 1990s when Charles Humphreys set it up in its current three-acre position. It is the third and best site yet; Italian alders and a beech hedge have reduced the west wind that prevails here, spring frosts have become less common, and the autumns come warmer than previously. 2003 was a standout year for the Humphreys, with a fine sparkling being made, and they also produce a light, dry, aromatic still white blend. Their *Three Squirrels* label is a reference to the ownership of Hazel End by the Gosling Family for 200 years. Since the 17th century a sign hung outside 19 Fleet Street, formerly Gosling's Bank, where Samuel Pepys reported dropping in for 'a pint of wine'.

114

9

THAMES
AND CHILTERN

Buckinghamshire, Oxfordshire
and Berkshire

The southern vales evoke thoughts of soft, sun-blessed green hills with tiny lanes, running rivers and pretty cottages. Tolkien's Shire in other words. And the area around the Chilterns certainly lives up to its billing, home to some of England's warmest weather and to some of its finest wines. It also has moisture-retaining soils and many aquifers which prevent vine stress during periods of drought. The beech woods and chalk grassland support a diverse array of flora and fauna; violets, primroses and bluebells carpet the ground in the woods beneath the canopy. Wild orchids grow on the chalk grassland amongst a yellow carpet of celandines and cowslips. Bird watchers should find plenty to interest them from skylarks to red kites, and if you're lucky you may even find grass snakes and common lizards basking on the slopes in the sun.

Oxfordshire vines

As ever in the UK, it is also the home of bizarrely named places. Particularly memorable are the roundabouts of Golden Balls and Mongewell, the rather ominous Gallowstree Common, the exotic Mapledurham and the chilled out hippy vibe of Tokers Green.

BUCKINGHAMSHIRE
Hale Valley

Boddington East, Hale Lane,
Wendover HP22 6NQ
Telephone: 01296 623730
wine@halevalley.freeserve.co.uk

Antony and Carol Chapman's small vineyard makes still and sparkling wine and is open to visitors during English Wine Week and by prior appointment. As far as I am aware it is Buckinghamshire's only commercial vineyard.

OXFORDSHIRE
Bothy

Oakley Park, Frilford Heath, Abingdon,
Oxfordshire OX13 6QW
Telephone: 01865 390067
Shop open: Friday–Saturday
10.00–17.00 and the first Sunday in
each month (10.00–16.00). Tours are
welcome but pre-book (min 12, max
30). Also open both weekends during
English Wine Week
www.bothy-vineyard.co.uk

2005 was not a good year for Oxfordshire wine producers in general. The Liwiçkis at Bothy vineyard experienced their worst ever year, with the late May frost completely destroying the crop. And then in 2006, generally an excellent year, the overly warm, wet September led to an attack of 'sour rot' diminishing the crop by 25%. Still, careful selection of grapes at harvest means that they have still been able to produce some good wine to sell in 2007, and their persistence will undoubtedly pay off, given Bothy's well-established reputation.

Bothy has 6,000 vines in total, the most successful of which have tended to be the Ortega and Optima grapes that excelled in 2004, probably the best vintage in Bothy's 29 year existence. Not only did that year bring a good clean crop but Richard and Siân Liwiçki actually made the wines themselves for the first time. The resulting Optima/Ortega blend, the *Renaissance*, changes radically from year to year, the 2003 being rich and deep with nectarine and dill aromas and a peach and cream palate akin to a southern Rhone white. It ages gracefully. The *2004 Oxford Dry* meanwhile was a much drier and more Sauvignon Blanc-like wine.

There are problems with wildlife here, but even so the local beasts and birds, excepting the rabbits that burrow through the soft sandy soil and weaken the vines, are encouraged most of the year. The exception is at harvest time, when the Liwiçkis employ a motley array of bird screechers, helium balloons shaped like birds of prey, bangers, shimmering CDs and netting to try and keep both the hedgerow birds and the high flyers away from their precious

116

crop. Full ripening now occurs most years, which was not the case when Bothy began. All this creates a need for voluntary help, and the social side of running a vineyard was one of the reasons Richard originally wanted to buy the vineyard; he had been helping out the previous owners voluntarily himself to learn more about the making of wine.

The Battered Birds and the Boozy Bees

Grapes in the wild turn into wine purely from the action of wild yeasts on the sugars and there are many stories from all over the world of drunken animals, from confused bees unable to find their way back to their hives to elephants leaning up against trees because they are unable to hold themselves upright. One can only feel sorry then for the starling, a particularly voracious grape-eater, which is the only animal that can't get drunk! Apparently its immunity to the effects of alcohol is due to having an enzyme capable of breaking down alcohol around 14 times faster than humans. Perhaps this explains the starlings' bitter refusal to accept sobriety in gorging on as many grapes as quickly as possible.

In Oxfordshire, at now defunct Boze Down vineyard, the labels of the wines (one of the best labels in the country I reckon!) were festooned with a drunken badger, courtesy of the little blighters that ate most of their first real crop of grapes back in 1997. The solution in Boze Down's case was a combination of electric fencing and high trellising (Geneva Double Curtain), which at any rate turned out to be the best form of trellis for the grapes – O happy coincidence! The badgers are now restricted to the windfalls, and good luck to 'em I say.

Brightwell

Rush Court, Shillingford Road,
Wallingford OX10 8LJ
Telephone: 01491 832354
Group tours only
www.brightwines.co.uk

Just on the south side of the River Thames, north-east of ancient, pretty Wallingford lies Brightwell, one of the most promising young English vineyards. Situated on a flinty chalk-clay in the sheltered bowl of the upper Thames Valley, it is run by Bob and Carol Nielsen, an enthusiastic and energetic couple. Not only do they keep the huge number of vines well tended and trimmed but there are beautiful flower gardens all around, birds of prey eye you from their cages, and there are some ace pigs. As if that isn't enough for them they are instrumental in the local vineyard association, and the UK wine awards were held here at this lovely site in 2006. The vineyard itself is wide-spaced, and luxuriously green, the sun scattering long shadows everywhere.

All the wines here are good, but I would particularly highlight the *Oxford Rosé*, 100% Dornfelder: a vivid reddish pink, with delicious cherry and raspberry aromas and dry refreshing flavours of redcurrants and pink grapefruit. One for those who like their rosé close to the red side of the spectrum. Their red is also good, and with bitter cherry flavours is reminiscent of an Italian wine. Lastly, the *Flint 2005* is delicious, with greengage and gooseberry flavours. If you like Sauvignon, try this.

Right. Brightwell vines

Below. Those pigs!

Fawley

Henley, The Old Forge,
Fawley Green RG9 6JA
Telephone: 01491 577998
Tours by appointment

Fawley, another rolling Oxfordshire vineyard established in 1985, has a problem with pigeons. Perhaps it's the proximity to so many thick beech woods* that top the Chiltern Hills but they are particularly greedy here, scoffing down grapes with gay abandon. 2003 was particularly good here, with fine still wines, and 2002 made a luscious sparkler. 2005 by contrast demonstrated the other side of the viticultural spectrum of yin and yang, with the entire crop wiped out by an outbreak of powdery mildew. The spread of this will not have been helped by the higher humidity that has been experienced in recent years in this part of the country, one of many effects of global warming that are not beneficial to grape growing in this country.

* These are the best woods for finding edible mushrooms. The dense tree-lined walkways have such thick foliage that it can cut off up to 80% of the sunlight. They are also a sign of chalky soil and adorn the downlands across the South.

Global warming and its effects

The world's climate is changing rapidly – you only have to ask growers of vines. As to how this might affect production just consider that the bulk of Australian wine production areas exist at an average temperature of 24.5°C. If the predicted 3°C rise occurs, their grapes will turn to raisins!

What about the UK you ask? Well, according to DEFRA statistics, all ten of the hottest years on record have been during the period 1990–2007 which would be no surprise to anyone who has been growing grapes for more than twenty years. At Ridgeview, where they have their own weatherman, Mike Roberts says that in the 1960's, there were no days over 29°C, in the 70's one or two in three of the ten years, the 80's a handful, but since 1994 every year has

had several, and they are becoming more and more prevalent.

There are many other changes too, from the higher humidity mentioned at Fawley to the 'lumpy weather' brought to my attention at Painshill in Surrey (see separate vineyard entry). At Glyndŵr vineyard in Wales, Richard Morris, whose family have farmed potatoes in the area for years said that they have kept careful diaries of rainfall for years. And while he said that if climate change was not such a hot topic, he might not have noticed any change, when it came down to it he had found that autumns were generally wetter, while January and February were drier. He also commented that for the first time ever his vines were looking a little stressed because of the June/July heat; they are used to temperatures of 20°C, rather than 27°C plus. Interestingly too, the figures for this year show that July was the driest since 1911, which was the last good vintage (one of the few!) for the historic Castell Coch vineyard in South Wales.

BERKSHIRE
Stanlake Park

Stanlake, situated within Windsor Great Park, has a rich and fascinating history that reaches back to the 12th century when it was named Hinton Pipard. Its name was changed to Stanlake Park in the Tudor period and its first vines were planted in 1979 when it was known as Thames Valley Vineyards. The neat vines, including unusually, the Gamay grape famous for Beaujolais, ripen well in the warm Berkshire sun and thrive in the loamy, well-drained soil. With an on-site winery, in high yielding vintages like 2006, Stanlake Park can process 150–200 tonnes of grapes and make more individual wines than most. Around a dozen different wines can currently be bought from the cellar shop at the vineyard, which is open every day. Over the years, these have included some of the finest red and sparkling wines in the UK.

The original manor house here was timber-framed and partitioned with wattle and daub. This manor remained until about 1590 when the political situation in Britain settled after the Wars of the Roses and landowners were confident in spending money to re-build using brick. In 1502 the estate was owned by Sir Reginald Bray, who helped to arrange funds for Henry VII's invasion of Britain and was with Henry when he defeated Richard III at Bosworth. Legend has it that he picked Richard's crown from the bush where it had fallen and passed it to Henry, thus starting the Tudor Dynasty. Sir Reginald had been appointed under-treasurer of England in 1485 and as an architect he is credited with altering and re-building parts of St George's chapel in Windsor Castle. After his death, Stanlake passed to the wife of another eminent man of his day, Sir William Sandy (later created Lord William of the Vine). He was a soldier and signed the letter to Pope Clement regarding Henry VIII's divorce from Queen Katherine.

Other owners of the estate have included Francis Windebank, Secretary of State to Charles I, and Richard Aldworth who fought gallantly for the Royalists at the battle of Newbury and at the siege of Bristol. Charles II is reputed to have stayed at the house to be able to rendezvous with his mistress Nell Gwynne. It is believed that one of the major battles in the revolutionary fight between James II and the forces of William of Orange took place close to Stanlake Park and thus the inscription on the clock tower of the stable block at Stanlake Park reads 'Revolution 1688'. In memory of this some of the Stanlake wines are named *Clocktower*. Richard Aldworth-Neville was born at Stanlake and was the editor of Samuel Pepys's Diary.

Twyford, Reading RG10 0BN
Telephone: 0118 9340176
Open in winter: Monday–Saturday
11.00–17.00, Sunday 12.00–16.00
Restaurant: Monday–Saturday
11.00–17.00, Sunday 12.00–17.00
www.stanlakepark.com

Stanlake's eccentric and colourful history seems to have seeped into the water, and perhaps the wine. Nearby Westbury vineyards was owned by Bernard Theobald, an eccentric bearded man whose fervent belief in the potential of the UK for viticulture combined with an experimental nature to bring the Geneva Double Curtain training system to the UK. This was in addition to the use of unconventional grape types, an idea adopted by John Worontschak, the Stanlake winemaker who learnt his trade with the mighty Penfold's in Australia and who has been at the forefront of innovation in the UK wine industry (and various other places in the world) for many years. Attention to detail, including less dense planting methods and the invention of training systems appropriate to the climate by Jon Leighton have ensured high sugar levels and a fearsome reputation as a great winemaker.

A particular reputation for great reds has emerged, perhaps a consequence of Thames and Chiltern's position as the warmest UK region, and I have indeed had some fine reds here, particularly the Pinot Noirs. For me at the moment however, it is their *Pinot Blush 2006* that stands out, a rosé with moody character showing off a type of wine that the British are increasingly brilliant at making. It is indeed blushed in colour, with strawberry and orangey hints on the nose and palate and ethereal, delicate flavours reminiscent of really good Sancerre Rosé. Tasty.

WESSEX

Hampshire, Isle of Wight, Channel Islands, Dorset and Wilkshire

The ancient Saxon kingdom of Wessex is a mixed bag as a wine region, but is generally temperate due to an interesting pattern of isotherms that swirl together just south of the Isle of Wight. This is one reason that Hampshire is one of the counties most densely developed with vineyards, although bar Wickham they are generally pretty small. Wiltshire too is burgeoning as a viticultural county, though its soils and terrain differ markedly from the hilly limestone Chilterns in the north to greensand and the massive flatland of Salisbury plain in the south. All said, this is a promising region wine-wise, and vineyards are likely to continue to proliferate hereabouts.

HAMPSHIRE

Beaulieu

This is one of the true homes of the great UK wine revival. The abbey itself, reputedly one of the most haunted places in Britain, was founded by Cistercian monks in 1204 and had its own vineyard which lasted for some considerable time. Then in 1956, the Gore-Brownes rented a house beside Beaulieu called The Vineyards and duly established their own vines there. By the 1960s their initially tentative experimental vineyard was turning out thousands of bottles of *Beaulieu Abbey* wine. Margaret Gore-Browne even wrote a book on the subject, the entertainingly named *Let's plant a vineyard: 6000 vines, 600 or 60 or 6* and also planted vines in South Wales (without much success it must be said). After the estate passed over to the National Motor Museum, it became attached to the lovely gardens, and can be visited by prior appointment.

John Montagu Building, Brockenhurst, Beaulieu SO42 7ZN
Telephone: 01590 612345
www.beaulieu.co.uk

21 June 2006

The hot slow dust of the southeast, houses blur into one great pub-less estate, with road names like Primate Road and Calabrese, trying desperately to alleviate the stifling suburban boredom. Shedfield, Botley, Boarhunt, a fruitless search for Titchfield wines.

Bishop's Waltham was better, and I found some Northbrook Springs wines at a little restaurant/wine shop which would have been robbed of all its stock if it had been in a city. Ten minutes passed as I wandered round the shop alone before a member of staff appeared from upstairs. Grape designs are all over the town and the Bunch of Grapes funeral service and Vine Street seem to urge me on through historic connections. Indeed William of Wickham's home was at Bishop's Waltham ...

Bishop's Waltham

Tangier Lane,
Bishops Waltham SO32 1BU
Telephone: 01489 896803
Groups only. By appointment

Situated on the intriguingly named Tangier Lane, Bishop's Waltham is a little haven set away from the bustle of modern life. The owner finds relaxation in the vineyard as it keeps him away from his computer screen, a therapy from his day-to-day business. And it has been long-term therapy, the vineyard having been planted in 1982. From a quality point of view the best years for Bishop's Waltham were in 1985 and 1987, while yield was largest in 2006; their own favourite recent wine has been the 2005 Pinot Noir. Over 25 years, they've noticed that spring comes two weeks earlier, and autumn correspondingly two weeks later, equivalent to an extra month on the growing season. Unusually for this part of the country, the grapes are not sent away to be made into wine but are processed and bottled on site.

Birchenwood

Birchenwood Farm, Brook,
Lyndhurst SO43 7JA
Telephone: 02380 812595
Open during English Wine Week

The quaintly named Birchenwood lies just west of Southampton, in among a small cluster of New Forest vineyards and was planted by Joan and Frank Briggs in 2001. They began harvesting in 2004, with a small yield, while 2005 was hit by a rainy autumn and late spring frosts. Very little wine was made that year, but it was good quality. The 2006 was still maturing in Vat 6 at the time of my visit, awaiting its testing, but a good yield may have been diluted by another bout of seasonal rain. The Briggs make their own wine, and if you're staying within the lovely green dome of the New Forest, Birchenwood is open during English Wine Week (late May/early June).

Coach House

Roger Marchbank is the Chairman of the UK Vineyards Association, a familiar and approachable figure in the world of English and Welsh wines. This ex-BT manager almost fell into growing grapes and making wines when he bought a house in West Wellow, Hampshire. Back then the land that now comprises the vineyard was an acre of field with someone else's horse grazing on it. The horse was neglected, and so the Marchbanks asked the owner to take the horse somewhere it would be cared for properly. This suggestion was ignored, upon which the owner of the horse kicked up a fuss. The Marchbank's lawyer said that rather than fight a court case they should instead plant something, and as nearby Wellow vineyard (then a major force in UK wine) were wanting extra grapes, they planted up in 1987. Two years later Wellow vineyard had gone bust, but by then Roger had got the bug, and never looked back. He looked after his vineyard part-time while still going out to work for eight years, and nowadays looks after not only the UKVA and Coach House vineyards but makes wine and helps take care of four other smallish vineyards in Hampshire (Setley Ridge, Bewley, Marlings, Birchenwood). Coach House derives its name from the

Coach House grapes ripening

pub over the road which was the coaching inn lying precisely 12 miles between Salisbury and Southampton. His own house was part of the livery stables.

Roger has problems with foxes that will eat grapes all night long, but at least they help to keep the rabbits off the young vines. Happily, Bacchus and Reichensteiner don't attract much attention from the wasps as they ripen in October, by which point the pests are usually gone. Talking of vintages, he comments (and is not alone in this) that 2003 brought loads of sugar but no flavour, while 2004 by contrast was a big well- balanced crop and was probably the best year so far. 2005's crop was pretty much a disaster; a late spring frost hit on 6 May at -3°C decimating the leaves and the crop not only here but in a swathe of vineyards through Hampshire, Berkshire and Oxfordshire. With earlier budding than up north they were hit hard here and Coach House lost its entire crop, just like Bothy vineyard in Oxfordshire. With his geologist's cap on, he comments that in the long-term the world is heading for another Ice Age, but there are definite changes in weather patterns, hotter, earlier summers being one of them. Still, he suggests we shouldn't forget that it is not just 2003 that was an unbelievable year, but 1968 and 1947 as well; in the late Middle Ages we couldn't grow grapes, because, historically, the Thames used to freeze over regularly.

Roger loves winter pruning when you can pick which days you go out, and with the vintage over feel the sense of creating something for the coming year. He believes that a big part of the UK wine scene will always be hobby vineyards like his own which produces around 1000 bottles a year. In the future he thinks there

UKVA

The UK Vineyards Association, formed from the six regional associations and a grouping of the large producers in the UK, is the organisation to which grape growers and winemakers belong in order to share information, to have a voice in Westminster and Brussels, and to promote their products. The association has overseen the changes that have taken UK wine from small beginnings in the 1950s to over 300 vineyards today in a growing UK market. The St George's Day trade tasting is now firmly set as part of the wine trade year and English Wine Week as part of the rural products year. The Wine of the Year Competition is our internal celebration of quality and success and the results list and award stickers bear witness to the wider wine world that our wines are now worth taking seriously.

The following are the officially sanctioned quality statuses for UK wines.

Quality/Regional wines – tested. You will often see 'psr' on bottle labels. It is a required EU term meaning 'produced in a specified region.'

Quality Sparkling wines – untested. The lack of testing needs changing, and there is a definite movement towards this.

UK table wine – untested, no grape varieties or vintage allowed on label.

will be roughly 30 good wineries of some size and that the UK will produce about three times as much still wine than it currently does. Contrary to old-fashioned views of French and English rivalry the UKVA and the French Independent Vignerons are close and given that we are in the same EU wine band (for the purposes of wine rules and regulations) as the Loire it makes sense to come together more. Roger doesn't think that a proposed EU planting ban (brought on by over production of wine in other countries) will cause as many problems as has been foreseen either. He does worry a little that the predicted boom in English sparkling wine may not actually have the market that is needed for all the planting being done and he still thinks that white and rosé wines are probably the way forward for the UK. Asked about his favourite wines, he recalls *Northbrook Springs Aromatic Dry 1996*, *Eglantine North Star*, *Thames Valley Heritage Fumé 1998* ('an amazing oaked wine, something we will learn to do better and better') and *Chapel Down Pinot Noir 2003*. Even so he isn't sure whether we will manage reds very well generally. In conversation with him, his passion for UK wines is immediately obvious and his contribution to them is undoubted.

Court Lane

After a quick shower back in the sweltering depths of London I sat down to try out *Court Lane's Ropley Classic 2004*. I was amazed ... deep burnished shining-yellow in colour with a delightfully fresh tropical fruit smell lifting from the glass and flavours of grapefruit and melon, fuller than average and far better for six quid than most worldwide wines. It is particularly amazing once you learn that it is 54% Müller-Thurgau, a variety I have generally found to be pretty uninspiring. The addition of Reichensteiner and in particular Huxelrebe, probably makes all the difference. In any case, it was the perfect end to a hot sweaty day, most of it spent in the car. Clearly, Stephen Flook, the 70-year-old owner and winemaker at Court Lane knows what he is doing. No wonder that El Vino, the long-established Fleet Street vintner has the sole agency for the UK.

Court Lane was originally just a garden planted up with 40 vines in 1975. Stephen's vineyard is not generally open to the public, though he does do occasional tours and will see people if contacted beforehand. Nevertheless it is a fascinating example of the old-style UK hobby vineyard done right. It lies on a gentle south-western slope and production averages 2,000 bottles a year. The soil is clay loam over flinty chalk and despite its altitude of 125m above sea level the frost is not usually too bad. In temperature

Ropley, Alresford SO24 0DE
Telephone: 01962 773391
Visits by prior arrangement

Left. Court Lane's barrel press

Right. Leaving Court Lane: resplendent poppy fields

checks over 15 years he has recorded 1,000 'degree days', a measurement of how much heat is needed to grow grapes for wine, on only two occasions (see *General Topography* on page 41 for more about this). Pheasants wander through the vines like they own them and pigeons are an unusual pest, descending in huge flocks 'just like locusts' to devour the ripe grapes. Generally, the vineyard is a quiet, lonely place filled just with birdsong and Stephen, which suits him, especially at the end of June when the smell of flowers break through the vines. But his expression changes to a smile when expressing his particular love for the harvesting when the place is filled with 18 people all chattering and gathering together afterwards for a shared meal. Prior to retirement, Stephen was a chartered chemical engineer and still does all the testing on his own wines, as well as for some other vineyards. He used to make elderberry and elderflower wines and was inspired to try viticulture when he came across Gillian Pearkes' book on UK viticulture. The small modern winery was built in 1993.

Northbrook Springs

Beeches Hill, Bishop's Waltham,
Southampton SO32 1FB
Telephone: 01489 892659
Open: Easter–Christmas, Saturday
11.00–17.00; Sunday 13.00–17.00
Christmas–Easter, Saturday
11.00–16.30. Phone beforehand.

Northbrook Springs was planted in 1989 on the warm, free-draining, southern slope soils of the Hampshire Downs. They have experimented for a long time with differing styles of wines from oaked whites to sweet wines and the quality here is very high. Since they received the benefit of noble rot in 1994 they have been one of the few UK vineyards to consistently make dessert wines. The current owners took over in 2000 and have had good vintages since. The wines are sent afar to Cornish Camel Valley to be made. Their *Aromatic Dry 1996* was a particularly fine wine, which had aged into a refreshing, delicately limey beauty after 10 years, yet more proof that British wines are well able to compete with worldwide whites in ageworthiness. More recently, their *2002 Sparkling* was also excellent.

Somborne Valley

2003 was Somborne Valley's best year so far with an exceptional Pinot Noir and sparkling wine. Presumably, that year the badgers kept their sniffling snouts out of the grapes, they are pretty much the only real pest in this run of little vineyards that dot west Hampshire. Well, I say little, though actually Somborne is one of the largest at 20 acres and if the plan for 50 acres and their own winery by 2009 comes to fruition they will then be a large estate.

Hoplands Farm, Kings Somborne, Stockbridge, Hampshire SO20 6QH
Telephone: 01794 388547
Retail outlet on site

Sour Grapes

This vineyard is a hangover from the Thomas's old house, with which they inherited seven acres of grapes. When they moved in 2001, they missed the vines and decided to plant up an acre of vines (450) with red Triomphe and white Seyval grapes. To their extreme misfortune, just as they were awaiting the fruits of the recent long hot summers, their house burnt down in March 2006 and the whole of the 2005 harvest was lost in the blaze.

Oak Tree House, Michelmersh, Romsey SO51 0NQ
Telephone: 01794 388547

The 2006 vintage was too much for them to handle, but they did rally the troops around and picked the Triomphe and so at least there will be some red from their *annus horribilis*. They're now just hoping that the taste makes all the effort worthwhile. And, despite these difficulties, they are putting the best foot forward and in the future intend to build a winery and open to visitors.

Webb's Land

At the Queen's Golden Jubilee celebrations at St James's Palace in 2000, English wine was being served and the wine in question was *Webb's Land 2000 Fumé*, undoubtedly a memorable moment for Philip Peters. He also recalls the *2000 Sparkling* being a particular triumph, which was unusual as in most UK wine-growing regions 2000 was a pretty awful vintage. He acquired the 14-year-old working farm and vines in 1998 and has since had various successes. Wines are currently sent to John Worontschak to be made at Stanlake Park.

Webb's Land, off Tanfield Lane, Wickham PO17 5NS
Telephone: 01329 833633
Open for visits by prior arrangement

Winchester Vineyard

Winchester SO23 7EA

This is a small enthusiastically-run hobby-vineyard of the type that often starts people off on larger-scale plantings. The Winchester vineyard consists of two allotments; the 82 vines sharing their space with raspberries, strawberries, redcurrants, blackberries, plums, apples, rhubarb and assorted vegetables and herbs. The winery consists of the kitchen and the winemaking is done using a handpress. The wine goes into recycled bottles. Titles of wines include *Titus's Tipple*, named after their cat and *Alfred's Blood* after King Alfred who governed Wessex from Winchester. Vintages vary sharply, 80 bottles in 2004, 11 in 2005 (hit by late frosts and pigeons) while 2006 should produce over 200 bottles. The Chisholms reckon that the vineyard has cost them between £1000–1500 including allotment rent. They are keen to promote a new movement, allotment vineyards and these do indeed seem to be a more and more common feature of the UK wine scene at the moment. Indeed it is the enthusiasm and joyful experimentation of small vineyards such as these that have helped keep the UK wine scene on its upward curve over the past 50 years.

Wickham

Botley Road, Shedfield,
Southampton SO32 2HL
Telephone: 01329 834907
Open: February–December,
Monday–Saturday 10.30–17.30;
Sunday 11.30–16.30
www.wickhamvineyard.co.uk

Top. Spacious sunlit rows of vines. The historic oaks pictured in the background are not helpful to the vineyard, quite the opposite in fact; they shade them, take nutrients from the soil and are a home to insects and birds. The latter problem is partially solved by the use of Flash (the dog), bangers, noisy things on strings and shouting children.

Bottom. The winery: note the manholes at the base of each tank.

From the high plateau of the New Forest, where horses grazed behind my tent, I descended into Hampshire. Suddenly the villages were not villages so much as commuter points for London with fewer pubs and churches and less sense of independent life than further west. Even the vineyards feel better organised, less ramshackle and more business-like.

To be found just past Reading Room Lane, Wickham is no exception, established in 1984 and now run by Angela and Gordon Channon. It has a nifty tape-recorded tour through the large, pretty estate, making it ideal for lone visitors, especially with such a good selection of wines. The tour also takes you to the modern well-equipped winery, which you will see in action if you go at the right time of year. In addition there is a restaurant and a nature reserve of mixed and wet alder and wetland which sports meadow flowers, great spotted woodpeckers, deer and sparrowhawks.

The tour focuses partially on the history of UK wine and wine drinking. Close to the vineyard Roman pictures of drinking cups were discovered at an unearthed pottery kiln, while Hambledon, only a few miles away, was the site of the first UK commercial vineyard to be planted in the 20th century. The site itself is only

20m above sea-level, protected from southwesterlies and is very fertile. Its 12 acres produce 30–35,000 bottles of wine each year, making it one of the larger vineyards. Having said that, extensive work has been needed, first to drain the heavy clay (as vines really don't like getting 'wet feet') and recently they have resurfaced a nearby slope in order to make it south-facing, a mammoth task. Wickham uses very high training systems and wide spaced rows; this helps protect the vines from ground frost.

Wickham Medium (Würzer grape) has a lovely fresh aroma and an easy honeyed herbaceousness to the palate. If you fancy something really different (and a bit pricier), the *Sparkling Demi-Sec* (a little sweetness) split my tasting group of friends down the middle, sort of toffee-ish and rich, yet at the same time with a hint of prawn cocktail crisps. Well, I did say it was different. The wines here are sold at the House of Commons and Vinopolis.

Ageing Wine

No man ... having drunk old wine straightway
desireth new: for he saith, The old is better.
                                        St Luke ch.5, v.39

Well I'm not convinced of this as a universal truth myself, as most wine is made for drinking young. Nevertheless, many of the wines you will come across at UK vineyards will be older than the previous year.* This is because many wines, in particular sparkling wines and reds, benefit from being put away to age in oak barrels or big stainless steel vats for anything from one year up to eight. Many, including still whites also benefit from bottle-ageing (on their side, in a dark, cool place) at home.

The theory of ageing whites is this. If you split white grape types into aromatics (Sauvignon, Viognier) and neutrals (Chardonnay, Riesling, Chenin), then it is the wines made from the latter types that will age well, but in actual fact, there seems to be no such rule for the UK. Theoretically Madeleine Angevine ages well, but not unless you can get the acidity high enough which is often a real problem. I have had beautiful aged Kerner and Huxelrebe. Bacchus, which is ferociously aromatic, can age superbly or not at all well, depending on acidity and how it has been made. In fact UK wines, perhaps because of their

marginality and tendency to underripeness seem to need bottle-aging. You may well be amazed by the change in a UK white three years after you bought it. Mature wines are full of details that are not there in younger vines and it is well worth laying the wines down for a few years if you have the patience and space.

Oak barrels at Wickham give light vanilla flavours to wines but at a price of over £400 a time!

* Though not as many as in other countries due to the aforementioned high demand for UK wines. I lost track of the number of times people were unable to say whether their wines aged well as they had sold out of everything each year!

ISLE OF WIGHT

Adgestone

Adgestone is one of the oldest vineyards existing in the UK. Almost in its 40th year, it was begun in 1968 and the owners still make their own wines in the cellars. Interestingly I was told that the best year thus far was in fact 2006, so the wines on their way this year should be very good indeed and may even match up to the success of the *2003 Barrel Aged Red*, probably the best wine of theirs that I have tasted. This picturesque vineyard, set in 10 acres of outstanding natural beauty, is open all year round, so if you happen to be on the Isle of Wight do go and visit. It is overlooked by Brading Down, with its nearby Roman villa, where it is believed the Romans used to grow grapes 2,000 years ago.

Upper Road, Sandown PO36 0ES
Telephone: 01983 402503
Open: Easter–October, 10.00–17.30;
November–Easter, 10.00–16.30,
Tuesday–Sunday
www.adgestonevineyard.co.uk

Rosemary

Rosemary is a surprisingly large British vineyard, covering 30 acres and would undoubtedly be better known if it was on the mainland. That said, it has the benefit of the mild island climate, always a draw for people of all ages. Its valley situation helps retain summer warmth and offers shelter from the southwesterly winds. The gentle vineyard slopes allow excellent frost drainage in the spring to protect the newly-budded vines whilst the soil, a clay-silt loam overlying greensand, is not only free-draining but also retains sufficient moisture for healthy growth.

You are free to stroll around the vines, enjoying the surrounding views and there is a *'Vine to Wine'* video, showing a typical year in the vineyard. The winery is available throughout the year for you to browse around and contains display boards on the wine-making process. Particularly interesting is that Rosemary's winery is in operation on selected days throughout the year. If you are interested in visiting them during a operational day just ring to find out dates. Whatever your tipple there's something for everyone here, from red wines, ciders and bottle-fermented sparkling wines to liqueurs, country wines and apple juice. Rosemary even sell an excellent selection of traditional island-produced mustards, garlic and biscuits.

Smallbrook Lane, Ryde PO33 4BE
Telephone: 01983 811084
www.rosemaryvineyard.co.uk

Oak-ageing

Oak-ageing brings a very different character to wines and is something which is becoming more common in the UK, though we are still in the process of discovering which grapes combine best with wood. The wooded, grilled or smoked aroma is more delicate if the wine is matured in casks rather than exposed to oak chips. Barrels must be properly seasoned before they are used and the wood introduces particular aromatics into wine which are whisky lactones (coconut), vanilla aldehyde (vanilla), and engenol (cloves). English oak is too slow growing (and therefore too expensive) to be a viable ageing wood.

CHANNEL ISLANDS

La Mare

St Mary, Jersey JE3 3BA
Telephone: 01534 481178
Open: April–October,
Monday–Saturday 10.00–17.00
www.lamarevineyards.com

Just outside St Mary on Jersey, La Mare is an old vineyard and drinking their *Domaine La Mare Barrel Fermented 2003*, I could swear I was drinking a decent white Burgundy; it has all the character and finesse of good Chardonnay with a lovely, bright, yellow colour, a slight gold sheen and a nose of vanilla, flowers and a hint of asparagus. The palate has a buttery oakiness; rich but not overly so with a slight floweriness, orange zest and citrus flavours and good length. Tingly. You would never guess that this was a UK wine, let alone that it is made of Seyval Blanc and Phoenix grapes. It matched the lemony goat's cheese we were eating superbly. Perhaps this Frenchness is due to its proximity to France, but then one would expect a Loire Sauvignon-a-like, as is the case in mainland Britain. Perhaps it suggests a good future for oaked Seyval and the as yet little-tried Phoenix. They also make *Bailiwick Red* and an unoaked white.

La Mare itself is a farm of great antiquity; prehistoric flints are frequently discovered here, indicating man's presence thousands of years ago. The earliest buildings here date from the 1600's and the fine central farmhouse, built of the lovely pink granite for which the island is famous, is dated 1797. For much of the 19th century its land was devoted to apple trees beneath which grazed the farm's herd of Jersey cows, giving way to potatoes and cauliflower in the 1900's. Robert and Ann Blayney planted Jersey's first commercial vineyard at La Mare in 1972 and developed it to include not just vineyards but also the Jersey Distillery (apple brandy is a speciality and cider is also produced). La Mare has a beautifully peaceful ambience and good facilities for visitors with a restaurant and tours of the 22-acre vineyard and winery. On a final note of curiosity, their Rosé sparkling is named after the Lily of Jersey, Lillie Langtry.

DORSET

Horton

Horton Estate, Wimborne BH21 7JG
Telephone: 01258 840258
Courtyard shop open at weekends from
10.00–16.00 for tasting and sales.
Closed January–February
Phone beforehand

Dating from 1985, this is Dorset's largest vineyard, producing white, red and sparkling wines. Brian Burch founded Horton but retired in 2000, selling on the vineyard to Neil and Sara Forest. Their red (Pinot Noir-based) is notably good, and from personal tastings this most difficult of grapes seems to do surprisingly well in Dorset. They also use oak maturation, which combines notably well with

Kerner, while their Bacchus is often turned into sparkling wine. There are picnic areas and a well-equipped winery situated beneath Horton Tower.

Purbeck

Since the retirement of the previous owner in 2006, this intriguing vineyard, set up to produce good reds on the Jurassic Kimmeridgian soils of South Dorset, has been taken over by Rob Steel. The Steels love this part of the country, famed for its beaches, cliffs, Swanage and Corfe Castle (just down the road from the vineyard) and jumped at the chance of a change of lifestyle. The Swanage railway chugs along beside the vineyard; it really is a lovely place to visit. In the past, the best wine has been the Pinot Noir and they are hoping to build on this success whilst also making whites and perhaps even sparkling wine. Everything is done at Purbeck itself (as Rob puts it: 'low food miles') and there is a new website.

Valley Road, Harmans Cross,
Corfe Castle, Dorset BH20 5HU
Telephone: 01929 481525
www.purbeckvineyard.co.uk

Sherborne Castle

1996 was Sherborne Castle's greatest vintage, 15 years after planting both yield and quality were very high. The *Bacchus/ Reichensteiner* produced that year was particularly good. The vineyard was begun as an alternative to arable and dairy farming and the wines are made at Bagborough vineyard by Steve Brooksbank. They have noted recently that sugar levels have been higher in the grapes but are not certain if this is due to climate change or to the application of trace elements as folian food. The latter allows leaves to remain greener for longer with resultantly higher photosynthesis, leading to higher grape sugars.

Wake Court Farm, Bishops Caundle,
Sherborne, Dorset DT9 5NG
Open: by appointment only
www.sherbornecastle.com

WILTSHIRE
A' Beckett's

In 1995, Paul and Lynn Langham were sitting in the next village along from where they now live and work watching the boys play and wondering what to do with their lives. In late 2000, they bought the farm that lies beside the Tudor Farmhouse and is known as A' Beckett's. It already had 600 apple trees and 60 Victoria plum trees and the Langhams added six acres of vines the following year. The vines quickly took root and some of them grew over eight feet in their first season. The weather during 2001 was

High Street, Littleton Pannell, Devizes,
Wiltshire SN10 4EN
Telephone: 01380 818153
www.abecketts.co.uk

Two Vicars Bless the Success of 5,100 New Vines

In a symbolic ceremony reminiscent of ancient traditions set down in France and Germany, two local vicars will be blessing the planting of 5,100 grape vines, on a former fruit farm at Littleton Pannell near Devizes on 23 April – St George's Day. Paul said: 'Having the vines blessed by our local ministers is symbolic of fruitfulness, growth and productivity. The vines will suit our climate conditions very well as they come from Northern France and Germany, where conditions are very similar to our own. With the varieties of grape that we are using, we intend to produce red, white and sparkling wine. In the meantime, we will be watching and tending our vines and look forward to being blessed with success when our first bottle is popped in 2003.'

Business Link News, (23 April 2001)

ideal for the young vines, with plenty of sun and rain and a long autumn to help the new growth ripen. 1300 posts were put in and the combined length of wire used from start of vine to end of last vine amounted to five miles.

The Langhams currently grow Auxerrois, Reichensteiner, Seyval Blanc, Pinot Noir and Dunkelfelder (for colouring). The August day I visited on was a much more typical English summer's day than I had seen through June and July, cooler with sunshine coming and going, as opposed to the baking heat of the previous months. I sat with a coffee on a pub-style table outside their house, looking out over the green fertile dip that Paul envisages one day being a valley of vines. I know what he means, it is easy to imagine an English equivalent to the slopes of the Cote d'Or here. He is actually engaged in trying to persuade the farmer opposite him of the benefits of grape growing. Judging by the success of their white wines I can see why he might decide to follow suit (local Waitrose stores will soon be stocking A' Beckett's wines).

Their efforts are aided by the looming hill nearby, which while not as high as Plumpton's 1,500ft-high Sussex ridge, is still enough at 7–800 feet to create a rain shadow and thus shelter them from the westerly winds. So while nearby Devizes, with its Wadworth brewery (which still has its own beer cart and Shirehorse to hold up traffic) often gets heavy rain, they rarely see it here. The greensand soil here is similar to much of southeastern England and it seems to suit not only the white grapes but the reds too, judging from the grapes I saw which were well into ripening. Proof comes in the pudding; the delicious *2004 Estate Blend* (Auxerrois/Reichensteiner)

Flowers and smoke over A'Beckett's sunny rows

needs serving ice-cold for its fruity gooseberry flavours and mineral edge to be as refreshing as an icy river after a dusty days' hike in the desert. Lynn says she thinks the Pinot Noir dominated *Estate Red* tastes like Christmas in a glass and she's right. With its supple meaty tannins, cranberry fruit and slight nuttiness, it is one of this region's best reds. It will be even better in a few years; at present its over-exuberant acidity is its only flaw.

The Langhams are very involved in the local vineyard association and are a good example of the younger people who are the future of the UK wine industry. The major pests faced are badgers who the Langhams try to entice away from the ripe grapes with badger gates and cat food. 'If I could speak badger, I'd tell 'em to sod off,' says Paul. Plans for the future involve not only increasing the acreage, but also adding a visitor centre, shop and winery. If they have come this far in so short a time, I believe that they will achieve this and I very much hope that 'Vine Valley' will be a reality in the not too distant future. Certainly the climate and the beauty of this vineyard bode well, not to mention the quality of the wines which are currently made at Wickham in Hampshire. They have absolutely no regrets and are actually making money from the enterprise. 'Otherwise,' says Paul pragmatically, 'we couldn't be doing it.'

Bow-in-the-Cloud

And Noah he often said to his wife when he sat down to dine,
'I don't care where the water goes if it doesn't get into the wine.'
Wine and Water (1914), GK Chesterton (1874–1936)

Noahs Ark, Garsdon,
Malmesbury SN16 9NS
Telephone:01666 823040
wine@bowinthecloud.co.uk
www.bowinthecloud.co.uk

Bow-in-the-Cloud has several things that make it unique. As you drive along the single-track country lane keep your eyes pinned for a lovely old cottage, beside which is a lamp post the like of which you may not have come across since reading *The Lion, the Witch and the Wardrobe*. Upon its side hangs the brightly-coloured wooden vineyard sign depicting Noah's Ark and the rainbow of God's covenant, the Bow in the Cloud. The name was decided on by the readers of *The Sunday Times*, whom Keith Willingale, previously a naval engineer, had decided to consult and the wines that they now produce, *Cloud Nine* and *Arkadia*, were named in the same way. Bow-in-the-Cloud consists of five acres of Schönburger, Bacchus, Seyval and Phoenix and last year the vines produced around 8,000 bottles of white wine, which is mostly sold at farmer's markets and from a butcher in Malmesbury.

Keith produced his first Bacchus in 1994, just 69 bottles off 116 vines. He has since found Seyval Blanc to be a blessing because of its reliability, with Bacchus taking the most time and energy. That and the Schönburger (which was starting to turn its lovely orangey colour on my visit) are always threatening to get mildew. A blue ex-vineyard tractor found in a barn in Somerset and an unusual but effective William's spray attachment for the back have made work in the vineyard a thousand times easier. It is not only disease that is a problem but animals as well. 'We get everything,' says Keith, with some exasperation, 'deer, hares, pheasants, foxes, badgers ... and squirrels.' 'Squirrels?' I replied, unsure that I had heard correctly. Apparently, the EU is currently using Bow-in-the-Cloud as part of its evidence to allow culling of squirrels. 'The squirrels gnaw the young bark,' explains Keith. As far as he knows and I know, it is the only squirrel-afflicted vineyard in the UK. Despite the squirrels, the last few years have seen good crops here in North Wiltshire, aided by Keith's innovative methods. You can tell that he loves this technical side of farming grapes, his naval engineering skills being used to good effect in a unique training system which uses a grooved post with T-pieces that can be moved once the vines reach a certain height. Not only this, but he finds that when he plants vines and more than one grows, he lets them carry on growing and it doesn't seem to harm them. So I saw five vines rising where one might expect one normally, but all still bearing fruit without difficulty. The final novelty I saw was that some of the young vines had rolls of flat plastic around them, an idea borrowed from the UKVA, but which effectively gives each vine its own little greenhouse and protects it from pests and herbicides.

Climate change seems to be bringing added warmth, which is lucky because it has also brought earlier November frosts which necessitate earlier picking here. *Cloud Nine* is a Bacchus/Schönburger/Seyval blend which is herbaceous, lemony, with a hint of spice and a really clean finish. The 2004 was still too young when I tried it and will benefit greatly from two more years of bottle age, after which it will have mellowed into a graceful lovely wine. On the back is the following legend:

Above. Vines are wrapped in polythene for protection and warmth

Opposite. Smoking dog in Malmesbury

CLOUD NINE
It is reputed that the ninth pair of creatures to enter Noah's Ark
were two crows who loved to boast about 'a day on the grape.'
They chattered away in their top-of-the-ark nest crowing that
the juice of the 'lubbly bubbly' was like 'us nines on clouds'.
This was the origin of the expression 'being on cloud nine'.

Fonthill Glebe Wines, incorporating Test Valley Vineyards and New Forest Wines

The Winery, Teffont Evias,
Salisbury SP3 5RG
Telephone: 01722 716770
Contact vineyard first before visiting
www.fonthillglebewines.co.uk

This well-established vineyard emanates from the late seventies and together with associated vineyards in Hampshire produces a diverse range of wines from sparkling Seyval to Pinot Blanc. Sales are from the winery and from local farmer's markets, not least Salisbury, where they can be found every Saturday.

Quoins and Little Ashley

Contact to buy wines: Alan Chubb
Telephone: 07835 265082
alan@quoins.demon.co.uk
www.quoinsvineyard.co.uk

Quoin's first vintage came in 2005. It was a satisfying start after struggling with the depredations of botrytis without the aid of commercial sprays (it is an organic vineyard). Despite these difficulties a rather good Rondo red was turned out from this southernmost outpost of Cotswold limestone, near to the Saxon town of Bradford-on-Avon. Legumes and grass cover are grown between the vines and this helps soil fertility, reduces weeds and increases the insect predator population. The wines are made at nearby Mumfords vineyard and Alan Chubb began his viticultural life by helping out and managing his neighbour's vines at Little Ashley. They still look after that vineyard as well, though Little Ashley is not organic and sell the wines in addition to their own.

Wylye Valley

Crockerton, Warminster
Telephone: 01985 211337
Open: January–April, Saturday only
10.00–17.30; May–December,
Monday–Saturday 10.00–17.30

The river Wylye which flows at the bottom of the valley is famed for trout fishing and each wine here has been named after a fishing fly. Thus they have *Coachman, Teal & Green* and *Watson's Fancy*. Here, they do not blend the grapes but make varietal wines from the cool-climate varieties Regner, Kernling and Seyval Blanc. Like A' Beckett's, the soil is a free-draining greensand and the vineyard lies in the shelter of the river valley near Warminster. These nine acres of vines are capable of producing 15,000 bottles a year. Friendly service and a free tasting make this a worthwhile stop-off point if you're anywhere near Warminster or Salisbury Plain.

The shop, with vineyard behind

II

THE WEST COUNTRY

Somerset, Devon and Cornwall

This region is milder than the east coast, though the farthest-flung regions suffer difficulties due to westerly winds. I have found the general consistency of West Country wines to be impressive by comparison to other areas, most have good length and often exotic, warmer flavours than in other places. This is a little paradoxical given that it is no warmer and indeed often much cooler than other areas to the east. There also seems to be more of a willingness (partially due simply to topography) to plant on steeper hillsides and this adds character and definition to the wines. This point needs to be noted if the UK wine industry is to prove that it can grow good enough grapes to produce the great wines of which I believe it is capable. Interestingly, many of the finest wines in the world are west coast, not east, as these areas tend to be cooler and less humid.

SOMERSET

Bagborough

Stephen Brooksbank has been producing cider and wine in this part of Somerset since Pilton Manor vineyard closed down some years ago. The former Pilton winemaker still produces wines for many smaller vineyards all around this part of the country and certainly knows what he is doing; Pilton Manor wines used to win many awards. The farm that he works from is not really an appropriate site for growing vines and instead Stephen rents land, French-style, at North Wootton, near Shepton Mallet. Winemakers like Stephen have kept the quality of many a vineyard's wines up over the long years and have been responsible for discovering the best ways of utilising the weird array of grapes the UK possesses.

Pylle, Shepton Mallet,
Somerset BA4 6SX
Telephone: 01749 831146

Dunkery

Wootton Courtenay,
Minehead TA24 8RD
Telephone: 01643 841 505
www.exmoor-excellence.com

At Derek Pritchard's Dunkery vineyard, the largest in Somerset, ten varieties of grapes are grown including five red varieties. Most of these wines, including the reds age incredibly well and have particularly fine aromas. Tucked away in an Exmoor village, the vineyard shares its tenure with an abundance of wildlife; buzzards, red deer, roe deer, badgers, foxes, pheasants, partridges, green woodpeckers, goldcrests, long-tailed tits and large flocks of goldfinches are regular visitors. The magnificent Exmoor views all around make this a worthwhile visit, as do the wines, some of which are simply fantastic and are carefully aged and made on the premises. A range of other local products can be bought at their Exmoor Excellence shop, while their own wines can be bought in many of the little shops around the Exmoor area. Their *1998 Reichensteiner* was fabulous, like a morose, windswept winter's day suddenly torn apart by vivid summer sunshine. If you want a wine with a zest for life this is it.

The steep slopes of Exmoor

Mumford's

Mumford's is a family-run business whose grapes are grown on the four-acre vineyard just east of Bath. Vinification is done in the purpose-built winery. They produce several varieties of white wine, rosé and an outstanding English red. These are available from local outlets, including Waitrose in Bristol, Bath, Cheltenham and Cirencester, as well as direct from the vineyard or by mail order (phone or e-mail for details). The unusual vineyard name is derived from Simon de Montfort who is believed to have owned land in the area. The labels have a Roman theme because two Roman roads to Bath pass near Mumford's and a Roman coin was found beneath a vine.

Shockerwick Lane, Bannerdown Road, Bath BA1 7LQ
Telephone: 01225 858367
Visitors to the vineyard are welcome, as are tour groups, but telephone first.
www.mumfordsvineyard.co.uk

Oatley

Oatley are a small but ambitious commercial vineyard with a favoured site on a well-drained, fairly low-lying southeast slope in rolling countryside between the Quantock Hills and the Bristol Channel. Two dry white wines a year are normally produced by Iain and Jane Awty from Kernling (the grapes of which can ripen to a pinky red colour) and Madeleine Angevine. They aim for interest and character, rather than blended consistency, so there can be significant differences in the wines from year to year. But the varietal characteristics shine through to give two distinct 'series' of wines, named *Leonora's* and *Jane's*. The wines have won 13 awards in 15 years of entries to *Wine Magazine*'s International Wine Challenge, the world's largest blind wine tasting.

Cannington, Bridgwater TA5 2NL
Telephone: 01278 671340
Visitors welcome but phone first
www.oatleyvineyard.co.uk

Staplecombe

Since 1981 Martin Cursham has been having a lot of fun at Staplecombe vineyard in Somerset, growing grapes and making wine to earn a crust. His best year has been high-yielding and high-quality 1989, when he made his favourite wine, a single varietal Kerner. 2003 was excellent for quality but had a poor yield, while 2006 had an excellent yield, but indifferent ripeness. Perhaps this latter comment may suggest that some predictions of 2006 being a great year may be premature despite the enormous crop brought in at most vineyards.

Burlands Farm, Staplegrove, Taunton TA2 6SN
Telephone: 01823 451217
Summer afternoons only, phone ahead

Rolling Devonshire countryside

DEVON

For all further information on vineyards in Devon visit this excellent website.
www.discoverdevon.com/site/food-and-drink/vineyards

Blackdown Hills

Oaklands Farm, Monkton,
Honiton EX14 9QH
Telephone: 01404 47442
Seasonal 10.00–18.00 by arrangement
www.blackdownhills-vineyard.co.uk

A good stop-off point if you're on your way down to Dartmoor or Cornwall. Stretch your legs after the drive to Devon with a cheap walk-and-taste tour which takes you around the fields with lovely views and Dumpdon Hill as a fine backdrop. There is also a guided tour of the vineyard and winery available by appointment. This includes a wine tasting and an informative talk on the process from vine to wine and lasts approximately two hours. The wines are named *White Monk* and *Red Monk*.

Down St Mary

The Old Mill, Down St Mary,
near Crediton EX17 6EE
Telephone:01363 82300
Open: 1 April–31 October and
1 December–24 December,
Tuesday–Saturday 14.00–17.30
www.english-vineyard.co.uk

Situated in the rural heart of mid-Devon, on a steep sun-filled slope above the River Yeo (not the Somerset one), Down St Mary was planted in 1986. Here the soil changes from the south Devon red clays to a warm shale. A public footpath at the top of the vineyard shows off the typically pretty views and if you search carefully you may find the badger sett, the inhabitants of which are rather destructive. In their shop/tasting room, you will receive a warm

The bridge at Down St Mary

welcome from Bernard and Penny Doe, who have gone from volunteering to run a stall for the Southwest Vineyards Association (while someone was away) to running the whole operation. They took over in 2001 and immediately grubbed up the Siegerrebe that was there, preferring to plant Pinot Noir, Pinot Meunier and Dornfelder in order to produce fizz, red and rosé.

They are about to release a single varietal Madeleine Angevine, which is to be named *Maddy*, after one of their large friendly dogs (she was named for the grape variety and likes to chase her own shadow) and their labels have won awards for design, for which the credit goes to Bernard. Other names are as interesting as the labels, with their Kirton wine named after the old name for Crediton, which used to be the Bishopric before Exeter stole its limelight.

The *Bottle Aged Classic 1996* (Huxelrebe/Reichensteiner/

Sharp terraces increase the
intensity of the sunlight

Bacchus blend) was fascinating, with a heavily-honeyed, apricot
nose and a strange, dry, palate. As Penny said, 'It's what happens if
you lie in a dark room for 10 years, you go weird.' I liked it a lot, kind
of reminded me of something fitfully, softly decomposing, like
newspapers in rain. Of the modern wines, I particularly liked the
Downe Reserve, just off-dry with a honeyed nose and a rhubarby
palate, presumably on account of the unusual Schönburger/
Madeleine blend.

Down St Mary are also closely connected with the local Higher
Living vineyard, whose grapes they take on and which is extremely
steep having been converted from sheep and cattle pasture after
foot and mouth disease.

Kenton

Helwell Barton, Kenton EX6 8NW
Telephone: 01626 891091
Open: May–September, 12.00–16.00
including weekends and bank holidays
(closed Thursday and Friday)
www.kentonvineyard.co.uk

Kenton lies on the west side of the beautiful Exe Estuary, nestling
in the foothills of the Haldon Hills. Planted in 2003 on an old farm,
the south-facing slopes and sandy soil along with the mild and
sunny climate are ideal for grapes. Matthew and Jo left behind
careers in law and medicine and moved from London to the West
Country in 1998 with their young family, ready for the challenge of
growing vines and making quality wine in the English countryside.
Matthew had planted some rows of vines in their old orchard

garden and after extensive research into the realities of growing vines in England, he swapped intellectual property law for a tractor suit and enrolled on the wine studies course at Plumpton College, East Sussex. Here, like so many other new UK viticulturalists, he learned grapegrowing and winemaking hands-on in the college's vineyards and winery.

Kenton now has over 4,500 vines producing thousands of bottles of wine annually. Visitors are welcome to enjoy the wines and vineyard and to participate in the many events and activites that go on here, including wine tastings, food- and wine-matching events and grape picking at harvest. Wines are made on site in a purpose-built winery and Kenton currently produce a white, red and rosé. A decked sun lounge overlooks the vineyard, yet another place to enjoy the beauty and tranquility of Devon's rural setting with a glass of wine. Devon must surely rate as one of the best counties for vineyard visiting in the UK.

Manstree (Boyces Farm)

I had to go back to Manstree on my own on Thursday morning, as we had failed to find the place on Tuesday (the one low point of an otherwise fabulous day that included paddling in the sea, a gorgeous meal and a fantastic bottle of 2001 Margaret River Cabernet). Somehow, through tiny lanes and winding hills, past Noglands Farm and the pungent smell of the bulk potato farm I found my way there and went for a wander down the vineyard, which is dwarfed by the much larger and rather appealing pick-your-own farm. The latter has just about every conceivable type of fruit from tayberries to tummelberries and numerous beautiful handbaskets of flowers. Unfortunately I visited too early for strawberries and gooseberries, all delayed due to the cold spring.

There is a well set-up, free vineyard walk and tasting here (depending on what's in the fridge), as you wander up and around the rows of vines and fruits. It must be a superb place to be a little later in the summer when the grapes are ripening (currently they are just flowering, though the flowers are beginning to turn to miniature bunches of grapes) and there is fruit all around. The flowers need dry breezy conditions in late June and early July for pollination. Unusually, a quarter of the vineyard is on a north-facing slope, on which are placed the early-ripening Madeleine Angevine and Siegerrebe varieties. Though these ripen 7–10 days later than the same varieties on the southern slope, in summertime they actually get more sunshine in the early morning

Bottle Shapes

Wine bottle shapes have changed radically in the UK over the past few years. The tall thin Hock bottles of old have now just about disappeared (a bit of a shame I think) due mainly to their association with cheap German wines like Liebfraumilch and Blue Nun and in have come the shorter, fatter, Bordeaux and Burgundy styles. Perhaps the UKVA should encourage a bottle designing competition for a distinctive UK bottle reflecting the individual flavour of the wines and matching the creativity of our labels.

New Barn Farm, Manstree Road,
Shillingford St George,
Exeter EX2 9QR
Telephone: 01392 832218
Open: March–December,
Tuesday–Sunday, bank holidays
10.00–17.00
www.boyces-manstree.co.uk

Above. Flowers, fruit and vines exist together at Manstree

Right. The rather ominous tale of Manstree, as told on the label

MANSTREE

English Regional Wine 75cl
Produce of the United Kingdom
..every man shall sit under his own vine.." Micah 4v4
Made from grape varieties grown at and bottled for
Manstree Vineyard, Shillingford St. George, Exeter, Devon. 01392 832218

Best Served Lightly Chilled

Manstree is the name of the road that passes the Vineyard and also that of the nearby field, indicating that there was once a gallows there for the execution of sheep stealers and other felons.

Today, vines now flourish on the warm Southern slopes of renowned Red Devon Soil, producing fine white wines.

and late afternoon and the wide rows let in more light and counter disease. An experiment with Chardonnay failed, as it doesn't seem to like the red Devon soils much, preferring southeastern greensand and maybe this explains the prevalence of sparkling Seyval in these parts.

Planted in 1979, this vineyard has two names; the first comes from the Boyce family who have owned the site for 12 years. Manstree is explained on the wine label above, a rather dark but exciting tale that conjures up images of days gone by. The wines are made at Yearlstone and Camel Valley, one being the *Mayval Medium Dry*, a blend of Madeleine and Seyval, hence the name.

We drank the *Manstree Essling Brut Non Vintage* (12%) on a beautiful evening in the quiet of our campsite, after a long walk on

Dartmoor. Made using the Méthode Traditionelle from Seyval Blanc, the same grape that Camel Valley use for their sparkling, it couldn't have been more different. To be honest I wasn't expecting much from an £8 bubbly that Manstree have stopped producing, but this stuff was awesome, a lovely yellowy colour with good mousse (bubbles) and a rich, lithe, lemony, mildly yeasty nose and palate; if I had more time and money, I would have gone back and bought up the rest of their stock. We accompanied it with prawns in mayo and paprika, rich and full-flavoured, but not enough for the wine, which overpowered them. Manstree is sited in an area known as Devon's Frying Pan because of the atypically low rainfall and it clearly works wonders on the grapes. Devon seems a cheery place generally, full of tanned people and lorries with dust graffiti that have a sad face beside the word Monday and a happy face beside Friday – not your general 'Clean me.' style of wit here.

Oakford

White, red and rosé wines on four acres in the beautiful Exe Valley, 10 miles north of Tiverton, Exmoor edge. Visitors are welcome but phone first.

Holme Place, Oakford,
Tiverton EX16 9EW
Telephone: 01398 351486

Old Walls

Old Walls Vineyard is situated on steeply sloping, south-facing land overlooking the village of Bishopsteignton and the river Teign. The name is partly inspired by the 13th-century Bishop's Palace of which all that remains are small parts of the once impressive walls. There is evidence of a vineyard here dating back to Roman times but the present vineyard was begun by the Dawe family in 2002. They have planted a good selection of grape varieties, the Pinot Noir early variety seeming to be very much at home in this climate. Mind you, they've already had to transplant some mature Reichensteiner vines due to poor moisture retention on slopes of up to 35°.

Old Walls Road,
Bishopsteignton TQ14 9PQ
Telephone: 01626 770877
Open: at weekends for tours and tastings but please ring first
www.oldwallsvineyard.co.uk

The wines themselves are on sale at Old Walls Vineyard shop and winery where tastings are on offer, not to mention lunch in the tearooms and a terrific terrace view. To the delight of the family the wine produced from the first harvest in 2004 was awarded 'English Quality Wine' status. The *2004 Red* has real depth of colour and is smoky and full of soft red fruits. The red, white and sparkling wines are made in their own winery which was completed in the autumn of 2005 and the 2006 vintage was the largest so far.

Pebblebed

The Wine Cellar, 46a Fore Street,
Topsham, Exeter EX3 0HJ
Telephone: 01392 875908
Visits by arrangement. Shop open
for sales, Saturday 10.00–13.00,
or by appointment
www.pebblebed.co.uk

Pebblebed Rosé 2004 is an astonishing wine, like drinking pure delicious crisp rhubarb. It was the vineyard's first commercial vintage and deservedly won a Gold Medal at the English and Welsh Wine competition. A bright future beckons and the enthusiasm and knowledge of head honcho Geoff Bowen (an environmental geologist) is tangible. The vineyard has been built up from a tiny community vineyard in 1999 to a total of 22 acres today. Pebblebed is so-named because of the giant, raging rivers that transported and deposited hard quartzite pebbles across the Triassic desert forming the deep pebblebed ridge that extends across parts of East Devon. Today these remarkable pebbles are visible on the beach at Budleigh Salterton and are unlike any other rock found in southern England. This is undoubtedly one of the best organic vineyards in the UK and with each of three sites spread over south Devon bringing different qualities to the wines, there is a real sense of *terrior* as well. Pebblebed consists of sites located at Ebford, Clyst St George and at West Hill, near Ottery St Mary. The different sites may be better suited to different grape varieties and the diverse locations help to spread the risk from natural calamities such as frost or hail. Geoff's approach is to seek land that is best suited for viticulture, wherever it may be located.

The potential to have grapes from different vineyards also adds considerable interest from a winemaking perspective. By vinifying in small parcels from the various vineyard sites and sub-sites, Geoff is able to identify the unique character and personality contributed by each locale. Such wines may be blended where judicious, or can be kept as separate single-vineyard cru examples. The philosophy throughout is to create a range of Pebblebed wines that is distinctive and reflects the personality of the respective *terriors*.

They are not afraid to experiment here and are one of a handful of vineyards currently testing the potential of Cabernet Sauvignon and Merlot in the UK. Indeed, these experiments may not seem so daft if Geoff's prediction that the amazing growing seasons of 2003 and 2006 will be the norm in ten years time comes to pass. Interestingly the rosé is primarily made from the white grape Seyval Blanc, which I have sometimes found to have a rhubarby tint to it and the new vintages of 2005 and 2006 were both tasting great. This is one of the few rosés that I would actually recommend ageing a year or two (presumably something to do with the Seyval base) to make the most of their deliciously crisp, dry, pink, grape-

The idea of terroir relates to the specific effect that a particular place and all the elements that go into it (aspect, soil, people, grape type) has on the wine that is made. It is about the production and celebration of wines unique to an area or site and highlights the interrelatedness of people, the land and viticulture. It embraces all the facets of a locality, from general climate down to specific soil structure of each tiny part of the vineyard. The Benedictine monks of Burgundy even went so far as to taste the soil to see what the differences were. This is in sharp contrast to a more New World view of grape type being the all-important factor, a view which has tended to produce the opposite effect of homogenising wines into having to taste varietally pure.

Personally, I am a terroirist; a nation's wines ought to reflect (to my

overly Romantic mind), its rural reality, its personality as a locale of a certain nation. What I desire from wine is something exciting, interesting, different and this is something the UK wine industry has in spades. But what it currently needs more of is great wines which reflect the country's personality.

Wines that smell of orchards, or of apple pie and cream to warm your innards in the cold of winter, or rhubarb crumble. Or reds that are elegant and strawberryish, or plummy or raspberry-packed with that smell of English roses, earth and drifting woodsmoke. Delicate floral flavours, the smell of hedgerows, fresh cut grass, honey, a scent and taste equivalent of the English and Welsh countryside. We're certainly getting there. I have tasted wines such as these and they are beginning to be the rule not the exception.

So which of our varieties show different terroirs best? From my experience at the moment, the most widespread differences I have come across have been in the single varietal Bacchus and Seyval Blanc wines, though it really is just as much about finding the grape that works best on a particular soil and place.

fruit flavours. Their dry white is also lovely and a sparkling wine is planned for release for Easter 2008. The wines can be bought at many outlets around Devon (see website), but chiefly from the Wine Cellar in Topsham, just south of Exeter. In the future, they plan to do tours from Darts Farm and with their varied sites I would imagine it could turn out to be a fantastic visitor experience. A bright future beckons.

Sharpham Vineyard and Cheese Dairy

Sharpham is one of the most stunning vineyards in England. The thousand-year-old farm nestles on a steep hillside overlooking the River Dart as it slowly turns from estuary into sea. Overlooking the vineyard is Sharpham House, built in 1770 with monies from Captain Parnall's capture of a Spanish vessel. It was designed by Robert Taylor and further interest is found in the Jacob Lane sculptures dotted around the grounds. The wrecked ship SS *Kingswear Castle* rests in the water below, now a perch for the local herons and

Sharpham Estate, Ashprington,
Totnes TQ9 7UT
Telephone: 01803 732203
Open: March–November,
Monday–Saturday, 10.30–17.30
or by appointment
www.sharpham.com

a Buddhist training and teaching college sits beside the vineyard. As if that's not enough, Sharpham also has volcanic outcrops, an old lime kiln and a huge water meadow, with abundant wildlife ranging from shellducks and herons to peregrine falcons and Atlantic grey seals.

The vineyard has a sheltered position at 12–25m above sealevel, washed by the tidal waters of the Dart which keep the clay soils moist. Warm even for South Devon, which is known as England's Riviera for good reason, the well-drained red shillett soils generally help the vines to budburst by the last week of April. Madeleine Angevine grows especially well here, with Muscat-like characteristics and their Dornfelder consistently ripens fully. Wandering around this beautiful, if occasionally confusingly mapped-out vineyard, one's attention is particularly grabbed by the fearsome steepness of the slopes.

The vineyard manager, Peter Sudworth commented that they had to give up on part of the vineyard because it was too dangerous to take tractors down and it isn't hard to see why. The winemaker Duncan Schwab has grown up with wine, his father founding St Sampson's vineyard in Cornwall (now defunct) many years before and he and the other staff have created a friendly easy-going atmosphere that makes tasting these wines a particular pleasure, whether you are beginner or expert. The quality of wines is superb too, impressively consistent given that they produce around 40,000 bottles a year. One finds plenty else to be distracted by too, all the above plus a very reasonably priced restaurant with wines by the glass, or fantastically sited picnic tables.

It's hard work doing this vineyard tour!

As I said it's a very good selection of wines, with lifted aromas and notably lengthy finishes to the whole bunch. Our favourites were the *Bacchus 2005* which really was very Sauvignon-ish, lively zingy and much more tropical than those from farther east; like a cross between Sancerre and Kiwi Sauv. The *Sharpham Red 2004* has got to be one of the best reds in the UK. It is 80–90% Dornfelder with a splash of Rondo, but doesn't taste like a Dornfelder with its rich red colour foretelling the velvety brambly fruit which wash all over the palate. If you want something even more unusual you could always splash out on the *Beenleigh Red 2003* (£21.50), which is made from Cabernet Sauvignon and Merlot grown in polytunnels nearby and which has regularly scooped UK Red Wine of the Year. Great wine, if pricy. Age it in your cellar for ten years to get the best result. The cheeses were great too, handmade with unpasteurised milk from the Sharpham Jersey herd, especially the *Rustic with chive and garlic*.

I can't help but wonder whether the high quality and interest of the wines here is related to the steepness of the slopes. Not enough UK vineyards are planted steeply enough in my opinion. There is a reason the world's greatest wines are grown on hillsides.

Yearlstone

Bickleigh EX16 8RL
Telephone: 01884 855700
Open: April–October, Friday–Monday
11.00–17.00 or by appointment
www.yearlstone.co.uk

Yearlstone's leaflet bears the proud statement, 'You don't have to visit Bordeaux to discover more about the magic of wine'. Once you have struggled up the incredibly steep slope, you turn sharply into an avenue of deciduous whitebeams. After you get out onto the terrace over the Exe Valley, your breath is taken away by the sheer beauty of the view, the 30-year-old vineyard falling away down below you into a lush green valley, a silver river glinting, the smell of wildflowers in the meadows, ancient buildings peeking from far hillsides.

And you might dwell on the possibility that mild springs, warm summers and long, gentle autumns might encourage good fresh, aromatic wines, in touch with their beautiful surroundings. Or reflect on the fact that this vineyard was once owned by Gillian Pearkes, one of the founding mothers of English Wine and that for 12 years it has been managed by Juliet White (wife of BBC correspondent Roger White; one of the most promising winemakers in the UK) whilst wandering through the vineyard for free, or enjoying a guided tour, or perhaps a delicious quiche, or glass of wine in the café.

These are fine wines. Get past the rather confusingly numbered labels and you will find an excellent range of well-priced wines, each very different in style (something you will certainly not find at every vineyard). Even the two *Madeleines* (*No. 1 and 2*) were utterly different, the first all easy-going apples and freshness and the second, sweeter and with just a splash of Bacchus, soft and peachy. The *Bacchus*, aromatic and Sauvignon-like; the *Rosé*, salmon-pink, strawberries and cream; the *Red*, black fruits and tobacco hints. And my favourite, the lightly-oaked *Number 6*, a Pinot Gris/

Wildflowers cover the ground between the vines at Yearlstone

Reichensteiner blend, superbly balanced with hazelnut, peach and lemon flavours; fresher and less rich than an Alsace Pinot Gris, but rounded and beautifully representative of where it comes from.

The wind was howling around the hill when we were there, abnormally powerful and ripping down gates and flower displays at will. It was a contrast to the normally quiet and sleepy atmosphere that prevails here at Yearlstone, its latitude shared with the famed Mosel wine region (although with markedly milder springs and autumns). The soil is red Devon sandstone with some shale.

Juliet says she got into the whole thing through starting to drink and like English wines herself. She also comments that things have changed a lot around UK wines, most of their customers used to be little drunken men and at the start things were a little soul-destroying at times because of the lack of enthusiasm. Badgers eating her entire first crop of Siegerrebe didn't help either. But, things have really picked up since the last poor harvest in 1997, which although tiny, was of an extremely high quality. Small consolation when you're trying to make ends meet. Today, with its well-equipped winery and its talented winemaker proving to the old men that women can do it too, this vineyard is one which I would highly recommend visiting, especially if you doubt the worth of English wines.

The view from this high, windy hill is fantastic.

CORNWALL
Camel Valley

After a jaunt to the stunning Lydford Gorge on the western side of Dartmoor – cascading waterfalls, dark rock pools and the mellow sound of rushing water – we travelled across Bodmin Moor for the Camel Valley Grand Tour, which is one of the more expensive guided tours. It was worth it, though we probably saw less of the steeply sloping vineyard than is usual due to the sweltering June heat. Certainly, that rather short part of the tour was the only disappointment of what is otherwise a great experience.

Moving on to the mercifully cool winery we were given an excellent talk by our guide (one of the Lindo clan who own and run Camel Valley) during which questions from all were encouraged and answered with enthusiasm. Not only that, but you get a *very* generous tutored tasting at the end of the tour. Almost no one leaves without a bottle of something or other and the atmosphere sitting up on the terrace above the vineyard is most congenial to sitting and chatting with a glass of wine.

Camel Valley has famously been championed by Rick Stein (after the tasting, you could pop to his restaurant in Padstow and try the Camel Valley wines there with seafood), Matthew Jukes and many others. It is a fabulous setting with a great tour and atmosphere, but I did find the wines varied a lot in quality, perhaps due to decisions on the exact blend being made by a group and not a single winemaker. Don't misunderstand me though, as three of the wines stand out as among the very best in the UK. The *Cornwall Brut 2005* is my joint-favourite UK bubbly, very English and made of Seyval Blanc and Reichensteiner. The nose is delicate and pretty, an aroma that is really difficult to pin down, delicate orange blossom, a hint of petrol, like an aged Riesling. The palate on the other hand, with its tiny bubbles and lithe creaminess was all fruit, apple and elderflower, extraordinarily refreshing and great with seafood.

And it doesn't stop there as the *Bacchus Dry 2006* is also a grand drop, unquestionably one of my top ten whites. It has an amazing aroma of elderflowers and fresh-cut grass that bounds up your nose like a puppy under a hose on a hot day. The dry palate has a deep, wistfully lingering, light flavour with more elderflower and a touch of lime cordial. The *Red* and *Rosé* were both lovely too, but if you're finishing a meal with a spot of blue cheese, then the pick of the rest has to be the *Sweet Aperitif 2005*, not thick and treacly, but lightly honeyed and with a slightly cheesy (in a good way) smell about it. I must also express my approval for the screwcaps which

Camel Valley Vineyard,
Little Denby Farm, Nanstallon,
Bodmin PL30 5LG
Telephone: 01208 77959
Open: year round; Monday–Friday,
Easter–30 September; Saturday,
bank holidays, Sundays 10.00–17.00
Guided Tours, 2.30 weekdays;
Grand Tour, Wednesday at 17.00,
April–October
www.camelvalley.com

adorn the tops of these wines, by far the best way to keep these white wines fresh, aromatic and beautiful.

Camel Valley was also Winner of Winners for Cornish Distinctiveness two years in a row, something the company is very proud of it.

Top. Big leaves help to protect the grapes from the rain

Bottom. The tasting room, where generous measures are dispensed

Lambourne

A young vineyard. Visitors are welcome to call and arrange a visit from Easter to September and see Graham Sheratt's modern wine-making methods in practice.

Ruanhighlanes, Truro TR2 5NL
Telephone: 01872 501212
www.lambournevineyard.co.uk

Oak Valley

3,500 vines adorn the two acres that make up Oak Valley, deep in the heart of Cornwall and close to the Lost Gardens of Heligan. It grew from a trial of a few vines back in 1996 and the 2006 wines are looking the best yet. The vineyard is planted on a gentle south-facing slope in a shallow wooded valley of oak, willow, hazel and hawthorn and the soil is deep fertile loam. This can present problems in controlling the natural vigour of the vine in such a good soil and they are carefully pruned each year, following the Scott Henry trellising system.

The vines are now mature enough to respond to the excellent 2006 spring and a decent flowering period, with a final yield of six tonnes from only two acres. Oak Valley has its own winery and is open Thursday to Saturday in the summer and by appointment at other times. Pest control is aided by the resident buzzards taking out small birds and rabbits.

Bosue Vineyard, St Ewe,
St Austell PL26 6EU
Telephone: 01726 843159
Open: Thursday–Saturday
and by appointment
www.cornwallwines.co.uk

Polmassick

Originally planted in 1976, Polmassick vineyard was taken over by Barbara Musgrave in 1986 and is very close to Oak Valley if you fancy a double-vineyard tour. It is sheltered, with good drainage and soil and faces south-south-west. Here, they make all their own wines of varying types. Particularly memorable have been the 1996 (their biggest cropping year) sparkling wine (Pinot Noir/Kernling) and current favourite is the rosé named *Rudhya*.

Mellym Boyse, Polmassick,
St Ewe, St Austell PL26 6HA
Telephone: 01726 842239
Open: daily for tours and tastings
from end of May to the end
September 11.00–17.00

Rose bushes

Ever wondered why you often find rose bushes growing at the end of vines? A little like the miner with his canary, they act as an advance warning device against mildew because they show it on their leaves well before the vines do. This allows a counter-attack with spraying (usually with sulphur) at any point in the season.

12

WALES
CYMRU

Glamorgan, Dyfed, Ceredigion, Gwynedd,
Ynys Môn, Clwyd, Gwent/Monmouthshire

Well, Man must destroy to create according to Thomas, but here in Wales, Man – and Woman – have created wine against the odds and proved that good wine can be made here, from the Black Mountains to lonesome Ynys Môn (Anglesey). The far-flung parts of this region suffer from western winds and exceedingly high altitudes and thus the vineyards are concentrated in the warmer and (somewhat more sheltered) southeast of the country, around Monmouth and Glamorgan.

This bread I break was once the oat,
This wine upon a foreign tree
Plunged in its fruit;
Man in the day or the wind at night
Laid the crops low,
broke the grape's joy.

Dylan Thomas, 1936

Monmouthshire countryside

GLAMORGAN
Bryn Ceiliog

Fairfield, 14 Clinton Road, Penarth,
Vale of Glamorgan CF64 3JB
Telephone: 02920 711017
Bryn Ceiliog is open to small groups
(6–7 or less) by prior arrangement

As he wanders through the vineyard during winter pruning Ian Symonds has a permanent group of followers. Like Doctor Doolittle, finches and tits fly all around him waiting to be fed, used to his solitary presence in this isolated vineyard, a mile from the nearest dwelling in the middle of the Vale of Glamorgan. He started work in 1998 and by the year 2000 the Symonds had (rather appropriately) planted 2000 vines. Their main enemies are the variable Welsh weather and the mistle thrushes (also known as Storm Cocks because of their unique habit of facing the bad weather and singing) that devoured 500 kilos of black grapes in 2005.

2006 is looking like a top year for quality whites in the UK with a high yield. Prior to that the 2003 whites and reds (mainly made of Rondo) were of the best quality at Bryn Ceiliog. Ian's personal favourite wine was the *2003 White*, chiefly composed of Orion, with some Reichensteiner and Phoenix. The vineyard started for a variety of reasons. There was the vineyard-owning heritage of Ian's Spanish wife Fernanda, a perfect site and a wish to diversify away from the organically-reared, pedigree Welsh Black beef cattle which they still own.

Harvesting here is between the end of September and the end of October and while Ian says that the pickers love what they still remember of those days, he finds it very stressful. Harvest just seems to be one of those times of year that vineyard managers either love or hate. It makes sense really as it's make or break time for all of them.

Glyndŵr

Glyndŵr House,
Llanblethian, Cowbridge,
Vale of Glamorgan CF71 7JF
Telephone: 01446 774564
Glyndŵr wines are available to buy
from www.barrelsandbottles.co.uk

Richard Norris often sits nervously through the flowering stage of the vines in June and early July. It is at this time of year that the south Wales climate hits hardest, as westerly winds bring the sea mists rolling six miles inland to sit atop the rows of well-kept vines behind his house. When I ask him how he got into viticulture he laughs and suggests, 'a stupid idea?' It was a romantic notion which proved to be the hardest work imaginable and is, he says, 'a job that never ends'. His family were potato growers and merchants and already owned the land on which this, the oldest Welsh commercial vineyard was planted in 1982. Despite the fact that this area of Wales has a particularly mild climate (the second highest average mean temperature in the UK, after the Scilly Isles and not

Rare breed hens pecking in the vineyard

prone to frosts), he thinks the site is not ideal, suffering from the aforementioned westerlies and rolling fogs. It is nevertheless a very picturesque six-acre site, with rolling green hills for a backdrop and little ponds and water gardens surrounding the house.

With gently south-southeast facing slopes, Glyndŵr is also the only vineyard in Wales that has had much success with reds (excepting Worthenbury with their polytunnels). The reds were fantastic in 1995, 2004 and 2005, while the sparkling Seyval was creamily lovely in 1996 and the 2003 is looking good too – all golden-tinted though not quite ready yet. 2003 was good for white wines too, his personal favourite of which is the Siegerrebe/Maddy blend. He is now producing a good rosé wine too. In terms of ageing the wines also differ radically. As at nearby Llanerch, the whites here do not age terribly well and are for drinking within two years, while the bubbly is at its peak about five or six years in. The red on the other hand, a blend of Regent/Triomphe/Léon Millot, lasts indefinitely and is generally still good at least ten years after the vintage. One wouldn't imagine so, on tasting it, with its silky light tannins, but the 2005 does have good acidity, cherries, plums and a certain aroma on the finish that reminds me of toasted hazelnuts. Charming, and I know all too well the surprising delights of UK whites that have been aged, so I wouldn't be at all surprised if this bulked out in terms of depth and flavour. Apparently, the *1995 Red* had the character of decent Burgundy after ageing, but unfortunately the one I sampled was only a year old.

Richard loves May, when, unlike in warmer regions, his vines are still dormant. There is time to enjoy the peace and quiet, with little risk of frost here in the Vale of Glamorgan. Even when they do begin to sprout, they are slow to bud and open, the coronets unfurling gently, rather than with the speedy sprint of more easterly vines. At 25 years of age, the vines have less foliage and more fruit and usually produce between 8–15,000 bottles. Rare breeds of hen wander among the rows, along with pheasants and the dog. Later on in the year he adores the vendange (picking time) and seeing what the subtleties of that year's weather have produced. The wines are made at Three Choirs – Glyndŵr are their oldest client – and the label they are decorated with is of the Welsh hero Owain Glyndŵr. The vineyard is not open to the public, but there is a guest lodge at the house and they also sell vines, which are a better earner than the wines as they are untaxed.

A Balthazar (15 bottles worth) of Glyndŵr Sparkling Seyval Blanc

Llanerch

The future of Llanerch vineyard currently hangs in the balance – it is being sold and will no longer be owned by Peter and Diana Andrews who built it into the success story it is today. As Peter puts it, 'it was a hobby gone wrong,' an extension of horticulture on the Llanerch estate they already lived on. After their daughters had left home, they no longer needed meadows for ponies to roam in so they created gardens and planted a small vineyard beside the house. This was no mean feat, as Peter was still running a chain of chemists in the daytime, so he would return home and dig holes for his wife to plant into the next day. Diana, meanwhile, was engaged in learning viticulture and viniculture at Plumpton College in Sussex. For the next 15 years they produced and bottled all their wine themselves, operating from a converted byre. The first vintage of 1986 provided wines for their eldest daughter's wedding. They also converted the original 19th-century stable block into two self-catering cottages and these are available to rent; a lovely place from which to visit southeast Wales. The estate covers 20 acres and contains not only an informative vineyard walk but beautiful gardens and a woodland area. Here lie lakes with fish that come to gawp at you with curious eyes as you trip-trap over the wooden slatted bridge to the secluded islands. It is a restful place bedecked in flowers and commercially the situation is good too, being close to a large population centre.

The Andrews were the first people since the 19th-century Marquess of Bute to try planting a large-scale vineyard in the vicinity (Llanerch now produces a wine for Castell Coch). Their wines are now well-known, highly rated among UK wine buffs and have been served at various state functions. They are widely available from Welsh Sainsbury's and Asda stores and the House of Commons. The couple were also instrumental in getting Wales its own regional status and have done a grand job of publicising not only Llanerch, but also Welsh wines in general. Though Peter says that they have never had a disastrous year, the quantities of wine produced have nevertheless varied hugely. They have had as little as 7,000 bottles to a maximum of 35,000, an enormous discrepancy. Production usually lies between 15 and 25,000 bottles. Poor flowering and frosts are not too much of a problem, whereas ripening the grapes properly is, along with mildew and massive flocks of starlings decimating the harvest.

Peter has always enjoyed winter pruning, because of the challenging nature of shaping each vine ready for the next two

Hensol, Pendoylan CF72 8GG
Telephone: 01443 225877
Open: March–December 10.00–17.00, or by appointment
www.llanerch-vineyard.co.uk

Deleafing vines at Llanerch.

years, each vine being individual and different in its growth. He says with hindsight, that the only thing he would have done differently was to plant 60 acres instead of six. He feels that they have proved that it is possible to make good wines even in cold, moody South Wales and tasting the delicately strawberry-ish biscuity *Cariad* (which means *Love*) *Blush Sparkling* I am minded to agree. It went down a storm when I opened it at a July barbeque. A point of interest, the Celtic Cross logo that adorns the bottle, if observed closely consists of four wine glasses on a plate of grapes.

The vines are now beginning to hit their peak and the wines produced in the next few years should be excellent. Happily, the vineyard will definitely be continued by whoever buys it and the Andrews will undoubtedly be helping out the new owners with advice. Given that they have done pretty much everything themselves since they began the vineyard – including Diana taking an active supervisory role in the winemaking at Three Choirs – this will be invaluable to whoever takes on the daunting task of continuing their success.

Top. Flowers deck the entrance to Llanerch

Bottom. Tall windbreak trees shelter the vines

Castell Coch (Red Castle)

Also of vinous interest in the area is the afore-mentioned Castell Coch, the fairytale Victorian creation of the wealthy third Marquess of Bute who had the castle built in medieval Austrian fashion, turrets and all. His family had vast mining interests in the area and were very wealthy. The Marquess sent his head gardener off to do research in Bordeaux and Champagne and upon return he planted a large vineyard on what is now the site of a golf course and woodland. The grapes had difficulty ripening, but given they were red varieties this is perhaps unsurprising. The wines must have resembled sherry, with 15% alcohol as huge quantities of sugar were added in the fermentation and the wines were matured for three years in oak. They needed the sugar, as the grapes apparently reached full ripeness only seven times in 45 years. Nonetheless, Castell Coch wine seems to have fetched a good price for the time, though *Punch* magazine asserts that it took 'four men to drink it: the victim, two to hold him down and another to pour it down his throat.' Wartime sugar rationing put an end to the Welsh wines and by 1920, the 63,000 vines had all gone.

www.castellcoch.info

Cwm Deri Vineyard, Martletwy,
Pembrokeshire, SA67 8AP
Telephone: 01834 891274
www.cwm-deri.co.uk

Lampeter Road, Aberaeron,
Ceredigion SA46 0ED
Telephone: 01545 570234
Open: Easter–October 14.00–17.00
daily. Organised groups by
appointment
www.ffynnon-las.co.uk

DYFED
Cwm Deri

Country (fruit) wines only. Lots of visitor facilities.

CEREDIGION
Gwinllan Ffynnon Lâs

This is a small vineyard in the beautiful Aeron valley producing white wines and country wines. Aberaeron, the little fishing village close by, is where Dylan Thomas used to go drinking when he lived in a little cottage up the road. Among the wines made are a classically-made fizz, or to use my favourite Welsh word *bwrlwm* (meaning *bubbly*), a late harvest white and a red wine, *Cardi Coch* from black grapes grown under glass in the area. Fruit liqueurs are also available, including apricot, damson and sloe.

GWYNEDD
Eryri

Planted in 1986, Eryri's raison d'etre was to prove a point, that it was in fact possible to grow grapes successfully by the sea in a cold northerly Welsh climate. It worked. Eryri has had some very successful wines over the years, not least a well-regarded oaked *Rondo Red*. However, the Workmans are currently simply keeping the vineyard going until their son takes it over their wines are not currently available. With any luck, this unique vineyard will once again open to the public.

The Wine Snob

The Wine Snob
The wine snob almost always looks like Uncle Monty from Withnail and I: ruddy, a little porky and sour-faced. He knows what he likes and he likes what he knows and will tell you what he knows at any given opportunity. Generally, he hates screwcaps, fancy labels and people who know more or less about wine than he does. Since most wine snobs wouldn't even deign to try English or Welsh wine it leaves English and Welsh wine enthusiasts the freedom to enjoy them for ourselves. Cheers.

YNYS MÔN
Llanbadrig

Even for the UK, the location of Tom Barlow's vineyard is unlikely to say the least. The climate here on Anglesey is not good for growing, yet Llanbadrig has still established itself successfully. (I haven't had the chance to visit, as it was just too far along the coastal road and then over the Menai Strait for me to make it over there.) Tom began planting vines back in Manchester at the age of 14 and it has been a bit of a passion for him ever since. The creation of Gwinllan Padrig (Llanbadrig Vineyard), began with the first planting of a single vine in 1991 The grape type was Frankenhaller, which is a large juicy black grape, related to the Black Hamburg that used to be planted in greenhouses all over the UK. The success of that vine whetted the Barlow's appetite and each year thereafter more vines followed. However, the chosen varieties were not at all suited to the Welsh climate so they began taking a more structured approach trialling different grape types and areas of the farm. By 2005 about four acres had been planted, but lack of rainfall had a devastating effect on the crops in 2004 and 2005. They are now irrigating and two polytunnels have been erected over previously planted Merlot, Cabernet Sauvignon, Pinot Noir and Pinot Gris.

Guided tours of the vineyard and the winery are available (based in a derelict milking parlour) and there is a café doing cream teas. A campsite forms part of the farm, which is close to the beach and has open views out to Snowdon and the Isle of Man. Four wines are currently produced, including sparkling. Their website signs off with the following rather lovely statement:

> *Please try any wine before you leave. You are not permitted to purchase any wine until you are completely happy.*

Gwinllan Padrig, Cae Owen, Cemaes Bay LL67 0LN
Telephone: 01407 710416/ 01407 710999
www.llanbadrigvineyard.com

CLWYD
Worthenbury

Worthenbury was planted by Martin and Mary Seed back in 1991 after some debate about what to do with the large back garden, previously the horse-training ground of the beautiful Old Rectory which they had bought. Unfortunately, in June that year they suffered one of the worst summer frosts on record (4–5 June). That set them back a year, but undaunted they continued with Sauvignon Blanc and Gewürztraminer (because they were fond of those varieties) planting some in the open and some in polythene

The Old Rectory, Worthenbury, Wrexham LL13 0AW
Telephone: 01948 770 257
www.worthenburywines.co.uk

Above. Indoor vines under the …and (opposite top) … polytunnels

Opposite bottom. Inside a perfect polytunnel

tunnels because of their northerly latitude (53°) but soon realised nature was not going to do them any favours and they switched everything into the polytunnels.

To go along with their different viticultural practices, the Seeds grow Sauvignon Blanc (one of the slowest ripening varieties), Pinot Noir, Reichensteiner and Chardonnay, though sadly the Gewürztraminer never worked out and has been relegated to a token decorative vine outside. The polytunnels have a central heating-type system which is used to protect against the spring frosts and they gain a very clean, ripe crop with naturally high sugars and alcohol. Obviously, the tunnels smooth out seasonal variations and the vines receive far more heat than is usual in the UK. When picking their crop in October – a time of year they particularly enjoy – the grapes have a much lower acidity (5–6g/l) than is normal for UK vineyards (often 10–12g/l).

They are now having a *Pinot Noir/Chardonnay Sparkling* made and rate their *2004* and *2005 Sauvignon Blanc* as their best wines yet. I can't disagree. The 2004 is beautifully balanced, crisp and clean with a herbaceous edge and lingering peach and mineral finish. Its pale golden colour is cut with a very pale pink tinge, something I have noticed in a couple of other UK whites with a little age to them. Their *Sauvignon Chardonnay 2003* was certainly not ordinary either, reminding me very much of a decent Chilean blend, with soft grapefruit, melon and banana flavours and again, great length.

Wines are available to buy via their website.

GWENT/MONMOUTHSHIRE
Monnow Valley

Great Osbaston Farm,
Monmouth NP5 4BB
Telephone: 01600 716209
Contact before visiting

Here on the steep banks of the Monnow Valley lies a small vineyard planted in 1979 and extended to four acres in 1988. One mile out of Monmouth town, the area bears resemblance to a miniature Mosel Valley and this is portrayed to great effect on their elegant label. The grapes produce a dry to medium-dry wine that is fruity, crisp and full of character.

Parva Farm

Tintern, near Chepstow NP16 6SQ
Telephone: 01291 689636
Open: Summer 09.00–17.00,
winter 09.00–dusk. Usually open but
phone first for the tour and tasting.

Driving from the south along winding roads we arrived first at the hulking ruin of Tintern Abbey, a famous haunt of the Romantics. Poets and painters have always had a particular affinity with this place, set beside the river Wye among steeply sloping hills. It was a shame in a way that it has been so ruthlessly well preserved as Clare and I would have been happy to lurk among its ruined walls, but were instead reduced to eating our sandwiches on what looked like a ruined medieval toilet just outside the main Abbey.

Afterwards we made our way through picturesque Tintern village beside the road and river, with the sharp hillsides preventing any real expansion. Suddenly we saw a sign for a vineyard, a little way ahead. A sharp turn is required to get off the main road onto the farm track which trawls steeply up the hill to Tintern Parva Vineyard.

Struggle up the steep slope of Parva Farm Vineyard and you will appreciate the additional difficulties faced in every element of looking after their vineyard. One of the benefits of the location, however, is the amazing view from on high, looking out over Tintern Abbey and the curling silver glint of the river Wye. Colin and Judith Dudley have owned the farm since 1996, but there has been a vineyard in existence since 1979. Still, when they took over, the place was pretty much derelict, so figuring it would be a lot of work to rip out the vineyard, they decided that diversity was the way to go. Nowadays, they have not only the vineyard (which produces about 4,000 bottles of wine a year) but also a thriving plant and flower business (they met working at a garden centre together), Welsh cheeses to sell and a large collection of different animals, from their two dogs to a pig, sheep and ponies.

The winding river Wye seen
from the vineyard

I saw a sign on the way out of Tintern that I've never come across before: 'BADGERS 2 MILES'. Predictably the Dudleys used to have problems with badgers – Colin once found Judith crying over yet another bunch of grapes decimated by them – but they have disappeared over the past 12 months and the rabbits have gone too. The rabbit's disappearance seems to be down to a combination of mixamatosis and the foxes that have moved into the badger's old sett. Now the worst offenders are blackbirds that like Pinot Noir, fieldfares, that are coming earlier (used to be November) due to a lack of food in Siberia and the sheep, which are their own. While they clearly do enjoy the work, they say that they never really relax until the van door is shut on the last crate of grapes and it heads off to be vinified at Three Choirs. 'Every year brings a problem you've never seen before,' says Colin in a succinct description of why viticulture is always challenging and always frustrating. For one thing they never know whether the rains will hit them, since bad weather seems randomly to pick either the Wye, Severn or Usk river to travel up. When they do get a thunderstorm, downy mildew hits shortly afterwards. They actually grow 17 different varieties here and some of the vines are now 27 years old.

Colin and Judith Dudley

They sell 95% of their wines from the vineyard, perhaps aided by the close proximity of the Abbey and the lovely Wye Valley. The Dudleys are also key organisers of Welsh Wine Week, which has been set up to mirror English Wine Week, as Wales was excluded from it and from various other events. A high point of their viticultural career has been their wine going to Brussels for EU events, though Colin does comment that he thinks it is disgraceful that Tony Blair never stood up for UK wines in the way that other countries' leaders do. Another memorable moment was going to the SWVA awards in Devon one year, not long after starting and winning just about everything going. They didn't know where to look.

I opened their *Bacchus 2003* at an Iranian Restaurant for Clare's birthday and it was swiftly devoured by our friends, who commented on its crisp cleanness and distinctive flavours. Al said it smelled like a cricket pitch. Ageworthy too. Their blend is also excellent, just a hint of sweetness, peaches and apricots and something I couldn't put my finger on but was utterly delicious. The *Pinot Noir Rosé* was all strawberries and cream, a yummy summer wine. The *2002 Rosé*, which has done best for them in competitions was picked in October, after a -7°C frost. Perhaps it concentrated the flavours – these freak chances of nature often add that extra unexpected dimension to a wine. Finally, they also do mead, which is spicily delicious

Sugar Loaf

Dummar Farm, Pentre Lane,
Abergavenny NP7 7LA
Telephone: 01873 853066
Open: 1 March–31 October,
Monday–Saturday 10.30–17.00,
Sunday 12.00–1700.
1 November–23 December,
12.00–16.00. Closed Mondays
and all of January and February
www.sugarloafvineyards.co.uk

From Tintern we ambled the car along the narrow valley floor and up along the Golden Valley to a campsite near Hay-on-Wye which was staffed by a blind lady who had to ask how much the note we handed her in payment was worth. We had a beautiful forested campsite all to ourselves, though admittedly it was a bit chilly at night. On a trip down one side of the Black Mountains we visited another vineyard near Abergavenny. It is named Sugar Loaf after the large bread-shaped hill opposite it. We trundled up a high-hedged, steep road, hoping that we would not meet any oncoming traffic. When we did meet the inevitable tractor, they pulled over and we got past – just. The lane opened out at the top into what looked to be a promising extensive place with wood-timbered outhouses, a barn and some shops lending it a slight air of a grouping of Swiss chalets.

A self-guided vineyard tour is available and Sugar Loaf sell local cheese and vines too. Louise Ryan and Simon Bloor have recently taken over the vineyard. The shop looked as good as the outside with a well-laid out tasting area and we chatted to Louise who was extremely helpful – her enthusiasm for the whole business was quite clear, as was her knowledge of the wines – all relayed in a sexy Welsh accent too. The wines themselves are decent but not yet jaw-dropping. The red blend is named *Deri Coch*, which means *'Red oaks'*, as the Deri Hill above the vineyard turns red in autumn at harvest time. But theirs is a youthful operation and everything is in place for a great little winery (and successful tourist operation). My one reservation is that it is pretty high and exposed, away from the tempering influence of the river in sharp contrast to say, sheltered Tintern Parva, nestled in the Wye valley. Still, the tall trees

Vines with Sugar Loaf in background

Rant on Tasting Glasses

Why do so many vineyard tastings in the UK involve those horrible little plastic glasses that look like they should be used for mouthwash? They are environmentally unfriendly, the shape is wrong for focusing the nose and they're so small that you can't swirl the wine or smell them properly (and many UK wines have gorgeous aromas). They make tasting properly so difficult that it is doing the wines themselves a disservice. My advice is to take your own glass, preferably a heavy duty ISO.

surrounding the vineyard break up the wind and certainly they have proved they can grow grapes worthy of winemaking in this stunning setting.

Wernddu

It is not for kings to drink wine, or for rulers to desire strong drink;
lest they drink and forget what has been decreed,
and pervert the rights of the afflicted.
Give strong drink to him who is perishing and wine to those in bitter distress;
let them drink and forget their poverty and remember their misery no more.

A good wife who can find?
... She considers a field and buys it;
with the fruit of her hands she plants a vineyard.

Proverbs 31

Pen-y-clawdd, Monmouth NP25 4BW
Telephone: 01600 740104
Open: phone first
www.wernddu-wine.co.uk

Leigh and Frank Strawford began their vineyard after Leigh read this passage in the bible. The couple already owned the land and moved from their successful manufacturing business into growing grapes and making wine. They have, in fact, the only winery in South Wales, a considerable achievement given the youth of the vineyard. The site is, like so many in this region, very beautiful, with a view stretching out over green Monmouthshire hills. We sat outside and took tea, Frank smoking a pipe and watching the blue smoke drift gently above the stunted rows of Seyval, while beside them rose the fully grown producing vines of Reichensteiner and Siegerrebe. The soil here is a slatey Marl, a fairly unusual base in the UK and perhaps one reason why Seyval Blanc, normally a guaranteed winner, isn't doing too well. Indeed, Frank wishes that they had never planted it.

They planted in late March of 2002 and the ground was so hard that they broke three spades. They prune the vines each year in early spring and Frank says that the harder you prune the vines, the better they seem to respond. He did say they are lucky that the wasps (which he rhymes with 'asps') die in October and that is generally when their grapes are achieving full ripeness (exactly when the wasps would start on them). They still have the usual problems with mildew and botrytis though, especially as they are an organic vineyard (registered with the Soil Association) which makes things all the more difficult. This is one reason they built their own winery was that it is easier to comply with the SA's rigorous standards.

Sales-wise Leigh enjoys doing the Usk and Monmouth shows and the farmer's markets and Wernddu also make cider and perry. Potentially, there are 12 acres of vineyard land here, so this could turn into a reasonably sizeable vineyard if things turn out well. And

Wernddu Vineyard in
summer and ... winter

their first efforts are really not bad. I tried both their pure *Reichensteiner*, which was full of Granny Smith apple flavours, while the off-dry Siegerrebe/Reich blend was herbaceous and lemony. Both had ultra-keen acidity and I think they will both age rather well; give them another three years and the quality may well surprise. It is also handy to note that they have not yet managed to get the grapes to full ripeness and that as they find ways and means of improving this the wines will undoubtedly get better and better. The distinctive label on the wines is taken from a line drawing of their daughter that was done while she was away on holiday in France.

13

THE MARCHER COUNTIES

Gloucestershire, Worcestershire and Herefordshire

Since Roman times the Marcher counties have been a hub of agricultural activity and this has included viticulture. The area has a mild climate and is sheltered from the cold westerly winds and rain showers by the glowering Welsh mountains and also by various smaller ranges of hills that cut between fertile valleys like the Vale of Evesham or the Golden Valley. This is a region of golden cornfields, of independently-minded nonconformists, of apple orchards and Herefordshire Cattle. It is also an area where the local farmers' markets are historically strong and where people are used to getting good well-priced local goods.

The Hop Pocket Wine Company (see page 195) and Orchard Hive and Vine (www.orchard-hive-and-vine.co.uk) both have an excellent online selection of local wine, produce, cider and perry, mead, beer and ale and apple juice. Heart of England Fine Foods (www.heff.co.uk) covers food and wine.

GLOUCESTERSHIRE

St Anne's

Oxenhall, Newent GL18 1RW
Telephone: 01989 720313
Open: five days a week in summer, weekends only in winter.
Phone first before visiting

St Anne's is a relatively old vineyard. Planted in 1979, the best vintage since the current owners took over in 1995 (a 'heart over head' decision) came in 2003, when they produced a superb red. Their rosé is tasty and fruit-packed and they also produce country and fruit wines and sell vines and hampers. Here at St Anne's blackbirds and, unusually, chickens are the main pests. The vineyard lies on the route of the popular Spring Daffodil trail; pay them a visit if you're ever on the trail – flowers and wine with blossom flying and butterflies flitting, blankets of bluebells and daffodils filling the woodland floor nearby – what more could you want?

Opposite. Gloucestershire countryside

Sir Kenelm Digby (1603–65)

Prior to the coming of bottles and secure stoppages, keeping wine was a risky affair. Most wine could not be kept for more than a year and was drunk within a few weeks of production. Beaujolais Nouveau would certainly have fetched a much better price than it does now. The prevention of the growth of the oxygen-consuming aceto-bacter bacteria (which turned wine to acetic acid) has been one of the most important discoveries of wine history. The man who helped achieve this was a fascinating 17th-century Englishman.

Born in 1603, Sir Kenelm Digby was Renaissance man personified, achieving renown as a philosopher, scientist, pirate, naval commander, alchemist, gourmet, diplomat and (probably) a spy. He was the son of Sir Everard Digby, who was hanged, drawn and quartered for his involvement in the Gunpowder Plot of 1605 and husband of the beautiful and scandalous Lady Venetia Stanley. Well known for his studies in botany, biology and physics, he was a founder member of the Royal Society set up in 1660. He was also interested in alchemy, dabbling in bizarre potions such as a magical Powder of Sympathy which healed wounds remotely and a viper wine which supposedly preserved beauty.

He is credited with the invention of the modern wine bottle by discovering a method for making standardised glass bottles which were stronger, darker, thicker and, most importantly, cheaper than the finely blown glass bottles previously made. Bottles were used only for serving wine and only the richest could afford them. It was at Newnham-on-Severn in Gloucestershire that the prodigiously talented Digby discovered a way to raise the temperature of coal furnaces by employing a wind tunnel to melt glass using more sand and less potash and lime. The blackening of the bottle to brown or olive green by the coal fumes also protected the contents from the light. Stoppers made of glass were used at first then corks were introduced. Wine, thanks to Digby, could now last for years longer.

Today Sir Kenelm is probably best known for his early cookbook, The Closet Opened. (See recipe for Digby's Excellent Small Cakes on p228).

grubbing up the old vines. While pests are not too much of a problem, lots of grapes did mysteriously disappear at the castle vineyard in 2005 – no-one saw what was eating them but she suspected some kind of mammal.

Thornbury produce just the one type of wine, the *Medium-dry White*, a blend of Müller, Madeleine, Reichensteiner and Kernling, but with the replanting more variety may well occur in the future. The best way to see the vineyard and taste the wine is to come for lunch or afternoon tea at the restaurant. The grounds are not open to the public apart from hotel/restaurant guests.

Three Choirs

Newent GL18 1LS
Telephone: 01531 890223
Open: summer 10.00–17.00;
winter 11.00–16.00
www.threechoirs.com

Three Choirs is one of the biggest and best-known vineyards in the UK. It is also a brilliant excursion with a well-laid-out tour beginning with a video then moving through the winery and on to the vines, complete with information signs and a nature trail. As you can see from the picture, when we visited, it was a baking hot July day and we were dripping in sweat as we wandered around the peaceful vineyard. It's a fair old way around the place but well worth it as there is so much to see on the 100-acre estate. By then you may well fancy a meal at Three Choirs' excellent restaurant, which specialises in quality seasonal English food. There is a herb garden, loads of wildlife (which is positively encouraged) and a 'no

pesticides' rule. You can rent a vine too. When you wander around you'll note that the vines are covered in name plaques, a slightly surreal image.

Three Choirs is set in rolling Gloucestershire countryside, has low rainfall and a naturally warm climate and its wines get better by the year. No doubt this is mainly due to one of the UK's most renowned and award-winning winemakers, Martin Fowke, who is responsible for some of the best and cheapest wines available. They have lovely guestrooms too if you fancy an extended stay. Three Choirs was established back in the mid-seventies and with major expansion occurring in the eighties has been one of the major forces in proving UK wine's commercial potential.

My one complaint about Three Choirs would have to be the video, which concentrates rather bizarrely on the bottling process, not something I have ever heard people clamouring to find out about. It is very 8os in style and just doesn't match the standard of the rest of the estate, with its varied array of things to do, see, smell and taste. It is nevertheless my favourite of the larger vineyards to visit, with friendly welcoming staff and an easygoing atmosphere. They also brew their own beer, Whittington's which is well worth a sample. All of their wines are good and well-priced, but my personal favourites are the *Late Harvest 2005* Dessert wine which is just lovely – peachy, lightly honeyed, and long on the finish – and the new *Willowbrook 2006* (see UK Wines in the Supermarket at the end of this entry). Finally, they have just introduced the *Sparkling Red 2004* made from Triomphe. It's really tasty and makes a good alternative to Aussie sparkling Shiraz. Go see for yourself.

UK Wines in the Supermarket

While I would obviously prefer you to be buying wines direct from the vineyard gate, this is clearly not an option for many, so here is a quick rundown of what is available to buy and what is particularly good at the supermarkets in the way of UK wines at the moment.

Waitrose has the best range of the lot with wines purchased from different vineyards in different regions: Llanerch in Wales, A' Beckett's in Wiltshire and Somerset. Sainsbury deals with Chapel Down (look for the *Century Extra Dry* for some light bubbly goodness) who also produce an own-label *Dry White* for them. It is made of Schönburger and Huxelrebe and is a good introduction to those grape types with autumnal harvest smells (hay and hedgerows) and a palate of grapefruit, citrus and spice. Morrisons have the quaintly named Three Choirs wines *Parson's Leap* and *Willowbrook* at very good prices and the latter in particular (2006 vintage) is quintessential UK fare, water-clear, fresh and vivacious and packed with cut grass and lemon flavours. Majestic stock Nyetimber's briliant fizz, while Laithwaites carry their major rival Ridgeview's more traditional Champagne-style bubbly. Asda and Tesco both do their own-label English wines (which are made at Three Choirs) and sometimes have fizz available too.

UK Wine on the Web

Although there is no one comprehensive site, the following are pretty good for buying UK wines. **www.bestenglishwine.co.uk** concentrates on award-winning bottles, while **www.englishwine.co.uk** is excellent but concentrates mainly on the southeast wines. Otherwise see the introductions to each regional section where I have put the most relevant sites for each. Beyond that, it is a matter of going to the individual vineyard websites at the end of each entry.

In terms of information on UK wines and vineyards there are two excellent sites. The first is **www.englishwineproducers.com**. This is dedicated to publicising UK vineyards commercially and has a good all round selection including news, mini-websites of some of the best vineyards, interviews with characters from the industry and details of English Wine Week and vineyard events. The second, less glossy website is **www.ukvines.co.uk** and contains the most detailed summary of all the vineyards plus grape types and some other decent bits and bobs. While **www.english-wine.com** is bitty it does have a really informative news and history section.

WORCESTERSHIRE
Astley

The Crundles, Astley, Stourport-on-Severn DY13 0RU
Telephone: 01299 822907
Open: Monday, Thurday–Saturday 10.00–17.00, Sunday 12.00–17.00
www.englishwineproducers.com/astley.htm

'I was in shorts when this was made,' said my brother-in-law Mike last night. My girlfriend Clare remarked, 'Twenty-two years old ... that's amazing', upon tasting it. I was expecting it to be awful. True to the form of fantastic old wines, the *Astley Kerner 1984* we were tasting had a mischievous green-gold glint in its eye, winking from out of the glass, daring us to be unimpressed. None of the four of us could be though, with fresh acidity, a slight hint of petrol yet still a distinctively English nose and a palate of intense lime, lemon and a honeyed mineral complexity. It is the oldest English wine I have tasted and is a testament to the viability of UK wines for laying down.

It is, in fact a wine that existed even before the present owners of Astley vineyard arrived. Though I wouldn't be surprised if Jonty Daniels and Janet Baldwin chose to be considered keepers of the vineyard rather than owners. For they continue a tradition of grape growing at Astley that reaches back to the mid-seventies, when it was for a short while the most northerly vineyard in the world. The house and vineyard themselves lie in an idyllic setting with ringing birdsong and plentiful wildlife. Jonty commented that you get more benign towards hungry animals as you grew older (despite the tractor occasionally fouling on a rabbit warren).

This attitude is one I have come across many times in my travels, a slowly developing resignation towards wildlife and a realisation that there is only so much one can do to stop damage as a grower of vines. Most end up encouraging the good wildlife in order to get shot of the pests by natural means. Here, Roe deer wander through the vineyard every May. Theoretically, they could wreck the place but, as if in acknowledgement of Jonty and Janet's

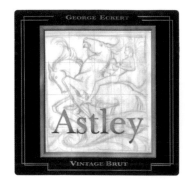

tolerance, they simply move on through. He describes with pleasure the elegant commanding gliding of the buzzards that are a permanent presence in the sky above their house. The same buzzards used to dominate their wine labels, the new versions of which are among my UK favourites. These are now based on a drawing by Jonty's father, a Paris café artist in the twenties and later a stills cameraman for the British film industry. And if you visit and happen to wonder where the name of the tasty *George Eckert Vintage Brut* comes from (citrus and mineral, good mousse, a bit different), it was his stepfather's name.

In terms of the vineyard itself, July is a hated time at Astley. The Kerner go mental, sprouting sideways in great clumps like a monstrous Afro hairdo; a wall-to-wall canopy of management that makes Jonty feel that he's 'always chasing the bus and never quite catching it'. Janet loves the warm earth and fresh flowers of March and April, tying in the vines before they go mad and listening to the birds fill the vineyard with song.

1984 was a magical year, Jonty remembers it not only for grapes, but for turnips, barley, peas; he was an arable farmer prior to redundancy, homelessness and then a vineyard in 1993 and a site which can produce a wine as delicious as the Kerner we tried must have something magical about it. Perhaps it is the history, the Severn Valley was a strong area for viticulture in Roman and medieval times and the steep south-facing slope of the Norman church at Astley is still known as 'The Vineyard'. Or maybe it is the soil; the name of their house is The Crundles, a local term for the outcrops of Triassic Red Sandstone which are a local geological feature and also give their name to Astley's *Triassic* blend. Perhaps it is the policy of good vineyard management; on a site of five acres one might expect to be able to get 12–15,000 bottles. Instead, Jonty and Janet restrict the yield and produce only 8,000 bottles. Then again it could be the redoubtable winemaking skills of Martin Fowke at Three Choirs. I think that it is the combination of all these factors, which the French refer to as *terroir* that make these wines what they are.

You won't be disappointed with the selection, varied (with vintage as well as style and grape variety) and most also age well. They range from the delicious citrus, medium-dry aperitif *Old Vine Kerner*, to the usually Sauvignon-like *Madeleine Angevine* (though I had one vintage that was a dead ringer for excellent German Riesling), through to the aromatically peachy but dry *Triassic* to the creamy, blue cheese match of their *Late Harvest* sweet wine. Try some and fall asleep to strange dreams ...

Tiltridge

Wednesday, 19 July 2006

It is the hottest day in recorded history in England. My frozen bottle of water has completely thawed out two hours after it came out of the freezer. The scenery looks amazing, lush green countryside, sweltering in Mediterranean heat. Peter and Sandy Barker transformed this former smallholding into a vineyard, close to the pretty riverside tourist town of Upton-upon-Severn, in the late 1980s. The wine names and labels are thematically-based variations around Edward Elgar and his works. The area surrounding is known as 'Elgar Country' because of the links with the famed composer and appropriately, this vineyard provides the toasting wine for the Elgar Society's events. Tiltridge lies in the shadow of the surprisingly tall and picturesque Malvern hills, which are green in summer and blue in winter. This is one of those vineyards where I have problems picking out a single wine to try. They are all excellent and all quite different ranging from the elegant light, beautifully coloured *Sonata Rosé* through the marmalade, lemon and vanilla of the *Variations Oaked Dry* (which would benefit from a couple of years in cellar) through to the broodingly intense *Dorabella Medium Dry*, with its unusual Huxelrebe-based orange, honey and hay palate and nose. Just the thing for that moment in late autumn when the nights start to close in and you want something after your meal rather than beforehand.

Bed and breakfast is part of farm life and in English Wine Week

Tiltridge Farm, Upper Hook Road, Upton-upon-Severn WR8 0SA
Telephone: 01684 592906
Open: Monday–Saturday 11.00–17.00; Sunday 12.00–17.00
www.tiltridge.com

Above. Big bunches of grapes forming at Tiltridge.

Left. The shop is elegantly situated at the end of the vines.

Noble Rot

Having struggled desperately for most of the year to keep the disease botrytis (known as Grey Rot) away from their vines, come autumn you might be surprised to find some viticulturalists who make sweeter wines actively praying for botrytis to appear. Early morning mists followed by warm sunshine encourage this type of botrytis, known in the wine world as Noble Rot (or botrytis cinerea). It has a curious effect on the grape, hanging on to the outside and devouring five-sixth's of the acidity, one-third of the available sugar and a third to a half of the water content. For certain types of grape left to hang on the vine until late in the autumn, this means a huge concentration of flavours and masses of sweetness. On the downside, the longer these are left out the more open they are to the worsening weather conditions of autumn, so it is always a risky stratagem. In the UK, native varieties such as Huxelrebe, Ortega and Optima are particularly susceptible to the beautiful ravages of Noble Rot and some lusciously honeyed dessert wines are now starting to be made.

they put on wine and cheese tastings and a guided tour of the vineyard, though you are free to walk around and try the wines at any time of year. They may well have a sparkling wine and a *Late Harvest Noble Rot Huxelrebe* out by the time you pay a visit too, so keep an eye out for these. What is fantastic about Tiltridge is that such a small vineyard – just one-and-a-half acres – produces such a fantastic range of different flavours in its wines. This, in addition to its friendly welcome and pretty site, make it well worth a visit in my book. Still, just in case this all sounds increasingly romantic, bear in mind that when the Barkers started the vineyard they had to live in a caravan for two years. Growing vines is not for the faint-hearted.

HEREFORDSHIRE
Beeches

Upton Bishop HR9 7UD
Telephone: 01306 886124
Visits by prior appointment only
www.beechesvineyard.com

Beeches Vineyard is a small, family run vineyard begun by Finnish native Ikka Boyd in 1991 with a planting of Madeleine Angevine, Triomphe d'Alsace and Seyval Blanc vines. The vines were planted on rough ground not suitable for farming. Fifteen years later the vineyard produced a dry white, a fresh rosé and a light, flavoursome red. Ikka and her husband John Boyd and their daughter Karin and husband Simon Wilkins now feel the vineyard is part of their lives – even their children join in the fun during the annual harvest. Beeches is also one of the few remaining original Georgian farmhouses in Herefordshire and is now a family home with vineyard attached, totalling 13 acres. The house has interesting period features including a cold store and large vaulted cellar.

Broadfield Court

Broadfield Court hosts corporate events with private and public social gatherings, wine production, outdoor activities and training, field sports and cultural entertainment. The estate is mentioned in the Domesday Book and is still a private farming estate of just over 1000 acres set in the beautiful rolling countryside of north Herefordshire. This tranquil setting is home to Bodenham English Wines. The shop and café in the 16th-century winery welcome all visitors to browse, taste and enjoy excellent, freshly prepared food and wine from Broadfield's vineyards. Other facilities include purpose-built rope and assault courses where you can express your adventurous side and field sports including a pheasant or clay pigeon shoot. They also host cultural events such as music, craft and garden festivals. There are four acres of old English gardens with a David Austin rose garden incorporating 37 varieties, a walled kitchen garden plus a variety of fruit trees and herbaceous borders. The house's six south-facing gables display some 600 years of history at a glance, dating from the 14th, 15th and 19th centuries.

In 1971 some 50 vines were experimentally planted by the founder, Keith James, with an additional 500 Reichensteiner vines the following year, continuing until the expansion programme was completed and covered 17 acres of Broadfield's finest south-facing slopes. The vines which have proved to flourish best include Huxelrebe, Müller-Thurgau, Seyve Villard and Madeleine Angevine as well as the original Reichensteiner. The juice is siphoned into Broadfield's own vats where it is fermented and bottled the following year. Six wines are currently made and the *Bodenham Broadfield Sparkling 2003*, made of Seyval Blanc is an absolute delight. It blends elderflower, lemon and cream like some divine liquid pudding. Broadfield offer wine tasting tours including lunches, teas and suppers for up to 50 people.

Bowley Lane, Bodenham HR1 3LG
Telephone: 01568 797483
Gift Shop & Court Café open daily from 10.30–16.00 in winter; 10.00–16.30 from Easter through the summer
www.broadfieldcourt.co.uk

Left. The Old House.

Right. The courtyard is a lovely place to sit and sip.

Coddington

Well, a strange name admittedly, but as you can see Coddington makes it into the top ten most picturesque vineyards' quite comfortably with its colourful array of summer flowers, its stream and carp pond and the serene woodland atmosphere taking you back to a time when life was conducted at a more graceful pace. We sat chatting beneath a blossoming tree, out of the baking sunshine. Denis and Ann Savage bought this lovely property ten years before he was due to retire as a paediatrician, with the intention of planting a vineyard. This they did, moving from their old hobby of making hedgerow wines on to growing grapes and even making the wine themselves in their own winery, sited in a barn up by the vineyard. The latter was planted over the farm orchard, unsurprisingly the best quality field. Among the memorable moments they recall are winning a silver medal for the first Bacchus they produced and also returning from holiday in Mexico and visiting the duty free at Heathrow to find their wine being stocked in Berry Bros & Rudd.

Clay on lime on sandstone. Sounds like a chant but the soil type is vital to the success of different grape varieties as their roots delve down deep into the layers beneath, soaking up the minerals below. Denis commented that the Bacchus – favoured among English wine connoisseurs at the moment – is really hard work, growing up and up like a forest, up to 10 feet in the air. It also suffers from powdery mildew. Ortega by contrast is bushy, while Pinot Gris is a sedate, easy (by comparison) grower. And we won't even mention the Kerner they used to grow ... At least the Savages don't have too many problems with the starlings any more and buzzards eat the rabbits and other small animals. Coddington does unfortunately lie in a frost pocket, though the frost quite often rolls down the vineyard into the wooded lower reaches. Anyway, the *Bacchus 2005* is definitely worth the effort and is my favourite of their four wines. It was consumed by me and my friend Liz with pasta that same evening in Hereford and we both thought it was delicious; fresh, gooseberry-ish and herbaceous. Ageworthy too, developing tropical flavours and depth with the years.

Four Foxes

Four Foxes is fairly large (eight acres) for a vineyard that isn't yet well known. Peter and Louisa Crilly took the place over about four years ago and are re-establishing the vineyard, once known as Hadley Court, that was originally started around 20 years ago. It

Near Ledbury HR8 1JJ
Telephone: 01531 640668
Open: March–December,
Thurday–Sunday 14.00–17.00
or by appointment

CODDINGTON

Bacchus
2005
Herefordshire Regional Wine

Top. The barn sits beside a sleepy pool with shady trees.

Bottom. The winery.

Four Foxes vineyard.

Longworth Lane, Bartestree,
Herefordshire HR1 4BX
Telephone: 01432 850065/
07974 504351
Open: Wednesday–Sunday
12.00–17.00 or by arrangement
www.fourfoxesvineyard.com

was renamed because someone used to count the foxes passing through the place, sharing it with a barn owl that swoops low across the fields in the evening. Both are probably good for removing pests, especially as the owl seems to be nesting up. Four Foxes lies beside Hampton Dean Nature Reserve, on a flood plain and they have a fine little visitor centre, good local food, a friendly welcome and a beautiful view. It was rather unkempt when I visited and will need some devoted canopy management if the wines are to reach their full potential on this lovely site. Still the *Madeleine Angevine* in particular does show a nettle-like promise, as does the *Sparkling Seyval* and the vineyard could have a good future ahead.

Frome Valley

Paunton Court,
Bishops Frome WR6 5BJ
Telephone: 01885 490768
Open: April–October,
Wednesday–Sunday 11.00–17.30
www.fromewine.co.uk

Frome Valley Huxelrebe is a quintessentially English Wine. It has the fresh-flavoured, sweet niff of a spring day after the grass has just been cut, something drawing one back to childhood and playing on new-mown lawns. The palate is pure, easy, dry refreshment with a mineral edge, but with no shortage of elderflower. It is the epitome of English whites with a fantastic finish too. Bear in mind that we were drinking the 2001, five years after the vintage and this bottle age is one of the things that aids most UK white wines. It is made on the banks of the River Frome in beautiful countryside at Paunton Court, where they grow 4,000 vines. The loamy marl soil clearly works with various varieties here, along with the magic of winemaking. As with most vineyards here and for miles around these grapes are sent off to Three Choirs for their transformation. The tasting room and shop are in an ancient threshing barn and outside a model vineyard demonstrates different grape varieties, each one grown on different trellises and showing various pruning methods.

The Hop Pocket Wine Company

This fantastic specialist has one of the best ranges of local wines, ciders, perrys, fruit wines and any other type of British alcoholic beverage you can imagine and is well worth a visit if you happen to be in the area. There is always a free tasting on and they even produce their own house wine, which is very tasty indeed (peachy and medium-sweet, Riesling-like but with English character and good with Chinese dishes). Run by Paddy Shave, an amiable and friendly ex-Oddbins Manager, you'll be hard pressed to pick from the amazing selection he keeps. Instead, you might prefer to tell him the kind of things you're into and good, well-informed advice as to what you might like will be forthcoming. The shop is also online if you are further afield. The complex in which the Hop Pocket resides contains a garden shop, deli, restaurant and massive gift centre.

Bishop's Frome, Worcester WR6 5BT
Telephone: 01531 640592
www.hoppocketwine.co.uk

Lulham Court

Lulham Court is a three-acre vineyard in the midst of a mixed family farm, surrounded by the wonderful Wye Valley in Herefordshire and has been producing wine since 1984. The array of wines is impressive, with six different varieties produced from Müller-Thurgau, Reichensteiner and Seyval Blanc grapes. Best of all here is their lovely apple-influenced Seyval *Sparkling 2002*, with a light toastiness perfect for accompanying light starters out in the open.

Lulham, near Madley,
Hereford HR2 9JQ
Telephone: 01981 251107
www.lulhamcourtvineyard.co.uk

Sunnybank Vine Nurseries

If you aren't content with reading about other people's travails in making wines here, one of the first places you should think of going to for properly grafted vines on a small scale is Brian Edward's Sunnybank Vine Nurseries. Just awarded full collection status by The National Council for the Conservation of Plants and Gardens, Brian has held by far the largest and most active collection of vines in the UK for a number of years. Active research into different vine type's performance is ongoing and new promising varieties are actively sourced and trialled. Sunnybank also produces a variety of its own decent wines as well.

Journey's End, Rowlestone,
Ewyas Harold HR2 0EE
Telephone: 01981 240256
There is an open day in September.
Mail order is available for vines
www.vinenursery.netfirms.com

St Weonards HR2 8QB
Telephone: 01981 580208
Open by appointment.
Cottages are available to rent
www.treago.co.uk

Treago

Sir Richard Mynors is quite a character. His family have lived at and owned Treago House and estate for 500 years and he grows and makes the wines himself on site. The wines range from a well-regarded sparkling with green apple and elderflower flavours to a soft damson red made from Cabernet Sauvignon and Syrah.

Treago sums up on its label the story of its origin. Grown and made at old Treago Hall by Sir Richard Mynors, who many would see as a typical old English eccentric (every so often he raises a choir from Herefordshire and conducts it himself in public performances), the bottle features the outer facade of the hall, castle-like and elegantly imposing. Since 1989, the best years here have been the last two, with large, good quality crops. The weather may have been good recently but the beasts have not – wasps caused the uprooting of all the estate's Madeleine Angevine, whilst netting has been necessary to protect red grapes from bird damage.

Here at this ancient house lies a one-acre walled garden, once planted with vegetables, which produced according to Sir Richard, 'a ridiculously large crop'. Now it produces triumphs like the *Bacchus/Seyval Blanc 2005*, entirely grown and produced on the estate, with a lot of work but a lot of fun too. The amount of fun had by Sir Richard is definitely aided by the owner's sense of experimentation. Astonishingly, from a one-acre vineyard he always produces at least six wines; a sparkling, dry white, lightly-oaked white, a medium dry, a rosé, a red and sometimes a medium-sweet wine. Not only that but the 2006 vintage proved good enough to make a Cabernet Sauvignon varietal and a sparkling Shiraz, both from tunnel-grown grapes.

Vine and Wine

Vine and Wine Ltd, 1 Putley Green,
Ledbury HR8 2QN
Telephone: 01531 660668
www.vineandwine.co.uk

Herefordshire is a centre for English viticulture in many ways. Not only does it have many good vineyards, Paddy Shave's excellent Hop and Pocket wine shop and Brian Edward's Sunnybank Vine Nursery but it is also home to Simon Day's Vine and Wine Consultancy. Simon grew up at Three Choirs vineyard and has since learned the trade in various capacities. If you are serious about starting up any sort of vineyard, Simon is on hand to help with site testing, advice on varieties and all and sundry regarding training systems and all other wine matters.

14

MERCIA AND
THE NORTH

Shropshire, Staffordshire, Warwickshire, Northamptonshire,
Leicestershire, Lincolnshire, Nottinghamshire, Derbyshire,
Yorkshire, Scotland

One of the most surprising things to me as I travelled around the UK was that so many of the best wines should come from this most northerly region. From the incredible *North Star* ice wine of Eglantine in Nottinghamshire to the fabulous *Heart of England Oberon Red*, I was constantly amazed. Mercia is a fascinating rag-bag of vineyards and diverse in every way, with soils ranging from light sand to heavy clay. It could perhaps best be described as a shaggy terrier in the company of Crufts' pedigrees. Beginning in Shropshire and the northern marches it continues across the true middle England of Northants, Warwickshire and Leicestershire, where every second pub is the *something and hounds* and every

The view from Windmill Hill.

place rings with battle names from the British Civil War like Naseby, Cropredy, Edgehill. Indeed, one of the best places you could possibly see this landscape is from the top of Windmill Vineyard, at 675 feet above sea level, from which point seven counties are visible.

From there it moves north, to the aforementioned Eglantine, the oldest vineyard in the country at Lincoln and picturesque Renishaw Hall in north Derbyshire; then on to the wilds of Yorkshire, where my infatuation first began. Grape growing is not a new thing even here – both the Cistercians and the Knights Templar used to grow vines successfully on the valley sides in West Yorkshire.

Heart of England Fine Foods (www.heff.co.uk) cover food and wine from Warwickshire, Shropshire and Staffordshire.

SHROPSHIRE

Halfpenny Green

Tom La, Halfpenny Green DY7 5EP
Telephone: 01384 221122
Open: 10.30–17.00
www.halfpennygreenvineyards

Halfpenny Green is by far and away the largest, most northerly vineyard in the UK. Family owned, at just over 25 acres and producing 60–65,000 bottles a year, Martin (father, the grower) and Clive Vickers (son, the winemaker) have really made something out of what was a large arable farm when they first set out. It may have started as a hobby, just half-an-acre, for Martin to see if he could make decent home-made wines from home-grown grapes. Eventually, the need for diversification encouraged this hobby into rather more than just that and now the Halfpenny Green has everything from a large visitor centre to a restaurant, a winery and a host of other associated craft shops on site (the deli does superb soups). There is even a fishing lake for those who fancy popping their rods in the boot – the others could join one of the 170 guided tours a year that the vineyard puts on. And all can enjoy the free tasting of wine! They also do corporate own-label wines and gift wines with self-designed labels for the likes of me and you.

Despite the size of the vineyard and its large production levels, they always sell out. A high proportion goes through local farmers' markets, though they also sell through Waitrose's midland branches. Well-placed in their position just outside the six-million strong populace of the Black Country and Birmingham conurbations, this is a considered and successful vineyard.

Clive Vickers loves springtime in the vineyard with its first tinge of green, exploding like Triffids into wild green-haired figures. One

of the advantages of being further north is that budding is slightly later here, thus providing less risk of early frosts decimating the crop. Asked about climate change though, he says that the weather had them worried in 2000 with its wet cold summer (11–12°C average temperature in July) and a winter that wasn't really cold enough to rest the vines properly. Having said that, the last few years have been fantastic and he comments that having perused his grandad's old farm records, people forget that weather also tends to go in 30-year cycles (the period it takes most people to

Inside the well-stocked shop and tasting room.

forget what went before that). I know what he means. Reading through Alan Rook's *Diary of an English Vineyard* from 1969, which chronicles the travails of Stragglethorpe vineyard in Lincolnshire, I come across many references to 'the wettest July for twenty years or the hottest summer in living memory'. Having said that he agrees that there do seem to be changes, especially with the disappearance of snow in winter and temperatures going up and up. Clive also enjoys the excitement of early harvest, the first grapes being picked at the end of September.

Most of the wines are named after the farm fields that form Halfpenny Green so we have *Tom Hill Huxelrebe*, which is grapefruity, the *Old Meadow Madeleine Angevine*, with apples, pear and a tight acidity that's beautifully refreshing. My favourite was the *Long Acre Schönburger* (it was clearly worth the problems they have with this variety) that had lovely, dry, peach and spice notes and a plump food-friendly feel to it. These wines are very consistent and most win awards at the UKVA competition.

Happily there is probably much more to be seen of Halfpenny Green, as the family farm is 800 acres and the Vickers do plan to expand the vineyard soon. They have also been improving the winery they built in 1994 and they are making wines for an increasing number of smaller midland, Marcher country and Welsh vineyards. They also bottle cider and perry, but have stopped doing functions and are moving towards selling more local produce. Despite being a large commercial vineyard, Clive feels that they have managed to keep something special about the feel of Halfpenny Green – they do not hire managers, the place is a family enterprise and you can tell from the way he talks that this is a passion as well as a business for him. Last year, they produced their first pink fizz, which sold out straightaway. It is to be hoped that they continue to maintain this progressive situation. In the meantime, pay them a visit.

Mulled wine: where it came from

I am known to be ... one that loves a cup of hot wine
with not a drop of allaying Tiber in't.
                    Coriolanus (1608), William Shakespeare (1564–1616)

The Germans used to (and still do) heat wine in a kettle on fires of vine prunings with a spoon of sugar dissolved in it. This habit was transferred to Britain through the church and gained popularity prior to the arrival of tea and coffee. The evolution of mulled wine into a popular drink is derived from these early practices.

Morville Hall

Ian Rowe was fascinated by vines ever since he was young, when he helped look after Black Hamburg vines (an old English greenhouse staple) at Morville Hall as a boy. He took a holiday to France in 1986, passing through many of the French wine areas and on his return planted a few vines in the garden. Finally, in 1989 he took over a small patch of ground and turned it into a proper vineyard. Over 18 years Ian has seen big changes in weather, budburst having moved from the end of April to any time in that month. Autumns are now longer and milder too, with the first real frosts no longer arriving until November. The result of all this is that harvesting the grapes is earlier too.

Their favourite wine is probably the *1998 Dry Müller-Thurgau/Madeleine Angevine* blend, which is still drinking beautifully, but the best year was actually 1996, when they got a ton of grapes and 560 bottles of wine from just 220 vines, superbly clean and well-ripened. The wines from this vintage won four trophies, four gold and five silver awards in regional awards, quite a feat for such a small vineyard. The worst year by contrast, was 2000 when poor flowering weather gave a patchy fruit-set which meant that among the decent grapes were many small unfertilised berries that became very sweet weeks before the other grapes had ripened, attracting legions of wasps. These ate two thirds of the crop and damaged the remainder forcing an early harvest in order to try and save something from the remains of their smallest crop ever. They did salvage a few drinkable bottles, but it was the only year that Morville Hall wines did not win any awards for their wines.

When the grapes do get past plagues of blackbirds, thrushes and wasps, the wines are made on the estate itself. While not open to the public generally, the vineyard can be seen when the Morville Hall gardens open to the public in early May in aid of the local church.

Morville, near Bridgnorth WV16 5NB
Telephone: 01746 714357
Ring for the open day details

Friday, 19 May

Altogether less promising weather, dirty clouds bringing sudden fierce attacks of rain, swooping like greedy seagulls on ice cream. This morning I drove Clare from London to Liverpool for a conference and now, as I drive southwards towards Shrewsbury through the Marcher country the Grey King smoulders in the west, threatening heavy rain. This baleful character from legend reigns over Cader Idris, one of the Snowdonian mountains. Apparently, the average cumulus cloud contains water droplets the weight of 80 elephants. I pass by places that seem to constitute some weird legend in themselves, as I find myself wondering whether I would find anyone on No Man's Heath, or a ringing sound at Bell o' th' hill, or God knows what at Steel Heath. I find myself stopping abruptly as I spot a place called Vineyard Farm, some kind of omen for my journey perhaps, but I spy no vines and take a picture of the gate instead and continue on my ghost-littered way.

Wroxeter Roman Vineyard

Wroxeter, Shrewsbury SY5 6PQ
Telephone: 01743 761888
Open: 11.00–17.30 daily.
Phone beforehand
www.wroxetervineyard.co.uk

They were right in the middle of bottling the new rosé at Wroxeter when I arrived. To find the vineyard make your way past the stark remains of some Roman baths (you could combine the two into a single visit) then on past some bird-filled hedges. Wroxeter, or Viroconium (Uroconium) as it was then known was once the fourth-largest town in Roman Britain, a place where vines grew some 2,000 years ago. The atmosphere here today is very much that of a working farm, no throwback hobby this, but a way of making a living. It is a feeling reinforced when talking to Martin, the son of David Millington, who originally set up the vineyard and who now shares the running of the business and the winemaking with Martin.

David is a Welshman and well known in the UK wine trade for his dogged pursuit of a court case that claimed the same rights for British winemaking as for any other agricultural practice, a right which seems patently fair and obvious. Somehow, his opponents were trying to maintain that grape growing and winemaking were somehow different from other types of farming and should be taxed differently. Thankfully he won the case and Wroxeter proves a good example of a sustainable modern UK vineyard. It does seem strange how little help the UK government have given to British viticulture over the years and in some ways it seems a minor miracle that vineyards here are booming given this refusal to properly support one of the very few instances of an agricultural sector that is actually doing well.

The most remarkable thing about Wroxeter Roman vineyard is its climate. One essential component of vine growth is sunshine and the more hours of sun a place receives the easier it is to grow vines and ripen grapes before the onset of winter. Most UK vineyards receive well under 1,000 hours of sunlight per year, a fact which had caused many people to write off viticulture here as a waste of time. While I think this assumption has been comprehen-

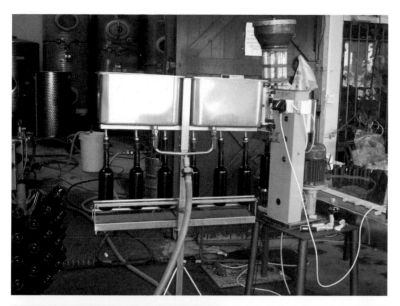

sively disproved, more sun certainly makes life a lot easier and
Wroxeter receives just over 1000 ripening hours each year. Not far
down the road, this changes to a far more normal 890 hours. This
strange phenomenon is caused by the Cambrian Mountains to the
west sheltering them from the fierce Welsh winds, forming a still
centre akin to Death Valley in the USA, though rather less scary.
Indeed, whilst I was there on an horrendous sullen day, the light
fluttered out while I was at Wroxeter, sunshine looping in and out
from behind the clouds as though to confirm this anomaly.

To put all this into perspective, Wroxeter receives about 110
days of light towards ripening – it takes only 65 days to ripen
Madeleine Angevine (which is why it is so popular in the more

Distant hills make for a dramatic vineyard setting.

northerly vineyards of the UK). They also regularly pick the grapes at incredibly high natural sugar levels (so no addition of sugar is necessary to boost the alcohol levels). One rather incredible effect of this has been that instead of having to wait the usual three years before the vines produce grapes it seems that they only take 18 months here. The young Solaris vines planted here last year – they are only the second vineyard in the country to plant this new cross – will be cropping this year. Similarly a year-and-a-half after they first planted back in 1991, they had their first vintage of both reds and whites in 1992, after diversifying away from the smallholding which the family had been working for 50 years. With regard to climate change Martin commented that rain has become torrential these days, with relatively few of the mild showers you used to get. Also the snow that used to come regularly after Christmas, no longer does.

The soil here is sandy and all round you can see hills in the distance, yet the vineyard itself is rather flat, with huge rabbits and hares tumbling in and out of burrows all around. The resident hawks take care of the birds, but wasps can be a problem as the grapes are generally high in sugar (again the result of all that light). It is beautifully cared for and a large and varied range of wines is produced by David and Martin in an innovative fashion at their own winery, using an old bulk tank they found for blending purposes. (Visiting Wroxeter is one of the most popular Boots 'Gift Experiences', a part of their rewards scheme!)

Is the climate here reflected in the wines? They certainly have less acidity in general, which makes them a more easygoing 'drink now' style, which also makes them less amenable to aging. The whites are fruitier and less herbaceous than general, though my favourite was the *Phoenix Dry* which did have a dry, herby, grassy palate which surprised me after a gorgeous, sweet, marmalade and honey nose. The *Roman Rosé 2005* was a brilliant peaches and cream swigger, while its sister *Roman Red* was similarly refreshing with oodles of sweet raspberry, cherry and vanilla.

STAFFORDSHIRE
Buzzards Valley

The only commercial vineyard in Staffordshire is Buzzards Valley. Here, you can book vineyard and winery tours followed by a tasting in the café, and maybe sample some honey from the beehives they keep too. Or you could go coarse or trout fishing in their nine lakes, eat at the restaurant (good vine wraps), browse their fine foreign and local wine selection, and even pick up a Christmas tree at the right time of year! Unusually too (especially for the Midlands) they make almost as many reds as whites (five) and the wines are very reasonably priced and very decent to boot, no mean feat when working with difficult cold clay soils.

Ivan and Pat Jones were originally dairy farmers but diversified into flower farming until the dried-flower business was super-seded by silk flowers. This led to them starting up the vineyard itself in 2001 on south-facing slopes which lie above beautiful woodland. Most of the Jones family are now involved in running the large complex that they have built up and in looking after the vineyard. If you are any where near Lichfield, Tamworth or Sutton Coldfield you should pay them a visit.

37 Shirrall Drive, Drayton Bassett, Tamworth B78 3EQ
Telephone: 0121 3081951
Tours by appointment all year round.
Phone for opening times
www.buzzardvalley.co.uk

WARWICKSHIRE

Come, come, good wine is a familiar creature if it be well used; exclaim no more against it.

Othello, William Shakespeare

Heart of England

The early death of David Stanley, the much-loved grower in 2006 was a tragedy for British wines. With their combined efforts, every wine he and his wife Meryl entered into competitions won awards. He loved wine, loved being on his own in the vineyard and loved the magic of the chemical transformation of grapes into wine, with all the plethora of different flavours, aromas and textures that process entails. David could visualise the grapes on the slope before they were there and indeed the Heart of England site, soaring above the pretty village of Welford-upon-Avon is far more akin to the *terroir* of great French vineyards than are most UK sites. Secluded and windy, this vineyard is very well-kept. The view stretches across the Cotswolds, the Malverns, the Vale of Evesham and Bredon Hill. Meryl has always particularly loved the vineyard

Heart of England Vineyard,
Welford Hill,
Welford-on-Avon CV37 8AE
Telephone: 01789 750565
Check whether it is open for visits beforehand
www.heart-of-england.info

Right. Wave-like vines cascading downhill.

Opposite. Wild flowers abound amid the young vines.

in June when the sunlight shines through the young leaves and the gorgeous views sweep clear across Shakespeare country. The site possesses higher than average sunshine and is on well-drained sandy loam with gravel subsoil. Badgers have been a particular difficulty since planting in 1991, as much for digging large holes that the tractors fall into than eating the grapes.

It was also a fine indication of how close-knit the industry is that so many other vineyard owners came to help out when David fell ill. The Stanleys had planned to build a new visitor centre and were busy expanding the acreage massively (a sparkling wine is now available and a rosé and late-harvest dessert wine had been planned), but the vineyard is now up for sale. I just pray that whoever takes it on will continue the Stanley's legacy as I believe that when the vines hit their peak in ten years time, the wines have the potential to be astounding.

What of the wines now? The reds are what this vineyard is known for and they do not disappoint, from their Shakespearean fairytale names to their elegant labels and the abnormally dense dark colours through to the flavours. The *Othello* is lightest, tasty and cherry-ish; then *Orpheus 2004* is all rustic and farmy with plums and cherries again and more body. The *Oberon 2003*? I could sit just smelling it all winter evening long – roses, damsons, sweet luscious blackberries, a hint of vanilla oak ... all present and correct. And the palate is a smooth, medium-bodied, brambley flavour with caramel, earthy notes and good length. This is confirmation that the UK can make excellent reds and not from Cabernet or Syrah, but from Rondo and Triomphe d'Alsace. The whites are excellent too, ranging from the beautifully fragrant *Phoenix*, a dry, mineral, citrus concoction to the *Arden Oak*, lightly nutty, green and rhubarby too.

Welcombe Hills

Vine Cottage, King's Lane, Snitterfield,
Stratford-upon-Avon CV37 0QB
Telephone: 01789 731071
Visits by appointment
www.welcombehills.co.uk

This newish vineyard near Stratford-upon-Avon is attracting good publicity and Chris and Jane Gallimore certainly take their wine research seriously. Last time I spoke to them they had just returned from a trip to New Zealand where they had been for two months trying to discover the secrets behind growing and making wine from that most difficult of grapes, the Pinot Noir. The vineyard was planted in 2001 and has been a great success thus far, with awards going to their *Bacchus 2005* and the soft, cherry-ish *Pinot Noir 2004* (clearly they're already doing something right with it). That said, the experimental sparkling *Bacchus 2003* has been their own favourite wine so far, though it sold out very quickly, so you won't get your paws on any very readily.

The recent stable, sunny weather has meant unexpected progress with their red grapes, good news given that Chris originally intended to plant vines in the Lot Valley in southern France. As it turned out they realised that the *terroir* on their own relatively frost-free land was actually reminiscent of Burgundy (clay with good drainage) and planted it up with Pinot Noir, Dornfelder and Bacchus. Initially, they would have loved to have planted Sauvignon Blanc and Chardonnay, but concerns about powdery mildew sensibly put them off this course and the wines they are making have proved remarkably good in a very short space of time.

The vineyard has an interesting history as well, standing on what was once part of William Shakespeare's own estate. Charles II escaped his enemies after losing the Battle of Worcester along a lane which runs where the vineyard is now situated. Their easy-drinking red blend is named *King's Retreat* after this event.

NORTHAMPTONSHIRE
Fleur Fields

Hill Farm House, Brixworth,
Northampton NN6 9DQ
Telephone: 01604 880197
www.fleurfields.co.uk

After a Tuscan holiday Bill Hulme and his wife, Flora decided to bring a little bit of sunshine life home and plant Fleur Fields vineyard. They had the perfect spot in mind, a south facing meadow at the top of the hill overlooking Pitsford Reservoir. With the help of friends and family the vines were planted over five years ago and now produce both still and sparkling wine. Contact the Hulmes and they will be delighted for you to taste these. Apparently, the wine is fresh, crisp with elderflowery undertones and honey and melon notes and is good served with blueberry pie, chilled. The labels are delightful too, with bright yellow flowers that cheer you up before the bottle is even open.

Vernon Lodge

It is a sign of the times that Mike Dean, proprietor of the small Vernon Lodge vineyard, should choose to describe the wines of his two best years (1996 and 2000) as having *depth and balance* and even more so of being *typically English*. With the latter term in mind, he finds that Madeleine Angevine (also known as the 'English grape') is best, while he also thinks Siegerrebe can be fantastic, packed with spicy fruit in a good year.

Even this far north, changes are occurring, with picking times in general having moved two weeks earlier than when Mike started. Like other vineyards in Mercia he has a small purpose-built winery to produce the wines, though his must be one of the earliest, built in 1983 to coincide with the first harvest here. In fact, it was visiting other UK vineyards as a member of the UKVA that encouraged Mike to try viticulture for himself, buying vines from the redoubtable Gillian Pearkes in Devon. Unusually for the UK, netting against birds has actually worked at Vernon Lodge, although this doesn't protect against the depredations of insects, in particular wasps, that puncture the grapes, suck the sweetness out and leave them open to rot.

Being the only vineyard for a long way around, Vernon Lodge has been the cause and beneficiary of village attention, with villagers helping out at the vintage and on pruning days, rewarded with bottles of the small quantity of wine produced. Indeed, the only day in the year that the vineyard is open is in conjunction with the village fête, held to raise money for the church ... quintessentially English, in other words.

Tiffield, Towcester,
Northamptonshire NN12 8AB
Telephone: 01327 350077

'Anglais Nouveau'

In 1985, *Motor* magazine organised a reverse 'Beaujolais Nouveau' run whereby the new vintage of English wine was taken to Paris in a weird and wonderful array of classic vehicles, a bizarre idea that personally I think should be revived. Mike Dean, of Vernon Lodge vineyard, who worked in the motor trade at that time managed to bag himself a luxury conversion of a stretched London taxi cab complete with chauffeur. Cool.

Windmill

At 675 feet above sea level, Windmill Hill Farm is one of the highest vineyards in England and has a view to match that altitude. Seven different counties are visible from the pretty vineyard, with its eponymous windmill and bee colonies, orchards, friendly dogs and hungry Jacob's sheep, which when they get out of their pasture, can be a danger to the vineyard. The whitewashed windmill itself is 200 years old, though there has been a mill on site since the 15th century. It ceased turning in 1905 when the local grain merchant went adopted steam and put 20 windmills out of business. It is now the residence of Doreen Hillier, who owns the vineyard and is also the winemaker (the winery is in the old farm buildings). She is a friendly, enthusiastic lady who will welcome you and happily chat about the vineyard and farm she has been running since 1985.

Windmill Hill Farm, Hellidon,
Daventry NN11 6HZ
Telephone: 01327 262023
Open: Easter–15 October.
December, Wednesday–Sunday,
12.00–18.00 or by appointment

They grow their grapes organically, though without official Soil Association status.

Commenting on the years past, she says that the late nineties were good for them and that conditions then seemed to suit the top of a windy hill. She and her partner Tom began growing grapes by accident as the property already had half-an-acre of vines, which they have expanded to 1¼ acres. They had both come from farming backgrounds and Doreen's mother and grandmother has made country wines and cider – she remembers being sent out to pick whatever was available when she was young. Along with a red, medium dry and dry white, rosé and sparkling wines, Windmill still make mead, cider and a range of different fruit wines at very good prices.

The Windmill, from which there is a stunning view.

LEICESTERSHIRE
Chevelswarde

Chevelswarde was the first organic vineyard in the UK, set up even before Sedlescombe in Sussex. They describe it as a type of middle-aged madness that drove them to start the vineyard, after John Daltry's previous career in engineering, designing large steam turbines. It was the vines that pushed them towards organic practice as in their first year they stuck to all the current advice which was to add plenty of potash and phosphates to the soil. As the vines sprang up big and fast, they thought they were onto a winner until they discovered the large collars around each and every node that betrayed the presence of disease. The vines died. They replanted organically with advice from the Soil Association. They make ends meet, but not quite overlap with the aid of a farm shop growing tasty vegetables.

John and his wife Ruth (who are both in their late 70s) have soldiered on through all the problem years and the added difficulties of organic viticulture and even decided to grub up the Müller-Thurgau (which meant most of their grapes) in 2002, replacing them with Phoenix and Regent. They wish they'd done this earlier now, but the benefits of this replanting and of the newly built winery should make themselves apparent now, as the new grapes will shortly be in the wines. John (who sounds a little like Wallace, from *Wallace and Gromit*, with a voice as rich as toffee apples) loves working in the vineyard and farm, as long as the sun is shining. Kittens bound around the place and you have to try the home-grown farm produce, most particularly the tomatoes, which are utterly delicious.

The Belt, South Kilworth, Lutterworth LE17 6DX
Telephone: 01858 575309
Phone first before visiting

Chevelswarde is the old name for South Kilworth and comes from Cyfel's (who was a Saxon chieftain) farmed clearing in the forest. Their old label had a fox staring at a rooster in a tree because they used to have poultry until a fox came and devoured them and also due to it being the symbol of Leicestershire. They also used to have two goats, which contrary to popular belief are unlikely to decimate a single crop as they prefer to try a bit of everything, being true omnivores.

Welland Valley

Marston Trussell, Market Harborough, Leicestershire LE16 9TX
Telephone: 01858 434591
Phone first before visiting

And so on through Leicestershire where I pull up a wide drive. When David and Jane Bates got married in 1968, their first house in Leicester backed onto allotments, one of which came with the property. While David had never really done any gardening, he grew vegetables and since there was a simultaneous boom in home

David Bates's vineyard lies in the heart of historic Midlands countryside.

winemaking, he decided to plant some vines in 1971 and began to make wine. Hankering after his own vineyard for when he retired, he put an advert in the paper in 1991 enquiring about land and got one reply back, one which he took up, buying 2½ acres of steep farmland. With his wheelbarrow and an old railway wagon (which became his first outbuilding) he planted up and made steady, pleasurable progress in both grape growing and winemaking.

At first he imagined he would be growing chiefly to make dry whites, but upon tasting one of his first efforts realised that while it tasted pretty poor as a still wine, it had that certain character sparkling wines require. As it turns out, their award-winning sparkling wine is still the main draw. Made in traditional Champagne style but with Seyval Blanc and Reichensteiner grapes, it is a very English bubbly, with bright acidity, sherbet-like texture and full, fruity elderflower and lemon character. In blind tasting, my friends from Oddbins thought that it was a good New World sparkling wine. Rather more surprisingly, their red is also excellent, with easy chompy strawberry flavours and hints of treacle and plum. I stood contemplating the lip-smacking thought of these two top wines combined into the forthcoming *Steeplechase Sparkling Rosé* as I gazed at the fantastic view, looking out over the countryside to the ridge where the battle of Naseby was fought many years ago.

LINCOLNSHIRE
Lincoln Medieval Bishop's Palace

Planted in 1972 with vines supplied by its twin City, Neustadt in Germany's Rhein Pfalz, Lincoln Palace vineyard is one of the most northerly in Europe. The cathedral's medieval bishops' palace was once the administrative centre of the largest diocese in England, stretching from the Humber to the Thames. Its rulers, the prince-bishops were both wealthy and enormously powerful, a fact reflected in the impressive architecture of the Palace, first begun in the late 12th century. Royalist troops later sacked the palace during the English Civil War. Lincoln's terraced hillside vineyard itself is part of the heritage garden and the form of the latter takes inspiration from the cathedral's medieval vaulting and spires, and the curves of the vines. Unfortunately pretty much all the wines go towards keeping Lincoln's dignitaries happy, so you are unlikely to get a taste, though you can go and visit the vineyard and take the nifty audio tour.

Old Bishop's Palace, Lincoln LN2 1PU
Telephone: 01522 527468
Open: most days between 10.00–17.00
www.english-heritage.org.uk

NOTTINGHAMSHIRE
Eglantine

I know a bank where the wild thyme blows,
Where oxlips and the nodding violet grows,
Quite over-canopied with luscious woodbine,
With sweet musk-roses and with eglantine.

A Midsummer Night's Dream, Act ii, Scene 1,
William Shakespeare

Ash La, Costock,
Loughborough LE12 6UX
Telephone: 01509 852386
Sales most days, phone first to check.
Organised group tours May–September
www.costock.fsnet.co.uk/
page21eglantin.html

'You can't produce decent wine north of the River Thames.' 'How many hot water bottles did you need to keep the grapes warm this year.' It was comments such as these from one particular southern grower that drove Tony Skuriat of the northerly Eglantine Vineyard in Nottinghamshire to call his world-class ice wine *North Star*. Still, as Tony puts it, in his slightly fractured eastern European accent, 'We don't pat ourselves on the back, we let others do it for us.' His face is deep and lined but bright blue eyes twinkle with excitement when he talks about sweet wines and viticulture. The blustery squalling day on which I visited only serves to reinforce the difficulty of growing grapes here, the ever-present dangers of frost, wind damage, rot and mildew seem much closer than in Devon or Kent.

Ice wine is made by freezing grapes and then pressing them, so that water crystals remain in the press and only the ultra-

concentrated juice trickles down. Whereas just-ripe grapes freeze at 0°C, fully ripe grapes only do so at -6°C. As one might imagine this reduces the amount of juice one gets considerably. In fact, instead of getting two bottles per vine, you are reduced to half-a-bottle from three vines. This makes the price, £15 per half-bottle seem rather more reasonable, especially given the production level for 2003 was only 1,000 bottles.

And the wine itself? *Eglantine North Star* (made with Madeleine Angevine grapes) is so unutterably gorgeous that you'll regret the last drop leaving your glass like a rose-gold morning disappearing. With an aroma that brings orange blossom, vanilla and a wisp of smoke, this is a real treat for the nose and the mouth. Honeyed, lush flavours of banana and orange and a lingering finish that stays with you, not for seconds, but minutes afterwards. This is truly memorable wine, the more so for being the only one of its kind in the UK.

Ironically, Tony has found this unique proposition to be quite a problem in competition, where, despite always doing well, it is always judged not as an ice wine but against other sweet wines, some judges commenting that it just doesn't have that botrytis flavour. Unsurprising really, since it isn't made of botrytis-affected grapes. Eglantine was named by Veronica Skuriat not after the 'Bedknobs and Broomsticks' character but after the smallest of the wild English roses (also known as the Sweet Briar) found growing along the hedgerows in some parts of the local countryside. Planted in 1979, the vineyard is accompanied by a beautiful flower garden, in which we watched a large bullfinch flitting and a mateless pheasant strutting. Tony has a massive collection of different vines from all over the world (200–300) and keeps bees whose honey makes a tasty smokey-honeyed mead (and homemade honey).

The main variety of grape grown is Madeleine Angevine, due to its reliability in these northern parts. Madeleine Sylvaner which is prone to noble rot if the grapes are left to hang on the vine, has also successfully produced a rather good botrytis dessert wine. It can be very difficult to control disease in the wet and the rain, especially if it's humid and mildew is a particular problem. One shouldn't underestimate the effort it has taken to get to this point; 40 years of learning since ex-teacher Tony had his first vines in the greenhouse, slowly expanding into the garden and then a five-year search for the correct site. Even now it is a three-year wait before they release a new vintage of *North Star*. Eglantine also make a creamy elderflowery dry white, a gorgeous ripe, red, cherry wine

Aurora Borealis wine

It was in the year of the East Midlands airport crash that *Aurora Borealis Rosé* was first made. They tend to press all grapes as soon as possible at Eglantine and the reds were the last grapes to be picked and pressed as they used to stain the old press (this stain won't wash off but disappears naturally after a year). The other members of the family had all tired of the process having worked all day long and had gone to bed. Tony was still there until late in the night and having pressed the last grapes into his first rosé wine, switched off the floodlights to see the Northern Lights* flickering their strange patterns across the sky. Hence *Aurora Borealis*.

* The Northern Lights have four forms; drapery, arc, band & corona.

Riesling

I love Riesling. Especially German Riesling, as do Tony and his wife, Veronica, befitting a couple who produce the UK's finest sweet wine. So I asked everyone I saw on my travels why no one in the UK is producing Riesling. Given that our latitude is very similar to the northernmost Riesling areas in Germany, I thought it was odd that no-one seemed to be trying. Apparently, at Easter, the great Mosel vineyards are no further ahead than the UK. But it seems that there is an all important hot spell in Germany that the UK lacks. It seems there is also a dearth of appropriate sites as even in Germany Riesling seems to do its stuff best only on extremely steep, slaty-soiled land. Tony has grown Riesling for quite some time now and said it ripened only once in ten years and even in 2003 had less sugar content than was ideal. Still, one of these days, someone may find the right site ...

with a touch of herbaceousness and a rosé and red that are utterly different and somewhat bizarre. This is due to the use of Cascade grapes, an unusual choice that have a flavour that has to be tried. Both have a creamy texture, but as to whether you'll like them or not, well, even I can't quite make up my mind.

DERBYSHIRE
Renishaw Hall

The Events Office, Renishaw Hall, Renishaw Sheffield S21 3WB
Telephone: 01246 432310
Visits by arrangement
www.sitwell.co.uk

For many years, Renishaw Hall had the dubious privilege of being the most northerly vineyard in Western Europe, lying 53°, 18' N of the equator. And where other vineyards have disappeared, Renishaw remains, vines lining what was once the Top Paddock, kept alive by the enthusiasm of the owner, the fantastically named Sir Sachaverell Reresby Sitwell and by one of the gardeners, Ray, through years of difficulty. The present head gardener, David Kesteven (known as 'Outdoor Dave'), young with a deep creased forehead and black rock-band ponytail, has given the old vineyard a new lease of life. Having rashly declared with youthful optimism at his job interview that he was sure he could learn about vines from books, it is only now, six years later that they are starting to produce good grapes and therefore good wines. As he says, the thing about gardens – and most particularly vines – is you have to get them planted and let them do their thing, patience is every-

thing. The last two vintages have been good ones, 2005 being memorable for David deciding to pick the grapes despite the fact that the BBC's 'Curious Houseguest' programme crew were due to arrive and film the vintage the next day. It turned out to be a wise decision as solid walls of rain that would have diluted the grapes arrived the next day and continued for two solid weeks.

Whilst the amazingly beautiful gardens are his first priority, the vines are a close second though they can be the bane of David's life, more difficult to care for than even the notoriously hard *Primula Oricula*. After all, as he says, at the end of the day, they have to produce something good enough to make into wine, which they certainly did not do for the vast majority of their existence so far. Still, with Tony Skuriat's help and George Bowden at Leventhorpe, it does seem as if Renishaw wine has a good future. Yields are five times higher as are the number of visitors and this lovely quirky English house deserves to live on for many years.

The design of the wine label was taken from a letterhead by Rex Whistler, the wartime artist, who was a friend of Sir Osbert Sitwell, Sir Reresby's uncle and the previous owner of Renishaw. The vinehouse is particularly beautiful and is inhabited by a variety that as yet no-one has identified, seemingly halfway between a white and a red grape (perhaps we have here the first genuine rosé grape?). Both the sparkling and still wines from the last couple of vintages have actually been rather good, the bubbly in particular is brisk and refreshing. Group visits are by arrangement and the place as a whole is well worth a visit, country air and drifting flowers mingling with careful design to bring the craft of gardening to life.

Driving back southwards, we hit swirling darkness in the form of pelting rain that forces every car to slow to 20 mph on the motorway ... then comes the hail, savage and destructive, belting on the roof and windows with such force we thought it might break the windscreen wipers. And what, I wondered had happened to the vineyards I had just been to? Would the vines that were further ahead be worse off than those only just leafing? There may not have been frost this spring but this sudden cold spell and the hail ... well, who knows?

YORKSHIRE

I end this guide where I began it, in God's own county, where I first discovered the joys of our own wines. Yorkshire is hardly usually associated with wine, though the monks at the great abbeys of Kirkstall, Fountains, Rievaulx and the rest almost certainly made some of their own (and grape growing can be traced all the way back to the Cistercian monks at Kirkstall Abbey in Leeds and the Benedictines in York). The rolling landscape is firmly associated with beer, from drunken monks to pints of bitter with Compo in the inappropriately named 'Last of the Summer Wine'. Still, these rolling hillsides may prove their worth in another way in the future. The land east of the Pennines is surprisingly sunny and rain-free and those slopes may well prove just the place for rows of vines here and the recent planting of two more vineyards may be a sign of things to come ...

RENISHAW

ENGLISH REGIONAL WINE

Estate grown at Renishaw Hall, Derbyshire.
Bottled by Mr. A. Skuriat at Eglantine Winery. LE12 6UX
for Sir Reresby Sitwell Bt, D.L., D.Litt.

Opposite. The Vinehouse.

Wine v beer: a clash of titans

Lo. The poor toper whose untutored sense,
Sees bliss in ale and can with wine dispense;
Whose head proud fancy never taught to steer,
beyond the muddy ecstasies of beer.

   Inebriety, George Crabbe (1754–1832)

The white sheet bleaching on the hedge,
With heigh. the sweet birds, oh, how they sing.
Doth set my pugging tooth on edge;
For a quart of ale is a dish for a king.

When Daffodils begin to Peer,
     William Shakespeare (1564–1616)

Part of our island history is the clash of cultures embedded and adopted into our drinking patterns. This is between the beer culture of the Saxon tribes and Viking north Europeans and the more occasionally hedonistic wine-drinkers of the South. The former celebrated drinking for the purpose of getting drunk, with beer and mead, a gift of the gods. The latter on the other hand, saw wine as an accompaniment to food, or part of religious ceremony, to be drunk in moderation and over a long period of time. This, of course, is a simplification (and who can blame the northerners for warming themselves up with a bit of alcohol), but as a rule it holds true and became a part of the class divide with the working classes the beer drinkers and the middle and upper classes, the Romans.

Pour out the wine without restraint or stay,
Pour not by cups, but by the bellyful,
Pour out to all that wull.

     Epithalamion, 250, Edmund Spenser (*c*1552–1599)

Helmsley Castle Walled Garden

Cleveland Way, Helmsley,
North Yorkshire YO62 5AH
Telephone: 01439 771427
Open: daily 10.30–17.00,
April–end October
www.helmsleywalledgarden.org.uk

Stuart Smith of the new Ryedale vineyard has also had a hand in setting up the small vineyard at medieval Helmsley Castle's walled garden. It is looked after by a group of volunteers in accordance with organic principles. Alongside the modern varieties sits a vinery displaying 34 varieties of Victorian grapes, and a cafe provides a pleasant place to sit, relax, and hopefully soon enjoy a glass of dry Yorkshire white wine.

Leventhorpe

Saturday, 2 April 2005

Bullerthorpe Lane, Woodlesford,
Leeds LS26 8AF
Telephone: 0113 2889088
Open: weekends 11.00–17.00 and
some weekdays but phone first.
Free tastings given … provided you
buy something!

A vineyard in Yorkshire? No, your eyes do not deceive you and actually Leventhorpe's micro-climate, with the Pennines stealing the rain, a south-facing slope to catch the sunshine and a little lake nearby, shows just why English wine can be made and made well even in Leeds. Clare and I arrived at Leventhorpe vineyard in Leeds to find a door with a large sign that stated, 'IF I AM IN THE VINEYARD SOUND YOUR HORN'. Almost French. George Bowden walked over with dark, worn features saying nothing and opening the door to his shed which was really the cellar/production room/tasting area. You may find George initially reticent, but show some true interest and he will reward you by talking so enthusiastically that before long you'll be setting up your very own vineyard. Just like me. Having tasted four good whites we wandered around the vineyard, which is packed with everything from Pinot Noir clones to Seyval Blanc to Madeleine Sylvaner, avoiding the dead animals underfoot. Upon returning down to the foot of the hillside, a brief question of mine prompted another 25-minute introduction to the joys of winemaking, from the Austrian wine scandal and dodgy journalists to the different tastes brought by added acids in Australian and Chilean wines. Memorably there was sound advice from George to Clare about me: 'Don't let him bore you.' (About wine that is.)

A year and a bit later I was back at Leventhorpe, the vineyard that first prompted me to write this book, to ask a few more questions and see how things were going with this vintage. Despite being behind by ten days in 2006 due to the poor weather of early spring, even these most northerly of vines had caught up in the scorching heat of June.

When I asked about bad vintages George puts it forthrightly, 'the only bad vintage that we had was down to me messing up.' Still it isn't just human error that causes problems. Annoyingly, wasps

and fieldfares took a fancy to his Madeleine Sylvaner, the best grape
at Leventhorpe, so much so that those vines have now been
removed. Recently, an eagle owl the size of a large cat has been
residing in the area and helpfully eating the rabbits and squirrels,
then rather distressingly moving on to pet cats and dogs. George
comments, with a wry glint in his eye, 'There's an irony there, the
hunter becomes the hunted.' Talking about organics he points out
that before pesticides the biggest cause of death in the world was
cancer developed through natural fungal infections. Not that he
suggests that all sprays are good, one spray was the source of quite
a few 'witches' hallucinations years ago.

George believes that picking correctly from the vast array of
different yeasts and acids is the key to good wine now. He thinks a
potential threat to wine here comes from pressure from New World

Copious bunches begin to form.

countries to ban chaptalisation, which would not be a problem provided they don't ban it wholesale but instead regulate it so that you can only boost alcohol by two degrees, which is all that most UK producers tend to add anyway. It would cause more problems in certain areas of France. Ironically, the southern hemisphere wines have their alteration methods too, notably irrigation and the addition of tartaric acid.

His Madeleine Angevine wines take four years to develop in bottle, something it is possible to taste as he keeps an *Estate Reserve* that is considerably older than the normal Maddy. Indeed this was a fine wine, with a delightful complex nose, all elderflower, cut grass, herbs and leaves. The palate was much fuller, with broad green flavours, a touch of peach and still had good acid levels. I also tasted two young Madeleines, the first of which had been picked ten days earlier than the second, the latter of which was slightly sweeter, with more body to it. Tasting some unfiltered pre-bottling wines was fascinating too – fuller and rougher-edged but more flavoursome than the bottled wines – the Seyval had a touch of rhubarb to it, while the barrel Madeleine had a real peapod character that it loses in bottle. A bit of a shame really, I liked that. Wines that had gone through malolactic fermentation had a much creamier texture. All the wines had good length too, not always the case with UK wines. They also make a sparkling Seyval, a red Triomphe d'Alsace and a Pinot Blanc.

Ryedale

Stuart and Elizabeth Smith not only provide an excellent supply of vines from their website The Vinehouse but have now ventured into the world of commercial vineyards with the setting up of Ryedale vineyard near Malton. Stuart has been growing vines in Yorkshire since 1977 and the plan is to concentrate on producing red, white and sparkling wine from the seven acres that lie between the Yorkshire Wolds and the North York Moors. The Smiths have around half organic and half conventional plantings in two fields, and when Ryedale comes into production in around 2009 the vineyard will open to the public.

Fairfield Farm, Westow,
York YO10 7LS
Telephone: 01484 865964
Not open to the public
www.thevinehouse.co.uk

Yorkshire Heart

Between York and Harrogate lies another new Yorkshire vineyard where Chris and Gillian Spakouskas planted up with both red and white varieties in Spring 2006. Like Ryedale vineyard, the vines should start to produce in 2009, so perhaps there will be a Yorkshire Festival of Wine that year!

The Firs, Kirk Hammerton Lane,
Green Hammerton, York
Not open to the public

SCOTLAND
Cairn O'Mhor

The fruits of my laboured search through the Internet for Scottish vineyards (a million and one evangelical fellowships later) were as follows. With much joy I celebrated my finds. Cairn O'Mhor fruit and leaf wines are made between Perth and Dundee. As their website states: 'What we do is gather up strawberries, raspberries, brambles, elderberries, elderflowers, oak leaves even, from all around, prepare them in different ways with water, sugar and various other ingredients to make a kind of sweet fruity soup, then we introduce our resident grape yeast into the barrels. Overnight these clever little organisms come to life and set to work converting the sugars in the mix to alcohol, breathing off carbon dioxide in the process which makes it go all frothy. After three days the must (what you call it) is hand pressed and when all the sugar has been turned to alcohol, the yeasts slip in to repose and gradually fall to the bottom of the tank. The clearing wine is drawn off from the top, filtered, bottled and stored in the dark.'

Cairn O'Mhor, near Errol,
Carse of Gowrie, Perthshire PH2 7SP
Telephone: 01821 642781
www.cairnomohr.co.uk

I have been told by my publisher that these wines are widely available (Scottish Asda stores stock them) and obviously from Cairn O'Mhor's website. He has assured me that the Elderberry wine is a good substitute for an after-dinner glass of port.

Moniack Castle Wineries

Moniack Castle Wineries
Inverness IV5 7PQ
Telephone: 01463 831283
www.moniackcastle.co.uk

From Eroll, a three-hour drive north along the A9 brings you to Inverness and it is some seven miles to the west to this city along the A862 to Beauly that you will find Moniack Castle Wineries near Easter Moniack. Again, this operation is one that produces its wines from fruit, flowers, berries and, interestingly, sap. They also make mead and sloe liqueur. The winery was started in 1979 by Philippa Fraser and is run by herself, her two sons Rory and Kit, along with Jonathan Garden and a local workforce.

One of the types of wines they produced, *Silver Birch*, was a favourite of Prince Albert when in residence at Balmoral. The operation is very much Internet-based but Jonathan Garden is very keen to talk to anyone interested in the wines.

Along with the nine country wines and liqueurs they produce there is also a range of marmalades, sauces and preserves. They also offer a guided tour on which you will see the fermenting room, filtering processes, bottling and labelling. After this you go through the cellars to the kitchen where the cooking of the preserves and sauces takes place.

The packaging and presentation is very good and the longevity of the business is testament to the appeal of these rural Scottish products.

So there you have it. The canny Scots don't even bother with vines and all that palavah. They just use the fruits they grow in huge quantities and let nature (and some sugar) do the rest. Brilliant. There is some evidence to suggest that the Romans were growing figs and grapes in Scotland and, there have been suggestions that if global warming continues apace then the southern mountain slopes of the Cairngorms and other Scottish ranges may well prove to be some of the best viticultural areas in the UK. We shall see ...

Appendix 1

FOOD AND
WINE MATCHING

We will eat our mullets,
Soused in high-country wines, sup pheasants' eggs,
And have our cockles boiled in silver shells;
Our shrimps to swim again, as when they lived,
In a rare butter made of dolphins' milk,
Whose cream does look like opals.

> *The Alchemist* (1610) Act 4, sc. 1,
> Ben Jonson *c*1573–1637

A lot of wine is intended to go with food and tastes wrong without it. At the same you should always drink exactly what you like and not drink what someone else tells you is the 'correct' wine. Just as no one has the same taste in food, neither will they in wine or in matching the two together. André Simon, the great wine writer always vouched that whatever drop you choose, food and wine are necessary partners, even that each is not quite alive without the other.

I cannot put it any better than Jean Brillat Savarin (1755–1826):

A meal without wine is like a day without sunshine.

So where to start?

Well loved he garleek, onyons and eek lekes,
And for to drynken strong wyn, reed as blood.

> *The Canterbury Tales* The General Prologue,
> Geoffrey Chaucer (1343–1400)

And who doesn't like a bit of garlic, onion and leek with a splash of strong red wine? You need strong flavours to match other strong flavours and delicate to match delicate.

What follows is my take on which British food goes with which British wine and when.

January

This is best done on New Year's Day when you might awaken with a hangover. Why not cure yourself with a fried breakfast combined with some orange-tinged fizz, *Nyetimber's Classic Blend 2000*. That should set you up nicely for the rest of the day.

February

Chicken tikka masala. Curries can be awkward to match, overpowering many a dish. You need something with a bit of bite to refresh you with all those spices charging in. Slightly sweeter wines often go well, as long as they aren't too herbaceous. Schönburger perhaps, or *Hop Pocket Medium Sweet*.

The matching of food and wine is not a scientific matter!

March

Spring not quite arrived? Fish and chips are great for warming you up and taking the rain-grey tint off things, particularly when combined with crisp, white, UK wines. Dry Seyval Blanc is best so plump for *Breaky Bottom's Seyval*, preferably aged a bit, food-friendly and with a gorgeous minerally edge to cut through the fat.

April

Ploughman's lunch: a firm slab of cheddar or stilton, apple chunks, pointless celery and oatmeal biscuits. Oh, and a glass of *Three Choir's Late Harvest*, a lovely sweetie to sip rather than swig.

May

Roast lamb, mint sauce, roast tatties. Forget Bordeaux, go for one of England's best reds, the beautiful, deep, brambly goodness that is *Sharpham Red 2004.*

June

Picnic. As the sun swings out and Wimbledon begins, what better way to celebrate than with a citric burst of sparkling Seyval Blanc. Bubbly of character with aromas of hedgerows and greenery, it will wash down your ham sandwiches, cheese, sausage rolls and cherry tomatoes beautifully.

July

Barbeque. *Frome Valley Huxelrebe* has a deliciously refreshing elderflower flavour, the perfect partner for just about anything you care to eat. Many English and Welsh rosés are also perfect for barbeque fair, with slight sweetness and strawberry flavours.

August

Celebrate the last month of summer warmth (at least it used to be), the month of weddings with a special treat, smoked salmon combined with its perfect partner, Bacchus. Bacchus is very food-friendly with enough weight for salmon and scallops and even turkey, duck, goose and pheasant. But for this particular food go with *Camel Valley Bacchus.*

September

Rhubarb crumble and custard. This goes well with all sorts of rosé, even the drier sorts, and I'd go for the elegant *Stanlake Park Pinot Blush*. Tasty.

October

Home-made winter vegetable soups are ace and match up well with a variety of wines from cheaper reds to off-dry whites such as *Astley Old Vine Kerner*.

November

Bangers and mash is a British classic Cumberland sausage being a particular favourite of mine with creamy mash, peas and thick onion gravy. Maybe even a slab of bacon too with a dash of mustard? Any red wine goes fantastically with this superbly warming wintry dish. Just fill up your glass, and stuff your face.

December

Turkey time so go for the awesome *Chapel Down Pinot Noir 2003*, a soft creamy red with cherry and cranberry fruits and a finish to die for.

Digby's Excellent Small Cakes

"Take three pounds of very fine flower, well dried by the fire, and put to it a pound and a half of loaf sugar sifted in a very fine sieve and dried; three pounds of currants well washed, and dried in a cloth and set by the fire; when your flour is well mixed with the sugar and currants, you must put in it a pound and a half of unmelted butter, ten spoonfuls of cream, with the yolks of three new laid eggs beat with it, one nutmeg; and if you please, three spoonfuls of sack [sherry]. When you have wrought your paste well, you must put it in a cloth, and set it in a dish before the fire, till it be through warm. Then make them up in little cakes, and prick them full of holes; you must bake them in a quick oven unclosed. Afterwards ice them over with sugar. The cakes should be about the bigness of a hand breadth and thin; of the size of the sugar cakes sold at Barnet."

Tip: cut the butter into the flour as one would for piecrust. Bake the cakes for about 20 minutes at 350deg.

For the icing: about a third of a cup of icing sugar and enough water so you can spread it.

Appendix 11
VINEYARD ADDRESSES AND OS MAP REFERENCES

In order to find the location of the UK vineyards that cater for visitors go to **www.streetmap.co.uk** and type in the 8-figure Landranger OS map reference that follows at the end of each entry below. So for Leeds Castle, type in TQ836532, and tick the Landranger reference button. Bingo! The location is revealed and you can then choose the scale of map you want to print out. Enjoy!

ENGLAND

Bedfordshire
Warden Abbey, Near Old Warden, Southill Park, Biggleswade SG18 9LJ
   TL144420

Berkshire
Stanlake Park, Twyford, Reading RG10 0BN
   SU800751

Buckinghamshire
Hale Valley, Boddington East, Hale Lane, Wendover HP22 6NQ
   SP879073

Cambridgeshire
Chilford Hall, Balsham Road, Linton CB21 4LE
   TL567489

Channel Islands
La Mare, St Mary, Jersey JE3 3BA

Cornwall
Camel Valley, Little Denby Farm, Nanstallon,
   Bodmin PL30 5LG
   SX031677

Lambourne, Ruanhighlanes, Truro, TR2 5NL
    SW897398
Oak Valley, Bosue Vineyard, St Ewe, St Austell PL26 6EU
    SW978475
Polmassick, Mellym Boyse, Polmassick, St Ewe,
    St Austell PL26 6HA
    SW972455

Devon

Blackdown Hills, Oaklands Farm, Monkton, Honiton EX14 9QH
    ST187030
Down St Mary, The Old Mill, Down St Mary,
    near Crediton EX17 6EE
    SS731044
Kenton, Helwell Barton, Kenton EX6 8NW
    SX945828
Manstree (Boyces Farm), New Barn Farm, Manstree Road,
    Shillingford St George, Exeter EX2 9QR
    SX900879
Oakford, Holme Place, Oakford, Tiverton EX16 9EW
    SS910213
Old Walls, Old Walls Road, Bishopsteignton TQ14 9PQ
    SX913740
Pebblebed, The Wine Cellar, 46a Fore Street, Topsham,
    Exeter EX3 0HJ
    SX965881
Sharpham Vineyard and Cheese Dairy, Ashprington,
    Totnes TQ9 7UT
    SX826578
Yearlstone, Bickleigh EX16 8RL
    SS938080

Derbyshire

Renishaw Hall, The Events Office, Renishaw Hall, Renishaw,
    Sheffield S21 3WB
    SK437785

Dorset

Horton, Horton Estate, Wimborne BH21 7JG
    SU037077
Purbeck, Purbeck Valley Road, Harmans Cross,
    Corfe Castle, Dorset BH20 5HU
    SY981804

East Sussex

Barnsgate Manor, Herons Ghyll, near Uckfield TN22 4DB
 TQ484280

Battle Wine Estate, Leeford Vineyards, Whatlington TN33 0ND
 TQ758185

Breaky Bottom, Rodmell, Lewes BN7 3EX
 TQ409063

Carr Taylor, Wheel Lane, Westfield, Hastings TN35 4SG
 TQ802158

Davenport, Limney Farm, Castle Hill, Rotherfield,
 East Sussex TN6 3RR
 TQ548278

Henner's, Church Road, Herstmonceux BN27 1QJ
 TQ641105

Hobden's, Wellbrook Hall, Mayfield TN20 6HH
 TQ572260

Plumpton College, Ditchling Road, Plumpton,
 near Lewes BN7 3AE
 TQ359134

Ridgeview, Fragbarrow Lane, Ditchling Common,
 Hassocks BN6 8TP
 TQ332177

Sedlescombe Organic, Cripps Corner, Sedlescombe,
 Robertsbridge TN32 5SA
 TQ776207

Essex

Bardfield, The Great Lodge, Great Bardfield, Braintree CM7 4QD
 TL693291

Carter's, Green Lane, Boxted, Colchester CO4 5TS
 TL985323

New Hall, Chelmsford Road, Purleigh,
 Chelmsford CM3 6PN
 TL836025

Sandyford Vineyard, Salix Farm, Great Sampford,
 Saffron Walden CB10 2QE
 TL641347

Gloucestershire

St Anne's, Oxenhall, Newent GL18 1RW
 SO699277

Strawberry Hill, 47 Orchard Road, Newent GL18 1DQ
 SO717289

Thornbury Castle Hotel and Tudor Gardens, Thornbury,
     near Bristol BS35 1HH
     ST633907
Three Choirs, Newent, Gloucester GL18 1LS
     SO713290

Hampshire
Beaulieu, John Montagu Building, Brockenhurst,
     Beaulieu SO42 7ZN
     SU385027
Birchenwood, Birchenwood Farm, Brook, Lyndhurst SO43 7JA
     SU283137
Bishop's Waltham, Tangier Lane, Bishops Waltham SO32 1BU
     SU542175
Court Lane, Ropley, Alresford SO24 0DE
     SU647326
Northbrook Springs, Beeches Hill, Bishop's Waltham,
     Southampton SO32 1FB
     SU553181
Somborne Valley, Hoplands Farm, Kings Somborne,
     Stockbridge SO20 6QH
     SU372298
Sour Grapes, Oak Tree House, Michelmersh,
     Romsey SO51 0NQ
     SU343263
Webb's Land, off Tanfield Lane, Wickham PO17 5NS
     SU561109
Wickham, Botley Road, Shedfield, Southampton SO32 2HL
     SU543134

Herefordshire
Beeches, Upton Bishop HR9 7UD
     SO643270
Broadfield Court, Bowley Lane, Bodenham HR1 3LG
     SO541534
Coddington, near Ledbury HR8 1JJ
     SO718426
Four Foxes, Longworth Lane, Bartestree HR1 4BX
     SO561412
Frome Valley, Paunton Court, Bishops Frome WR6 5BJ
     SO669500
Lulham Court, Lulham, near Madley, Hereford HR2 9JQ
     SO408410

Treago, St Weonards HR2 8QB
    SO491240

Frithsden, Hemel Hempstead HP1 3DD
    TL015099
Hazel End, Bishop's Stortford CM23 1HG
    TL494243

Adgestone, Upper Road, Sandown PO36 0ES
    SZ597865
Rosemary, Smallbrook Lane, Ryde PO33 2UX
    SZ594905

Barnsole, Fleming Road, Staple, Canterbury CT3 1LG
    TR279566
Biddenden, Little Whatmans, Gribble Bridge Lane, Biddenden,
    Ashford TN27 8DF
    TQ849362
Chapel Down/Tenterden/English Wines plc, Small Hythe,
    Tenterden TN30 7NG
    TQ853360
Groombridge Place Gardens and Enchanted Forest,
    Tunbridge Wells TN3 9QG
    TQ532377
Gusbourne Estate, Griffin Farm, Appledore, Ashford TN26 2BE
    TQ991326
Harbourne, Wittersham, Tenterden TN30 7NP
    TQ887286
Hush Heath Manor, Cranbrook TN17 2NG
    TQ756407
Lamberhurst Ridge Farm, Lamberhurst TN3 8ER
    TQ672356
Leeds Castle, Broomfield, Maidstone ME17 1PL
    TQ836532
Meopham Valley, Norway House, Wrotham Road,
    Meopham DA13 0AU
    TQ641653
Sandhurst, Hoads Farm, Crouch Lane, Sandhurst,
    Cranbrook TN18 5PA
    TQ807284

The Mount, Church Street, Shoreham, Sevenoaks TN14 7SD
     TQ521616
Throwley, The Old Rectory, Throwley, Faversham ME13 0PF
     TQ992556

Leicestershire

Chevelswarde, The Belt, South Kilworth, Lutterworth LE17 6DX
     SP610820
Welland Valley, Marston Trussell,
     Market Harborough LE16 9TX
     SP681858

Lincolnshire

Lincoln Medieval Bishop's Palace, Old Bishop's Palace,
     Lincoln LN2 1PU
     SK977717

Norfolk

Tas Valley, Forncett St Peter NR16 1LW
     TM155923
Thelnetham, Lodge Farm, Thelnetham, Diss IP22 1JL
     TM012774

Northamptonshire

Fleur Fields, Hill Farm House, Brixworth, Northampton NN6 9DQ
     SP747690
Vernon Lodge, Tiffield, Towcester NN12 8AB
     SP698514
Windmill, Windmill Hill Farm, Hellidon, Daventry NN11 6HZ
     SP519577

Nottinghamshire

Eglantine, Ash Lane, Costock, Loughborough LE12 6UX
     SK571279

Oxfordshire

Bothy, Frilford Heath, Abingdon OX13 6QW
     SU452987
Brightwell, Rush Court, Shillingford Road, Wallingford OX10 8LJ
     SU604916
Fawley, Henley, The Old Forge, Fawley Green RG9 6JA
     SU754862

Shropshire

Halfpenny Green, Tom Lane, Halfpenny Green DY7 5EP
S0830926
Morville Hall, Morville, near Bridgnorth WV16 5NB
S0668940
Wroxeter Roman Vineyard, Wroxeter, Shrewsbury SY5 6PQ
SJ565079

Somerset

Bagborough, Pylle, Shepton Mallet BA4 6SX
ST623395
Dunkery, Wootton Courtenay, Minehead TA24 8RD
SS941433
Mumford's, Shockerwick Lane, Bannerdown Road, Bath BA1 7LQ
ST789677
Oatley, Cannington, Bridgewater TA5 2NL
ST234398
Staplecombe, Burlands Farm, Staplegrove, Taunton TA2 6SN
ST206273

Staffordshire

Buzzards Valley, 37 Shirrall Drive, Drayton Bassett,
Tamworth B78 3EQ
SP159997

Suffolk

Gifford's Hall, Hartest, Bury St Edmunds IP29 4EX
TL844514
Ickworth House, Hollinger, Bury St Edmunds IP29 5QE
TL815615
Kemp's, Shimpling, Bury St Edmunds IP29 4EY
TL844510
Staverton, The Rookery, Eyke, Woodbridge IP12 2RR
TM330513
Willow Grange, Street Farm, Crowfield, Ipswich IP6 9SY
TM146565
Willow House Vineyard/Oak Hill Wines,
Fressingfield, Eye IP21 5PE
TM261775
Shawsgate, Badingham Road, Framlingham,
Woodbridge IP13 9HZ
TM297648

235

Wissett, Valley Farm Vineyards, Wissett,
  Halesworth IP19 0JJ
  TM356799
Wyken, Wyken Hall, Stanton, Bury St Edmunds IP31 2DW
  TL963717

Surrey
Denbies, London Road, Dorking RH5 6AA
  TQ167512
Greyfriars, The Hogs Back, Puttenham,
  Guildford GU3 1AG
  SU945483
Painshill Park, Portsmouth Road, Cobham KT11 1JE
  TQ100601
The Iron Railway Vineyard/Old Tramway Holdings,
  11 Vincent Road, Coulsdon CR5 3DH
  TQ290592

Warwickshire
Heart of England, Welford Hill,
  Welford-on-Avon CV37 8AE
  SP149505
Welcombe Hills, Vine Cottage, King's Lane, Snitterfield,
  Stratford-upon-Avon CV37 0QB
  SP210590

West Sussex
Booker's, Foxhole Lane, Bolney RH17 5NB
  TQ256231
Highdown (Centre For English Wine), Littlehampton Road,
  Ferring BN12 6PG
  TQ095036
Nutbourne, Gay Street, Pulborough RH20 2HH
  TQ081189
Nyetimber, Gay Street, West Chiltington RH20 2HH
  TQ081189
Southlands Valley, Mitchbourne Farm, Malthouse Lane,
  Ashington RH20 3BU
  TQ125152
Warnham Vale, The Old Barn, Northlands Road,
  Warnham RH12 3SQ
  TQ146350

Wiltshire

A' Beckett's, High Street, Littleton Pannell,
  Devizes SN10 4EN
   ST997544
Bow-in-the-Cloud, Noah's Ark, Garsdon,
  Malmesbury SN16 9NS
   ST960884
Fonthill Glebe Wines, The Winery, Teffont Evias,
  Salisbury SP3 5RG
   ST989315
Quoins and Little Ashley, BA15 2PW
   ST813625
Wylye Valley, Crockerton, Warminster BA12 8BQ
   ST867432

Worcestershire

Astley, The Crundles, Astley, Stourport-on-Severn DY13 0RU
   SO803673
Tiltridge, Tiltridge Farm, Upper Hook Rd,
  Upton-upon-Severn WR8 0SA
   SO836406

Yorkshire

Leventhorpe, Bullerthorpe Lane, Woodlesford,
  Leeds LS26 8AF
   SE372298

WALES

Ceredigion

Gwinllan Ffynnon Lâs, Lampeter Road, Aberaeron,
  Ceredigion SA46 0ED
   SN460619

Clwyd

Worthenbury, The Old Rectory, Worthenbury,
  Wrexham LL13 0AW
   SJ419461

Dyfed

Cwm Deri Vineyard, Martletwy, Pembrokeshire SA67 8AP
   SN035101

Glamorgan

Bryn Ceiliog, Fairfield, 14 Clinton Road, Penarth,
Vale of Glamorgan CF64 3JB
ST182708
Glyndŵr, Llanblethian, Cowbridge, Vale of Glamorgan CF71 7JF
SS984740
Llanerch, Hensol, Pendoylan CF72 8GG
ST051796

Gwent/Monmouthshire

Monnow Valley, Great Osbaston Farm, Monmouth NP25 5DL
SO501141
Parva Farm, Tintern, near Chepstow NP16 6SQ
SO530008
Sugar Loaf, Dummar Farm, Pentre Lane, Abergavenny NP7 7LA
SO287155
Wernddu, Pen-y-clawdd, Monmouth NP25 4BW
SO456074

Gwynedd

Eryri, LL45 2DZ
SH580266

Ynys môn

Llanbadrig Gwinllan Padrig, Cae Owen, Cemaes Bay LL67 0LN
SH383945

SCOTLAND

Perthshire

Cairn o'Mohr Winery, East Inchmichael, Errol PH2 7SP
NO249252

Inverness-shire

Moniack Castle Wineries, Inverness IV5 7PQ
NH555435

GLOSSARY

Acidity – Essential component of wine. Measured as a percentage of acid in grams per litre (g/l).

Botrytis – A fungus which rots grapes and is an enormous pain for most viticulturalists. A late form of botrytis (also known as Noble Rot or Pourriture Noble) acting on certain varieties leads to concentration of sugars and intense dessert wines.

Biodynamic – Style of organic grape growing which uses varying techniques include growing according to the phases of the moon, and the use of organically made sprays.

Body – Common phrase used to describe the weight of wine in the mouth. The more *tannin* and alcohol there is in a wine the weightier it will feel and the more body it will have.

Cane pruning – Method of pruning in which grapes are grown each year on new vertical shoots which rise from permanent horizontal canes.

Canopy – Actively growing shoots and leaves are referred to as the *Canopy*, while Canopy Management is trying to ensure that enough air and light gets through to ripen the grapes.

Chaptalisation – Addition of sugar to *must* to increase alcohol.

Dry – A dry wine is one in which almost all of the sugar has been fermented out of the wine.

Fermentation – Turning a base substance into gold! A chemical reaction whereby sugars in a liquid are transformed into alcohol, achieved by the actions of yeasts on grape juice.

Fining – The clarification of wine, traditionally achieved with the use of egg-white, filtration then being used to strain out the coagulated bits. The less filtering, the better, as each process reduces flavour intensity.

Frost pocket – A patch of ground where heavy cold air collects, and where frost damage to vines is much more likely.

Geneva Double Curtain – Common form of high training in the UK where each vine is grown into four branches paralleling each other, opening up the canopy to air and sunlight.

Gobelet – Form of *spur* training whereby the vine is allowed to grow various branches around a central stake without support from wires.

Grafting – In order to defeat the spread of *phylloxera*, vines are now grafted onto a phylloxera-resistant rootstock from an American origin vine (as these have proven resistance). The properties of different rootstocks in affecting yield, development and quality have recently come to the fore and choice of rootstock is now seen as extremely important.

Guyot (single or double) – Classic form of vine training, devised in France by Dr Jules Guyot, where one or two branches are grown horizontally, and each year vertical shoots are grown off it to bear fruit.

Hydrometer – Instrument used to measure the density of grape juice.

ISO – International Standards Organisation (standard decent tasting) glass.

Lees – Residue left by *fermentation*. Certain wines (notably sparkling wines) are left on the lees to develop particular flavours, yeastiness for example.

Maturation – Allowing wine to develop flavours by leaving undisturbed.

Mildew – Vine disease caused by a fungus, usually dealt with by spraying with sulphur.

Must – Unfermented grape juice.

Oeschle degrees (°Oe) – Scale for measuring the sugar content of grape juice.

Oxidation – A chemical change resulting from exposure of wine to air which does not usually improve flavour. This is why secure corks are essential.

Phylloxera – An insect that has been responsible for decimating vineyards all over the world. It attacks the root of the vine, killing it, but is now less of a problem due to *grafting*.

PSR – Quality wine status found on wine labels, and meaning *produced in a specified region*. Equivalent of French AC wines.

Racking – Siphoning wine between containers.

Refractometer – Instrument used to measure sugar content, and thus decide when the grapes are at optimum ripeness for the harvest.

Regional Wine – UK equivalent of French vin de pays wines. these wines conform to certain tested standards.

Rootstock – See *Grafting*

Scion – A vine grafted onto a different *rootstock* from its own.

Scott Henry – Popular UK training system named after the astronaut who invented it. Each vine has fruiting shoots going both upwards and downwards, giving higher yields than in general.

Smudge pots – Small pots with wicks that provide just enough heat to take the edge off frost at critical points in the year.

Spur pruning (Bush pruning) – Pruning down to short lateral spurs or shoots. Not generally used in the UK except in small garden vineyards.

Tannin – A grainy or furry substance commonly found in red wines. Tannin helps to give wine ageing potential and *body*. Maturation in oak also adds to tannin levels.

Terroir – French word describing the many things that make individual vineyards unique, including soil type, climate, winemaker, grape variety, aspect etc.

Varietal – Just means grape type e.g. Cabernet Sauvignon.

Véraison – Stage in ripening when the grapes begin to change colour.

Vinification – The making of wine.

Viticulture – The cultivation of vines.

Vitis Vinifera – Latin name for the wine grape. Most of the best varieties of grape for winemaking are *Vitis Vinifera*. Native to Europe.

INDEX